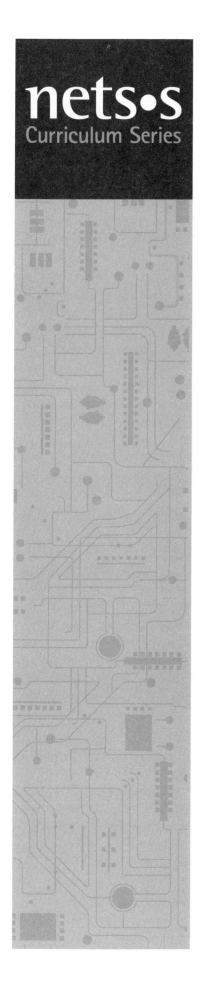

nets•s
Curriculum Series

National Educational Technology
Standards for Students

Multidisciplinary Units for Prekindergarten Through Grade 2

Jeri A. Carroll
M. G. (Peggy) Kelly
Tonya L. Witherspoon

The University of New Mexico
At Gallup

Zollinger Library

iste

nets•s
Curriculum Series

Multidisciplinary Units for Prekindergarten Through Grade 2

Jeri A. Carroll
M. G. (Peggy) Kelly
Tonya L. Witherspoon

DIRECTOR OF PUBLISHING
Jean Marie Hall

BOOK EDITOR
Lynne Ertle

BOOK DESIGN
Katherine Getta,
Katherine Getta Graphic Design

AQUISITIONS EDITOR
Mathew Manweller

BOOK PUBLISHING PROJECT MANAGER
Tracy Cozzens

LAYOUT AND PRODUCTION
Tracy Cozzens

International Society for Technology in Education (ISTE)
480 Charnelton Street
Eugene, OR 97401-2626
Order Desk: 1.800.336.5191
Order Fax: 541.302.3778
Customer Service: orders@iste.org
Books and Courseware: books@iste.org
Permissions: permissions@iste.org
World Wide Web: www.iste.org

First Edition
ISBN 1-56484-200-2

about iste

The International Society for Technology in Education (ISTE) is a nonprofit professional organization with a worldwide membership of leaders in educational technology. We are dedicated to promoting appropriate uses of information technology to support and improve learning, teaching, and administration in K–12 education and teacher education. As part of that mission, ISTE provides high-quality and timely information, services, and materials, such as this book.

The ISTE Publishing Department works with experienced educators to develop and produce classroom-tested books and courseware. We look for content that emphasizes the use of technology where it can make a difference—making the teacher's job easier; saving time; motivating students; helping students who have unique learning styles, abilities, or backgrounds; and creating learning environments that would be impossible without technology. We believe technology can improve the effectiveness of teaching while making learning exciting and fun.

Every manuscript and product we select for publication is peer reviewed and professionally edited. While we take pride in our publications, we also recognize the difficulties of maintaining quality while keeping on top of the latest technologies and research. Please let us know what products you would find helpful. We value your feedback on this book and other ISTE products. E-mail us at **books@iste.org**.

ISTE is home of the National Educational Technology Standards (NETS) Project, the National Educational Computing Conference (NECC), and the National Center for Preparing Tomorrow's Teachers to Use Technology (NCPT[3]). To learn more about NETS or request a print catalog, visit our Web site at **www.iste.org**, which provides:

- Current educational technology standards for PK–12 students, teachers, and administrators
- A bookstore with online ordering and membership discount options
- *Learning & Leading with Technology* magazine
- *ISTE Update*, online membership newsletter
- Teacher resources
- Discussion groups
- Professional development services, including national conference information
- Research projects
- Member services

Leading Authors

JERI A. CARROLL has more than 20 years of public school teaching experience in PK–2 in addition to 15 years of experience in early childhood teacher education. Dr. Carroll is currently professor of early childhood education at Wichita State University, where she works closely with early childhood and elementary preservice teachers and supports the professional development of inservice teachers in local districts. Several publications with Good Apple, Inc., and Teaching and Learning Company preceded her work with ISTE. She has served on the ISTE NETS for Teachers writing team and as a developer for ISTE NETS Online. She teaches courses in early childhood education and technology integration, and supervises student teachers.

M. G. (PEGGY) KELLY has 16 years' experience teaching in the public schools in kindergarten through eighth grade and has coordinated a parent cooperative preschool. She has taught at the university level for more than 15 years. Dr. Kelly is the co-director of ISTE's National Educational Technology Standards Project and has directed the development of the standards documents *Connecting Curriculum and Technology* and *Preparing Teachers to Use Technology*. At California State University, San Marcos, Dr. Kelly teaches courses in mathematics for elementary teachers and educational technology. She also supervises student teachers and works collaboratively with public schools on special projects.

TONYA WITHERSPOON has more than 10 years' experience working with students, teachers, parents, and administrators integrating technology into the curriculum at both private and public schools. Tonya is currently the Web developer for Wichita State University's College of Education and serves as a technology specialist for WSU's Project M3, funded by a Preparing Tomorrow's Teachers to Use Technology grant. Tonya also teaches workshops in clay animation, robotics and programming, multimedia, and online instruction.

CONTRIBUTING AUTHOR

LINDA MITCHELL is an assistant professor of early childhood special education at Wichita State University in the Department of Curriculum and Instruction. She has worked in the field of special education, with emphasis at the early childhood level, for more than 12 years. Dr. Mitchell is the associate editor of the *Journal of Critical Inquiry into Curriculum and Instruction* and serves on the editorial board of Young Exceptional Children.

contents

Section 3—Strategies for Managing Technology 221

Appendix

introduction

Our educational system must produce technology-capable students.

According to the ISTE National Educational Technology Standards (NETS) Project Overview (available at **http://cnets.iste.org**), "Parents want their children to graduate with skills that prepare them to either get a job in today's marketplace or advance to higher levels of education and training. Employers want to hire employees who are honest, reliable, literate, and able to reason, communicate, make decisions, and learn. Communities want schools to prepare their children to become good citizens and productive members of society in an increasingly technological and information-based world. National leaders, the U.S. Department of Education, and other federal agencies recognize the essential role of technology in 21st century education."

But does training in technology have to start in preschool? Young children at the computer? Young children online? Young children and any technology devices? Is technology useful in early childhood classrooms? Can technology be used in appropriate and meaningful ways in early childhood classrooms? The answer is a resounding "Yes!" and this book will show you how.

The NETS Project

The NETS Project was initiated by ISTE's Accreditation and Professional Standards Committee. ISTE has emerged as a recognized leader among professional organizations for educators involved with technology. ISTE's mission is to promote appropriate uses of technology to support and improve learning, teaching, and administration. Its members are leaders in educational technology, including teachers, technology coordinators, education administrators, and teacher educators. ISTE supports all subject area disciplines by providing publications, conferences, online resources, and services that help educators combine the knowledge and skills of their teaching fields with the application of technologies to improve learning and teaching.

The primary goal of the NETS Project is to enable stakeholders in PK–12 education to develop national standards for the educational uses of technology that facilitate school improvement in the United States. The NETS Project is developing standards to guide educational leaders in recognizing and addressing the essential conditions for effective use of technology to support PK–12 education.

The NETS•S Curriculum Series represents a continuation of ISTE's desire to provide educators with the means to meet the NETS. *Multidisciplinary Units for Prekindergarten Through Grade 2* is specifically designed to provide preschool and early elementary teachers with curriculum to meet the NETS PK–2 performance indicators while addressing content standards.

NATIONAL EDUCATIONAL TECHNOLOGY STANDARDS FOR STUDENTS

The NETS for Students are divided into the following six broad categories. Standards within each category are to be introduced, reinforced, and mastered by students. These categories provide a framework for linking performance indicators, listed by grade level, to the standards. Teachers can use these standards and profiles as guidelines for planning technology-based activities in which students achieve success in learning, communication, and life skills.

1. **Basic operations and concepts**
   - Students demonstrate a sound understanding of the nature and operation of technology systems.
   - Students are proficient in the use of technology.

2. **Social, ethical, and human issues**
   - Students understand the ethical, cultural, and societal issues related to technology.
   - Students practice responsible use of technology systems, information, and software.
   - Students develop positive attitudes toward technology uses that support lifelong learning, collaboration, personal pursuits, and productivity.

3. **Technology productivity tools**
   - Students use technology tools to enhance learning, increase productivity, and promote creativity.
   - Students use productivity tools to collaborate in constructing technology-enhanced models, preparing publications, and producing other creative works.

4. **Technology communications tools**
   - Students use telecommunications to collaborate, publish, and interact with peers, experts, and other audiences.
   - Students use a variety of media and formats to communicate information and ideas effectively to multiple audiences.

5. **Technology research tools**
   - Students use technology to locate, evaluate, and collect information from a variety of sources.
   - Students use technology tools to process data and report results.
   - Students evaluate and select new information resources and technological innovations based on the appropriateness to specific tasks.

6. **Technology problem-solving and decision-making tools**
   - Students use technology resources for solving problems and making informed decisions.
   - Students employ technology in the development of strategies for solving problems in the real world.

PERFORMANCE INDICATORS, GRADES PK–2

All students should have opportunities to demonstrate the following performances. Numbers in parentheses following each performance indicator refer to the standards category to which the performance is linked. ISTE has developed performance indicators for all grade levels. Listed below are only the PK–2 indicators, the specific focus of this book. For specific ideas on how to meet these indicators, see Appendix A.

Prior to completion of Grade 2, students will:

1. Use input devices (e.g., mouse, keyboard, remote control) and output devices (e.g., monitor, printer) to successfully operate computers, VCRs, audiotapes, and other technologies. (ISTE NETS•S, Standard 1)

2. Use a variety of media and technology resources for directed and independent learning activities. (ISTE NETS•S, Standards 1, 3)

3. Communicate about technology using developmentally appropriate and accurate terminology. (ISTE NETS•S, Standard 1)

4. Use developmentally appropriate multimedia resources (e.g., interactive books, educational software, elementary multimedia encyclopedias) to support learning. (ISTE NETS•S, Standard 1)

5. Work cooperatively and collaboratively with peers, family members, and others when using technology in the classroom. (ISTE NETS•S, Standard 2)

6. Demonstrate positive social and ethical behaviors when using technology. (ISTE NETS•S, Standard 2)

7. Practice responsible use of technology systems and software. (ISTE NETS•S, Standard 2)

8. Create developmentally appropriate multimedia products with support from teachers, family members, or student partners. (ISTE NETS•S, Standard 3)

9. Use technology resources (e.g., puzzles, logical thinking programs, writing tools, digital cameras, drawing tools) for problem solving, communication, and illustration of thoughts, ideas, and stories. (ISTE NETS•S, Standards 3, 4, 5, 6)

10. Gather information and communicate with others using telecommunications, with support from teachers, family members, or student partners. (ISTE NETS•S, Standard 4)

NAEYC Standards

In the late 1990s two national organizations, the National Association for the Education of Young Children (NAEYC) and ISTE, worked to address whether technology was appropriate for use with young children and which standards and objectives were achievable.

The NAEYC set the stage for the use of technology in early childhood classrooms with its 1996 position statement entitled *Technology and Young Children—Ages 3–8,* which stated, "Technology plays a significant role in all aspects of American life today, and this role will only increase in the future.... Early childhood educators must take responsibility to influence events that are transforming the daily lives of children and families." While it notes that research points to the positive effect that technology can have on children's learning and development, the NAEYC cautions, too, that technology can be misused. It is up to the teachers to use their "professional judgment in evaluating and using this learning tool appropriately, applying the same criteria they would to any other learning tool or experience."

Each numbered item below is taken from NAEYC's 1996 position statement. For specific ideas on how to meet these indicators, see Appendix A.

1. NAEYC believes that in any given situation, a professional judgment by the teacher is required to determine if a specific use of technology is age appropriate, individually appropriate, and culturally appropriate.

2. Used appropriately, technology can enhance children's cognitive and social abilities.

3. Appropriate technology is integrated into the regular learning environment and used as one of many options to support children's learning.

4. Early childhood educators should promote equitable access to technology for all children and their families. Children with special needs should have increased access when this is helpful.

5. The power of technology to influence children's learning and development requires that attention be paid to eliminating stereotyping of any group and eliminating exposure to violence, especially as a problem-solving strategy.

6. Teachers, in collaboration with parents, should advocate for more appropriate technology applications for all children.

7. The appropriate use of technology has many implications for early childhood professional development.

Essential Conditions for Technology Integration

Successful learning activities, such as the ones provided in this book, depend on more than just the technology. Certain conditions are necessary for schools to effectively use technology for learning, teaching, and educational management. Physical, human, financial, and policy dimensions greatly affect the success of technology use in schools.

The curriculum provided in this book is more effective when the essential conditions for creating learning environments conducive to powerful uses of technology are met. These include having

- vision with support and proactive leadership from the education system;
- educators skilled in the use of technology for learning;
- content standards and curriculum resources;
- student-centered approaches to learning;
- assessment of the effectiveness of technology for learning;
- access to contemporary technologies, software, and telecommunications networks;

- technical assistance for maintaining and using technology resources;
- community partners who provide expertise, support, and real-life interactions;
- ongoing financial support for sustained technology use; and
- policies and standards supporting new learning environments.

Traditional educational practices no longer provide students with all the necessary skills for economic survival in today's workplace. Students must now apply strategies for solving problems using appropriate tools for learning, collaborating, and communicating. The following chart lists characteristics representing traditional approaches to learning and corresponding strategies associated with new learning environments.

ESTABLISHING NEW LEARNING ENVIRONMENTS

Incorporating New Strategies

Traditional Learning Environments ➤ New Learning Environments

Traditional Learning Environments	New Learning Environments
Teacher-centered instruction	Student-centered learning
Single-sense stimulation	Multisensory stimulation
Single-path progression	Multipath progression
Single media	Multimedia
Isolated work	Collaborative work
Information delivery	Information exchange
Passive learning	Active/exploratory/inquiry-based learning
Factual, knowledge-based learning	Critical thinking and informed decision-making
Reactive response	Proactive/planned action
Isolated, artificial context	Authentic, real-world context

The most effective learning environments meld traditional approaches and new approaches to facilitate learning of relevant content while addressing individual needs. The resulting learning environments should prepare students to

- communicate using a variety of media and formats;
- access and exchange information in a variety of ways;
- compile, organize, analyze, and synthesize information;
- draw conclusions and make generalizations based on information gathered;
- know content and be able to locate additional information as needed;
- become self-directed learners;
- collaborate and cooperate in team efforts; and
- interact with others in ethical and appropriate ways.

Teachers know that the wise use of technology can enrich learning environments and enable students to achieve marketable skills. We hope that elementary educators will find the curriculum and other material provided within helpful in meeting these goals.

How to Use This Book

Multidisciplinary Units for Prekindergarten Through Grade 2 is divided into three main sections followed by a set of useful appendixes.

SECTION 1

Section 1 offers a series of essays that provide guidance on how to integrate technology into PK–2 classrooms. The main focus of these essays is effective classroom practice. Strategies are provided for designing your own technology-rich units, incorporating problem- and project-based learning into your lessons, supporting different learning styles with assistive technology, and assessing young learners.

SECTION 2

Section 2 contains four multidisciplinary themes developed around a centers approach to learning. Each theme has a unique topic (**All About Me**, **Communities**, **Food**, and **On the Go**) and each is divided into four units. In addition to long- and short-term lesson descriptions, each theme offers the following eight unit tools.

SPOTLIGHT ON TECHNOLOGY

Each unit highlights the use of one or more types of technology. For example, the **Food** theme focuses on software for spreadsheets and graphing, word processing, and drawing, as well as Internet sites. The Spotlight on Technology section explains how the highlighted technology can be incorporated into a variety of lesson plans that teachers may want to design.

WRITING ACROSS THE CURRICULUM

In every unit, children are given opportunities to write about what they see, experience, and imagine. Very young children vary in their ability to express themselves in written form. While some are able to write words and stories with coherence, others are struggling to express themselves with pictures.

The multidisciplinary nature of operating the classroom with centers and whole-group activities provides opportunities for children to write frequently. The subject of the writing varies from reporting to expressive writing. As centers are organized and a calendar of events is created, think about varying the writing activities from those that the whole class engages in at the same time to those that occur at the writing and other centers.

Additionally, as students become more able writers, consider having them keep a daily journal of their accomplishments at the centers. A simple writing prompt sequence of "What did I do today?", "What did I learn from what I did?", and "How do I feel about my work today?" enables students to regularly reflect on their work and record their thoughts. The journal provides a way to check student participation, monitor learning using self-reported data, and document consistent growth in writing.

TEACHER VOICES

Teachers want to know what other teachers think. This section presents stories and statements from other teachers on how the lessons have worked and what children have enjoyed or produced.

CHILDREN'S LITERATURE — Each of the four instructional units within each theme focuses on a multidisciplinary approach to teaching. Because reading and writing are so important in the early years, each unit offers a list of books that supports the lessons and activities.

WEB RESOURCES — Many of the units provide activities for which students would need access to the Web. The Web Resources "tool" offers teachers ways to incorporate the Internet into the units in meaningful and safe ways for young children.

TEACHING TIPS — It is always helpful to have suggestions on the best way to implement a lesson. The Teaching Tips "tool" suggests ways a teacher can get the most out of the lessons. This section provides insights into which teaching strategy might be most effective for you.

LESSON EXTENDERS — Sometimes lessons are so good, students and teachers don't want them to end. If that is the case for you, each unit offers a few suggestions for lesson extensions.

THEME CULMINATING EVENT — As the final unit tool, the Theme Culminating Event provides a short synopsis of the complete activity plan at the end of each theme. Use it to brainstorm preliminary ideas or set plans in motion for the final event.

SECTION 3

Section 3 provides additional essays that focus on classroom management issues. Incorporating technology into early childhood classrooms requires some advanced planning. These five essays discuss protecting hardware, using computers in different classroom settings, selecting peripherals and software, using the Internet safely and effectively, and coping with legal and ethical issues that surround technology use.

APPENDIXES

The appendixes provide several additional resources for the teacher. Included are classroom ideas for meeting the standards, and the standards themselves.

How to Use the Units

Each unit begins with sections entitled Unit Overview, Unit Objectives, and Standards Addressed in This Unit. Although only the English/language arts, math, science, social studies, and technology standards are cited in each unit, others standards (fine arts, physical education, and health) are also addressed in the lessons but not coded in the introduction. It is well recognized that rich early learning experiences involve stimulation of all the senses in ways that engage students and promote conceptual understanding.

Just after the standards you'll find well-rounded lists and fully developed sections entitled Children's Literature, Web Resources, Software, Getting Started, Motivating Activity, Whole-Group Activities, Multidisciplinary Activities, and Assessment. The use of technology is threaded throughout the discussions.

CHILDREN'S LITERATURE

A comprehensive selection of children's literature is provided to support the unit concepts. Far more literature titles are purposefully presented than can be used to provide opportunities to select the appropriate literature based on availability, activities prepared, and the specific focus of the unit. As time goes by, it is expected that some of the titles will go out of print and others will come along. Searching periodically for new titles to fit specific topics and student needs is a common teacher task.

WEB RESOURCES

Web sites that have been judged by the authors as appropriate for most young children are provided for each unit. All were available at the time of the printing of this book. Teachers are encouraged to preview the sites to determine the availability through the school filtering mechanism and the appropriateness of the sites for their specific group of children, the families, and the community. New Web resources are continually being developed for educational purposes. A search for new Web sites is always appropriate.

SOFTWARE

Several software titles are highlighted for use with each unit. In addition to word processing, drawing, and presentation software, content-specific software is also mentioned. It may be noted that several titles appear to be used frequently in this book. The repeated software tools are currently the most common found in early childhood classrooms and are applicable to various learning styles. It is a challenge to keep current in software, as the industry is continually developing new and more powerful tools appropriate for young children.

As with the list of children's books and Web resources, the software list is not to be considered specific and exhaustive. As time goes by, some of the software titles will go out of production and others will come along. Teachers are encouraged to use the software available to them in ways appropriate to young children and to search for new content-specific software on a regular basis.

In a few instances, the software section is expanded to include hardware, toys, CDs, and videos.

Teaching the Unit

GETTING STARTED

Each unit provides information for a parent letter introducing the upcoming topic and encouraging parents to share in the learning experience. Teachers are encouraged to customize the suggested information in the letter to keep parents informed of unit plans.

MOTIVATING ACTIVITY

The motivating activity launches the unit and helps students get involved in discovering more about the topic. From that activity, teachers and students together can generate questions and ideas that will guide the exploration of the topic.

WHOLE-GROUP ACTIVITIES

Some of the units provide ideas for whole-group activities. These activities are designed to generate student interest and promote cooperative and collaborative experiences in a large group. Not all units, however, are designed for whole-group interactions.

MULTIDISCIPLINARY ACTIVITIES

Each unit lists several activities in a variety of curricular areas (art, gross motor, health, language arts and reading, math, music, science, and social studies). Embedded in these activities are many opportunities for young children to build knowledge and skills to meet the curricular standards. As with most learning experiences designed for young children, it is not any one activity that will ensure that students are able to meet the standard. Multiple opportunities to learn can be scaffolded and must be provided.

ASSESSMENT

Two forms of assessment are provided given the likely differences in working with younger preschool children and the more able second graders. Each offers an assessment task.

The rubric for the younger students is based on the concept that young children are ready for different types of activities at different times and that they know the concepts best when they can teach others. It requires observation of the students to see whether they are interested, trying it, working on it, have accomplished it, or are helping others. Three or four objectives or standards are described in rows with levels of interest and accomplishment in columns.

The rubric for the more able students is based on the completion of objectives or standards and provides three levels of accomplishment—approaches target, meets target, and exceeds target. Three or four objectives or standards are described in rows with levels of accomplishment in columns.

TECHNOLOGY

Technology is an integral part of each unit; the use of technology is embedded in a natural and appropriate way into the sequence of activities. Some activities are designed for a whole group, some for small groups and centers, and some for individual investigation by an interested student. It is not expected that teachers will use all of the activities in any one unit, but only those appropriate to their group of students and the specific focus of the student's inquiry.

A Word of Caution

If you are a computer studies teacher or lab coordinator and have picked up this book to see what it has to say about early childhood and technology, we think it will help you see the support that might be needed by the classroom teacher as well as the types of technologies, software, and activities that might be appropriate for young children when they come into the computer lab. If this book seems too much like a classroom teacher's book, give it to the preschool, kindergarten, first-grade, or second-grade teacher, and tell the teacher that you would be glad to help with implementing any of the lessons in the classroom or in the lab.

If you are a classroom teacher and have picked up this book to see whether technology fits in your early childhood classroom, we think the variety of technology-supported activities will help you get started and see the possibilities. Computer technology belongs in the PK–2 classroom much in the same way as record players, tape players, VCRs, phones, and other devices. If you are overwhelmed by all that technology has to offer, don't put this book down. Walk it to your computer studies teacher or computer lab coordinator. Ask for help in setting up computer stations and activities in your classroom. We are sure the individual will be delighted to provide it.

Beyond This Book

Keep in mind as you read the units and activities, that the needs of every teaching situation could not possibly be addressed between the covers of this book. Take the examples contained herein and modify them to fit your unique circumstances and student needs. These sample lessons provide a lens for reexamining traditional lessons and discovering ways to infuse technology to enrich teaching and learning. As you are inspired to create new lessons and units, please share these with others by posting them on the ISTE Web site (www.iste.org). But that's not all!

Be proactive about sharing your good work with others. There are many lesson plan Web sites as well as school, district, professional association, and parent meetings at which to present new lesson plans and the resulting student work. Educators need to learn from their peers. Educators also need to inform parents of their efforts to integrate technology and learning, and inform the greater public about how schools are meeting the needs of students, parents, and the community.

References

ISTE. (1998). *National educational technology standards for students* [Online]. Eugene, OR: Author. Available: http://cnets.iste.org/students/s_stands.html

National Association for the Education of Young Children (NAEYC). (1996). *Technology and young children—Ages 3 through 8* [Online]. Available: www.naeyc.org/resources/position_statements/pstech98.htm

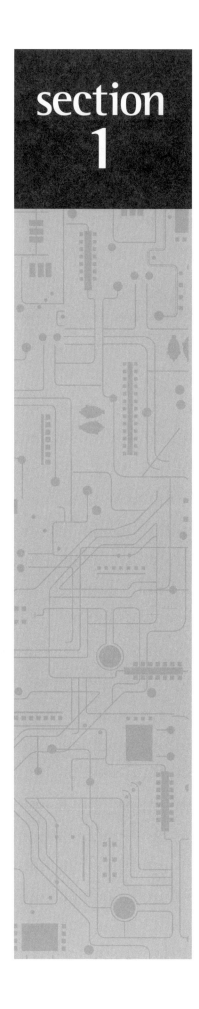

section 1

Strategies for Getting Started

chapter 1

JERI CARROLL

Designing Technology-Rich Multidisciplinary Units

Writing instructional units is a common task for PK–2 teachers. The topics, organizational pattern, and implementation take on different characteristics depending on the students, teacher, and context of the school. As technology has found its way into the early learning classroom, the method of developing instructional units has become more complex. As a way of providing insight into how the units in this book were developed, this chapter focuses on three models of developing instructional units: Integrated Thematic Units—The Historical Model with No Technology Used, Integrated Thematic Units—The Historical Model with Technology Added, and Fully Integrated Thematic Units.

Integrated Thematic Units

THE HISTORICAL MODEL WITH NO TECHNOLOGY USED

The Historical Model with No Technology Used is the least sophisticated of the three models. While using a project-based learning approach that allows for student-led exploration, the model limits itself to using traditional resources such as books, manipulatives and other educational tools. This model serves as a good starting point when developing your own units.

SELECTING A TOPIC

In a prekindergarten or kindergarten classroom, it is not unusual to find a set of centers, such as a blocks area, a housekeeping zone, a reading corner, a listening place, a puzzle location, and so forth. The materials in these centers are fairly standard and mirror the adult items one might find in the home. The play that occurs in these locations reflects the lives of the children playing in them.

Once the permanent centers in the classroom are defined, units of instruction are selected that provide an in-depth exploration of a small topic for a short period of time. Historically, these topics follow a calendar year and are predetermined for each week of the school year as part of the yearlong planning process. Little variation in topics occurs from one year to the next. Seldom do the units last more than a week; at the end of the week, books, materials, and supplies appropriate to the one-week unit are put away so that the books, materials, and supplies appropriate to the next unit can be set out.

With the emergence of NAEYC's position statements on the education of young children, curriculum design has begun to focus on the development of meaningful experiences for young children. It is suggested that topics emerge from the experiences of children in their schools, homes, communities, countries, and the world. For example, the topic of "snow" is now explored when snow falls, not the second week in January by a predetermined calendar. In fact, snow might not be explored in classrooms in the southern United States at all. Palm trees might be studied in tropical areas and not be investigated in Canada. Sea turtles might be explored in Hawaii, but probably would not be studied in Kansas.

There are many approaches to the selection and application of topics. The Reggio Emilia approach (explored in chapter 2) emphasizes that topics should emerge directly from the children's interests. The project-based learning approach allows students to work intensely on activities to completion, which may extend units longer than the traditional one week. The standards-based approach suggests that curriculum should begin with the standard and include activities designed specifically to help students address the identified knowledge, skills, and dispositions stated in the standard.

Each approach or combination of approaches has merit. The primary objective held in common by the approaches when developing instructional units is to focus on student interests and learning while meeting educational standards. The starting point for developing units, however, is widely debated, and a consensus may never be reached.

SELECTING BOOKS AND STORIES

Fiction and nonfiction books and stories provide a basis for many good lessons. Public, personal, and school libraries are often a source of books to accompany a unit. Bookstores offer access to the classic books for children, new titles, and works by new authors as well.

FINDING LESSONS

Without a curriculum guide, it is often difficult to locate activities on a specific topic that are appropriate for young children. Colleagues are always a good source of ideas. School supply stores often carry teacher resource books on general topics (learning centers, month-by-month activities) and even some topic-specific teacher resource books (weather, rocks, pets).

THE HISTORICAL MODEL WITH TECHNOLOGY ADDED

When computers are added to the classroom, the inevitable struggle occurs with trying to learn how to use the technology while teaching already planned instructional units. Figuring out ways for children to use the technology typically occurs after the teacher has base-level skills. How the technology is added to existing units depends on the teacher's comfort in trying new things, the existing models of effective use in place at the school site, professional development opportunities, and the technology support (formal or informal) available. Using a word processing package is usually the first place to start, followed by content-specific software and Web resources. Each new technology is added on to an existing instructional unit. How the technology integrates into the activities of the instructional unit becomes a product of time, experience, and constant modification.

USING WORD PROCESSING

Most computers for schools initially come with a word processing package. Setting up a computer with a word processing program allows students with emerging writing ability to copy, write, or create. While the first step for older children might be to allow them to use the word processing programs and work with the spreadsheet, database, and presentation components of those packages, young learners are more curious about how the letters get on the screen and form words. Word processing programs designed specifically for young children include rebus words, draw tools, large print, and many other features that allow for multiple uses in the classroom. Many teachers use the child-oriented word processor as a first step in introducing themselves to the technology and as a way of becoming familiar with a tool that their students will use. Many of these programs have tools for an adult level as well as a child level.

USING CONTENT SOFTWARE

An Internet search (using keywords "software reviews," "PreK software") will provide teachers with a selection of reviews of early childhood software, but these may not allow active exploration of all the software features. As with selecting books for the classroom, teachers need to preview software before the children use it—to determine whether it is appropriate, to ascertain the level of child-friendliness, and to examine which themes, activities, and standards it supports. Many software companies have free examination versions that function for a limited time. Increasingly, more developers' Web sites contain a fully functioning version of the software for limited access.

When selecting software, the following criteria should be considered:

- Content is nonviolent, age appropriate, and meets the developmental needs of the child.
- Software contains realistic representations of people (diverse cultures, genders, ages, families).
- Software is open-ended and discovery-based, and is controlled by the child.
- Software provides opportunities for children to work independently or with another child.
- Software grows with the child and becomes more complex.
- Software provides opportunities for creativity and problem solving. (Swick & Buckingham, 2000)

BEGINNING SOMEWHERE

After reviewing the software as outlined above, one might look at a catalog and become confused with the quantity of choices, with so many curriculum areas to be concerned about. As a beginning point, rather than expending a great deal of money on specific titles, look for software tools that have multiple uses. For example, Kid Pix and Kidspiration are two tools that have uses in many curriculum areas with products that can be re-purposed for a variety of settings. Kid Pix contains word processing and drawing tools that provide a creative environment for young children to record their thinking as well as to create solutions for open-ended activities. Like Kid Pix, Kidspiration can be used by the teacher for a whole-class activity or for individual and small-group work to brainstorm ideas, connect concepts, and just create. Both programs are multifaceted, easy to use, designed specifically for children, and allow students to create a myriad of products.

USING TOPIC-SPECIFIC SOFTWARE

Topic-specific software series are also available for young children, including Sammy's Science House (Edmark), Reader Rabbit (The Learning Company), and Living Books (The Learning Company). Each series has multiple titles, often spanning the curriculum, that have the same general format. Each series has been evaluated in many ways, and reviews are available on the Web. Young children react very positively to series software, as they are familiar with the format when presented with a new title. Children seem to need very little instruction and can focus on the content of the new title without being concerned about how to make it operate. Teachers have reported that children feel more comfortable exploring new features when they are familiar with the general operation. To be sure the series is what you are interested in, go on the producer's Web site, review the comments, and peruse the software sample.

FULLY INTEGRATED THEMATIC UNITS

Fully integrated thematic units were the authors' goals when developing the lessons in this book. Once teachers become familiar and comfortable with technology, the development of the theme takes a slightly different form. This book was created by combining the methods of instructional unit design previously discussed. When developing instructional units, this book's authors took into account

- national content standards for math, science, social studies, language arts, physical education, and the arts (visual, music, and dance);
- ISTE's National Education Technology Standards for Students and the PK–2 profile; and
- NAEYC's developmentally appropriate guidelines and position statements on technology, reading and writing, school readiness, and cultural diversity.

The standards provided a starting place for conceptualizing the units.

SELECTING TOPICS

As with the Reggio Emilia approach, topics for this book started with the child, focusing on the experiences all children might have. The initial brainstorming of topics began with what was known to be of interest to young children from personal experiences as parents as well as professional experiences as early childhood educators and technology specialists. The topics, therefore, include ideas that help young children make sense of the past, present, and future in the context of the world around them.

INTEGRATING THE
CURRICULUM

Selection of curriculum areas for this book's instructional units was guided by Howard Gardner's nine intelligences and the standard PK–2 curriculum. Literacy and technology are woven throughout each unit. Learning activities include individual, small group (center), and large group (circle) settings to develop self-discipline, perseverance, cooperation, and collaboration.

USING A UNIT
TEMPLATE

For this book, a unit template was designed that includes an introductory overview, objectives, standards, children's literature, Web resources, software, and teaching guidelines (a motivating activity, several ideas in different curricular areas including whole group and center activities, and assessment).

USING A
PLANNING GRID

To ensure that the array of activities covered were appropriate and comprehensive, a planning grid was developed that identified the unit topic in the far left column and identified the curriculum areas in the adjacent three columns. This grid provided a framework to brainstorm activities and ensured that all areas were covered adequately. Table 1 is an example planning grid for the **Community Places** unit in the **Communities** theme.

Community Places

TABLE 1

CURRICULAR AREA	WORKING	GETTNG AROUND	PLAYING
Art	• Create a collage of jobs	• Make picture maps	• Create a collage of places to have fun • Explore master paintings of people having fun
Gross motor		• Go on a walking tour	• Take a field trip to a fun place
Health		• Find locations of medical facilities	

continued on next page

Community Places

TABLE 1
continued

CURRICULAR AREA	WORKING	GETTNG AROUND	PLAYING
Language arts and reading	• Create stories about people on jobs and collect into books (word process)	• Gather stories of fun places to go in the community • Conduct a Web search for fun places to go in the vicinity	• Interview guests of various vocations (make videotape) • Collect stories about what the community used to be like (conduct oral histories on audiotape or word processor)
Math	• Conduct a stock market search on a major employer and follow the stock • Count how many of each vocation is in the community	• Make coordinate grid (use Tabletop Jr. software) • Graph modes of transportation for getting around the community • Measure the length of a walk, drive, etc.	• Calculate the cost of going places (use spreadsheet) • Discuss how to earn money to go someplace (use spreadsheet
Music		• Visit a local theater or concert hall	• Recite the poem "Rain, Rain, Go Away"
Science	• Explore how physics and chemistry are used in certain jobs	• Discover the effect of the environment on geography (look at digital pictures)	• Explore the physics of places—such as roller coasters • Discuss water parks and what makes them work
Social studies	• Find out about the major employers in the community— what do they do?	• Map the community • Use Yahoo! maps • Create treasure hunts • Study habitats in the community for animals and people (use digital camera, HyperStudio stack)	• Find the location of fun places using geography and mapping • Explore how families have fun, with a multicultural emphasis
Other			

Integrating Technology

How technology is integrated into a unit is highly dependent on those developing the instructional unit. Because PK–2 teachers often work together as age-level or grade-level teams, the unit development and infusion of technology is best a collaborative process. Productivity software, content-specific software, peripherals, and the Internet are all technologies that can be used with young children. What one teacher knows about word processing tools for young children may be enhanced by what another knows about a specific piece of software or a particular outstanding Web site. The Web has increasingly become a source for ideas, as it allows teachers to examine other teachers' work and commercial products. The Web was used extensively to find resources to support these units.

USING WEB-ENHANCED LEARNING EXPERIENCES FOR YOUNG CHILDREN

Using the Web with young children provides an additional learning experience that can take place in the classroom, in the computer lab, in libraries, and even at home. In most schools, the district uses filtering software that limits the type of sites that can be accessed. In addition, written statements known as acceptable use policies (AUPs) provide guidelines for student use of the Internet. It is highly recommended that all students, regardless of age, have a parent-signed AUP on file before using the Internet in the classroom.

Rather than using an adult search engine such as Google or Yahoo, teachers may find child-appropriate Web sites more easily using a child-friendly search engine. According to Mike Menchaca (2002, p. 26) in ISTE's *Multidisciplinary Units for Grades 3–5,* "The benefit of kid-safe search engines is that teachers, parents, and administrators can be certain that information found on the site will be appropriate for children. This can be a tremendous time saver for assignments that require students to find resources on the Internet. The drawback to kid-safe search engines is that, just as with Web portals, an agency can process information only so fast and newer resources added might not be available. Similarly, most search engines make determinations about the appropriateness of information but not necessarily about the educational utility of that same information. That is, a kid-safe search engine might determine that a site is safe, but that does not ensure that the information is educationally sound."

The following child-friendly search engines were used to locate Web sites for the instructional units. In addition, the Web site Kid's Search Tools (www.rcls.org/ksearch.htm) provides several child-friendly search engines for children that have been validated by librarians.

> KidsClick!: http://sunsite.berkeley.edu/KidsClick!
> Yahooligans: www.yahooligans.com
> Ask Jeeves Kids: www.ajkids.com

The KidsClick! site allows an advanced search that permits the user to set the reading level. To obtain Web sites for the units in this book, the reading level was set at "up to Grade 2" and "some or no pictures." When a specific site is suggested in a lesson for children to use, the site typically has a game, a story, or pictures related to the topic.

Some of the units in this book provide a list of sites that can be used with children. How to provide access to young children is a common dilemma. With Web sites that are intended for student access, options for access include posting the sites on a Web page or developing a word-processed document that allows hyperlinks. For example, in Word or Works, write simple instructions for the students and insert a hyperlink to take them to the place to find the answers. For the youngest children, a picture, graphic, or icon from clip art can be hyperlinked to the desired Web site.

YOU'RE NEVER FINISHED

The creative teacher always has alternatives for doing ideas proposed in any book. Where possible, blank space has been left at the end of the units for your notes and ideas.

References

Swick, K., & Buckingham, D. (2000). *Supporting learning with technology in the early childhood classroom* [Online]. Southern Early Childhood Association. Available: www.southernearlychildhood.org/position_technology.html

Menchaca, M. (2002). Everything you wanted to know about Internet filters. In *Multidisciplinary units for Grades 3–5* (pp. 21–28). Eugene, OR: ISTE.

LINDA MITCHELL AND JERI CARROLL

Project- and Problem-Based Learning— The Reggio Emilia Approach

Problem-based learning is a strategy that poses meaningful, real-life problems for students that guide their inquiry and learning. The role of the teacher in problem-based learning requires that they not only provide instruction, but rich resources, rich questions, and individual and group guidance as students work to solve the problem. The project-based approach to learning provides for an in-depth investigation of a topic worth learning more about, often originated by children's interests, with the teacher in the role of facilitator (Katz, 1994). The Reggio Emilia approach is an early childhood model that provides an opportunity for both problem-based and project-based learning in early childhood classrooms.

The Approach

The Reggio Emilia approach, developed specifically for early childhood programs, is based on an educational philosophy that views children as competent, creative, and curious learners who are intrinsically motivated to understand the complexities of the world in which they live (Rinaldi, 1993). Education is focused for each individual child in terms of the child's relation to the family, other children, teachers, the school community, and the societal environment. A basic principle of the approach is that the appropriate design of a school for early learning must be based on a community's values and beliefs and the needs of families within that community to be effective (Gandini, 1993).

The Reggio approach is grounded in constructivism with the belief that children learn best through constructing their own knowledge rather than through adult-to-child instruction (Staley, 1998). The approach is based on the theory and philosophy of leading theorists in the field of early childhood development and learning. Therefore, much about the approach is already familiar to educators of young children.

The Reggio approach includes several critical components, six of which are (1) learning spaces, (2) social exchanges, (3) projects, (4) art materials, (5) documentation, and (6) a collaborative teaching/learning style.

LEARNING SPACES

In the Reggio approach, spaces surrounding the school (neighborhoods, local landmarks) are seen as extensions of the classroom that may lead to questions or problems that become the basis for projects. In this book, we offer walks around the children's neighborhood and the school neighborhood, as well as virtual and real-world field trips to various places in the community. These, too, can be the beginnings for student-identified projects (Gandini, 1993). Students closely examine what they have in their schools, neighborhoods, and surrounding communities that help them more easily identify spaces and items needed for their learning experiences.

SOCIAL EXCHANGES

Social exchanges, such as shared activities, communication interactions, cooperation, and conflicts, are encouraged through the strategic placement of spaces, materials, and people (Gandini, 1993). Social exchanges are viewed as an important part of cognitive development. Our approach to integrating technology into early childhood classrooms suggests children often work together at a computer, sharing the responsibilities for using the mouse, keyboarding, and problem solving.

PROJECTS

In the Reggio approach, projects are in-depth investigations of a topic that evolves out of the child's interests. These interests might be triggered by engaging the child in books, activities, celebrations, or trips. Projects are ongoing, sustained, learning episodes focused on answering a question or addressing a problem. Discussions between children and between children and adults encourage children to construct and reconstruct ideas for themselves (Staley, 1998).

Helm and Katz (2001) provide several authors' examples of definitions and explanations of the project approach. One definition offered comes from Gandini (1997, p. 7):

"Projects provide the backbone of the children's and teachers' learning experiences. They are based on the strong conviction that learning by doing is of great importance and that to discuss in groups and to revisit ideas and experiences is the premier way of gaining better understanding and learning."

Additionally, Katz (1994, p. 1) offers the following definition:

"A project is an in-depth investigation of a topic worth learning more about. The investigation is usually undertaken by a small group of children within a class, sometimes by a whole class, and occasionally by an individual child. The key feature of a project is that it is a research effort deliberately focused on finding answers to questions about a topic posed either by the children, the teacher, or the teacher working with the children."

Add to those definitions and explanations the rich resources provided by technology. Research can take place in the classroom, where computers become a library through the use of the Internet. CD encyclopedias and dictionaries further guide exploration. Content-specific and age-appropriate software solves some questions and generates others.

Projects are not planned, as in themed activities or center activities, but develop as children ask questions or identify problems important to their own interests (Helm & Katz, 2001). Consequently, teachers may not know in which direction a project will head. It actually becomes a learning adventure for both the child and teacher.

The units in this book provide activities that will encourage students to identify their own projects which can subsequently be planned by teachers. The units start with a motivating activity from which questions or projects might evolve. The activities provide insight into ways to support and extend the projects and include ideas on using technology in seeking, analyzing, and communicating information.

ART MATERIALS

The creative use of space, materials, and people often centers on art mediums. Art materials are used to advance children's knowledge and to provide them with a visual mode for communicating. Simple drawing software, construction kits, and mapping programs offer students another way to investigate, understand, and communicate information.

Part of the Reggio environment is the atelier, a space used for art activities as well as ongoing projects. The atelier also provides opportunities for adults to gain an understanding of the processes by which children learn. An atelierista (art specialist) works in the atelier to prepare, provide, and provoke learning (Staley, 1998; Vecchi, 1993). The addition of appropriate technology to these spaces increases the methods and tools available to the teacher and the students.

DOCUMENTATION

Documentation of the learning and teaching process through slides, videotapes, photographs, children's art work and other products, anecdotal records, and transcriptions of children's words is seen as crucial in the Reggio approach (Vecchi, 1993). Documentation is used to provide evidence of children's interests, learning, and developmental skill levels; to inform parents and community members of school activities; and to aid in teacher inservice training that leads to further curriculum development and program improvement. Technology is already a critical element of this component. Photos, artifacts, and transcriptions of children's work can be saved in digital portfolios for the enjoyment of families and the assessment required by schools.

COLLABORATIVE TEACHING/LEARNING STYLE

The Reggio approach uses collaborative planning teams of parents, teachers, the atelierista, and the children to create the curriculum. All have input into the planning of learning activities. The use of e-mail; course software that includes grade books, discussion boards, and online chats; as well as school and teacher home pages increases the possibilities for this collaboration. This book provides ideas to motivate and support students, teachers, and parents in planning for the student-generated projects.

Classroom Vignette

Billie wanted so badly to bring his new pet, a goldfish, into the preschool classroom. Following the child's lead, Mrs. Smith set up a day for "show and tell." Sure enough, Billie brought the goldfish, equipped with a round bowl full of colored gravel and one piece of green, plastic foliage. To Mrs. Smith's amazement, the rest of her preschoolers, eight typically developing and two with special needs (one with Down syndrome and one with gifted abilities), were quite interested in Billie's goldfish. Many asked questions, such as: "Can I hold him?", "Where did he come from?", "Does he make any noise?" Using the project approach, Mrs. Smith asked the children if they would like to learn more about goldfish.

The next few weeks were full of fun projects, including reading about goldfish in books, searching for information about goldfish on the Web, seeing the various kinds of goldfish (**www.goldfishguy.com/Fish_Pictures/Fish_Pictures.htm**), eating goldfish crackers (**www.pfgoldfish.com**), examining goldfish artwork (**www.allposters.com/gallery.asp?aid=99864&c=c&search=7045**), and creating elaborate goldfish and fishbowls as artwork. The teacher even located the Goldfish Society of America (**www.goldfishsociety.org**).

One important part of the goldfish project came when Mrs. Smith put 10 live goldfish in her water table. The children were so excited. They began by simply watching the fish, but eventually the children began touching the goldfish. One child with special needs continued to try to pick up the goldfish. Other children became worried for the safety of the goldfish because of information they had learned from books and from the Web, so they worked collaboratively on how to solve the problem. Just how could goldfish be touched? They decided they could touch the goldfish with one finger and only on their tails. It was also OK to follow a goldfish in the water with one finger, but not to catch it. Still concerned with the safety of the goldfish, another child suggested that they should not keep the goldfish in the water table because they would probably die.

After going back to the computer and investigating places within the community, the children decided it was best to provide an environment for the goldfish in their classroom that was sensitive to the needs of the goldfish. The responsibility of taking care of the goldfish—placing fresh plants in the bowl, changing the water regularly, testing the water temperature, and increasing the oxygen level with a bubbler—left the children feeling quite successful in their goldfish project.

References

Gandini, L. (1993). Educational and caring spaces. In C. Edwards, L. Gandini, & G. Forman (Eds.), *The hundred languages of children* (pp. 135–149). Norwood, NJ: Ablex.

Gandini, L. (1997). Foundations of the Reggio Emilia approach. In J. Hendricks (Ed.), *First steps toward teaching the Reggio way* (pp. 14–25). Upper Saddle River, NJ: Prentice Hall.

Helm, J. H., & Katz, L. (2001). *Young investigators: The project approach in the early years.* New York: Teachers College Press.

Katz, L. G. (1994, June). *Images from the world.* Paper presented at the Study Seminar on the Experience of the Municipal Infant-Toddler Centers and Preprimary Schools of Reggio Emilia, Italy.

Rinaldi, C. (1993). The emergent curriculum and social constructivism. In C. Edwards, L. Gandini, & G. Forman (Eds.), *The hundred languages of children* (pp. 101–111). Norwood, NJ: Ablex.

Staley, L. (1998). Beginning to implement the Reggio philosophy. *Young Children, 53*(5), 20–25.

Vecchi, V. (1993). The role of the atelierista. In C. Edwards, L. Gandini, & G. Forman (Eds.), *The hundred languages of children* (pp. 119–131). Norwood, NJ: Ablex.

chapter 3

LINDA MITCHELL

Supporting Learning Differences Using Assistive Technology

All young children need to interact with their learning environments to achieve growth and development. Technology has great potential for supporting exploration and learning in young children, including those who have developmental delays or diagnosed disabilities (Stremel, 2000). Many assistive technologies (AT) designed for children with special needs are also appropriate in the early childhood classroom.

Young children developing fine motor, reading, and listening skills at different ages can be assisted by technologies such as screen readers, touch screens, alternative pointing devices, and software with audio cues. Clicker 4 is a verbal reading and writing program that uses pictures and speech to help students write and read sentences. Screen-reading software that reads the words aloud on a screen can be used for students with low vision. This software can also help emerging readers use software and the Internet. A pen scanner (a small pen-shaped tool that scans written text) can be used like a highlighter. A student can slide the pen across the words in a book or magazine and the pen scans the text. The text can then be transferred to a computer and read aloud or viewed as type and printed. A touch screen, graphic tablet, or other alternative pointing device can allow young students to navigate through computer menus much easier. Table 2, on the following two pages, examines a variety of assistive technologies.

All of these technologies are appropriate for young children, and they may be especially useful for children with diagnosed difficulties. Many children with learning differences need assistive technology to help them become more independent and to increase their learning opportunities. Steps in understanding and using AT include (1) defining the assistive technology, (2) assessing for needs, (3) planning its use, (4) funding, (5) teaching its use, and (6) implementing it.

Defining Assistive Technology

Assistive technology is defined in the Individuals with Disabilities Education Act Amendments of 1997 (IDEA, Sec. 300.5) as "any item, piece of equipment, or product system, whether acquired commercially off the shelf, modified, or customized, that is used to increase, maintain, or improve the functional capabilities of a child with a disability." Although AT can include a variety of devices targeted to meet individual needs for children with specific disabilities, such as hearing loss (e.g., hearing aides, personal FM units, TDDs, and closed-

Assistive Technologies Meeting Student Needs

TABLE 2

AT DEVICE	PURPOSE OF THE DEVICE	ASSISTS CHILDREN WITH THESE NEEDS
Screen readers and talking Web browsers	These devices read aloud the text on a screen. This includes the text in a word processing program such as Word, the text on a Web page, and the text within some software programs.	Low vision/blind Learning disabilities Auditory learners Cognitive delays Beginning readers Communication delays
Touch screens	These devices replace the mouse or other pointing device and allow the user to touch the place on the screen that contains the link or menu instead of using a mouse.	Motor disabilities (especially those with fine motor issues)
Alternative pointing devices	These tools replace the mouse as an input or selection device. These can be touch screens, switches (that can be operated by mouth, foot, eyes, or hands), or graphic tablets that allow handwriting or drawing with a pen-like pointer device.	Motor disabilities (such as those with cerebral palsy)
Software with audio cues	This tool works similarly to a screen reader but the cues are embedded within the software, which allows the menus and other text to be read aloud by the computer.	Low vision/blind Learning disabilities Cognitive delays Auditory learners Communication delays
Alternative mouse cursors or pointers	The cursor can be changed to a larger size or to an icon other than a pointer and show the path it is taking across the screen. The speed at which the mouse must be clicked or at which the mouse rolls can be changed.	Low vision Learning disabilities Cognitive delays
Pen scanner	This is a small scanner in a pen shape that can be used like a highlighter in a book or magazine. The pen scanner is slid across the text, and the text is scanned or digitized into the pen. This digital text can then be transferred to the computer to be read aloud by a screen reader, displayed in a larger font in a word processing program, or printed out.	Learning disabilities Beginning readers Cognitive delays Communication delays
Graphic tablet	This alternative pointing device allows handwriting and drawing to be entered into the computer using a pen-like pointer.	Motor disabilities Cognitive delays Communication delays
Screen magnifiers	This software enlarges information. Most screen magnification software has the flexibility to magnify the full screen, part of the screen, or a particular screen location (by providing a magnifying glass view of the area around the cursor or pointer).	Low vision Motor disabilities Cognitive delays

continued on next page

Assistive Technologies Meeting Student Needs

**TABLE 2
continued**

AT DEVICE	PURPOSE OF THE DEVICE	ASSISTS CHILDREN WITH THESE NEEDS
Small or large mouse	Mice come in different sizes, with different touch buttons and different configurations. Some mice have balls or wheels built within the mouse that are rolled underneath the mouse. Other mice, called trackballs, have the wheels on the top and allow for the thumb or fingers to roll the wheel. Some do not have wheels or balls—they use an optical sensor and are called optical mice. They are more precise, easier to use, and don't pick up dirt and grime like mice balls. Some mice are squeezable rather than push-button.	Motor disabilities Cognitive delays
Voice to text	Speech or voice recognition software translates the spoken voice into text. The software must be trained to individual voices and dialects. The software can be installed on a computer or a handheld device.	Low vision Motor disabilities Cognitive delays Communication delays
Text to voice	This is what screen-reading software does—it takes written text and changes it to voice. This task can be accomplished with screen-reading software if the text is already digitized or on the computer (one example is the software program Clicker 4). The task can be accomplished by a pen scanner if the text is in print and must be digitized first.	Low vision Motor disabilities Cognitive delays Beginning readers Communication delays
Special needs options within the operating system	Both Windows and the Mac OS have options and preferences that can be changed to be helpful for special needs. The cursor can be changed to a larger size or to an icon other than a pointer and show the path it is taking across the screen. The speed at which the mouse must be clicked or at which the mouse rolls can be changed. Both Windows XP and Mac OS have speech capabilities built in.	Low vision Motor disabilities Cognitive delays Beginning readers
Alternative keyboards	One alternative is a skin that is laid over the traditional keyboard to make the letters bigger and easier to see. Intellikeys is a keyboard that is made of a few pictures than can be pushed to navigate or control a computer. These pictures or overlays can be changed depending on the type of software or the type of student using it.	Low vision Motor disabilities Cognitive delays
Alternative printer	A Braille embosser is a printer that creates embossed text in Braille. A Braille translation software program translates the text from the computer into Braille and "prints" to the Braille embosser.	Low vision/blind
Refreshable Braille displays	This is an electromechanical device that renders Braille dots with tiny, independently controlled pins. The device reads the text that a computer sends to the monitor and displays it as Braille.	Low vision/blind

caption television) or cerebral palsy (e.g., scooters, walkers, manual or powered wheelchairs), other categories of AT include devices that meet basic learning needs for children with delays or diagnosed disabilities. Examples include electronic communication devices, laptop computers, speech synthesizers, computer software designed for early learning experiences (e.g., math, reading, spelling, writing), touch screens for computer monitors, keyboard overlays, switches or joysticks to maneuver a computer, and computer simulations.

Assessment and Assistive Technology

The first step in identifying which AT devices may be useful for any individual child is to assess the child to determine current strengths, abilities, challenges, and needs. An AT device should be considered only following assessment that has determined a device's ability to improve the child's performance and function within his or her daily routines and learning environments. When selecting AT devices it is important to consider family members' desires and priorities for the child (Simmons, 2001). Bowser and Reed's (1998) outline offers a process that can guide a child's assessment team in identifying AT needs and devices.

Planning for Assistive Technology

After identifying the specific AT devices that are needed by a child, those devices need to be written into a child's Individual Education Program or Individualized Family Service Plan (for children who qualify for early intervention or special education). This plan becomes the guide for providing AT within a child's specific special education services, supports, and accommodations. Additionally, one needs to consider how to fund the AT devices.

Funding Assistive Technology

Paying for AT devices requires both family members and professionals collaboratively locating possible sources of funding. Some families have insurance companies that allow for AT devices, particularly if prescribed by a physician. For families not supported by private insurance, solutions to funding problems may need to be more creative. Although IDEA requires that AT be provided when needed, it does not require local education agencies or infant-toddler programs to purchase all required items (IDEA, 1997). In fact, local education agencies and infant-toddler programs are typically only payers of last resort. Other possible sources to investigate, but which usually require eligibility to be established first, include community development disability programs (typically located through the state Social and Rehabilitation Services Agency), community service organizations (e.g., Kiwanis, Knights of Columbus), churches, nonprofit organizations (e.g., United Way, March of Dimes), and Medicare. Luckily, many states have AT lending library programs so that a device can be borrowed and tried out before one decides whether to purchase it.

Teaching the Use of Assistive Technology

Once an AT device is obtained, its use must be taught, not only to the child but also to family members, professionals, peers, and others who interact often with the child. This is especially true if the AT device is used for communication. Opportunities for practice must be incorporated into the child's daily routine (Simmons, 2001). Many times, the more functional the use of the device, the more quickly it is learned and used by the child.

Implementing Assistive Technology

Children provided with AT demonstrate positive gains in many of their developmental domains (Hutinger & Johanson, 2000). For example, providing a child with a computer to use for interactions between the child and an adult or the child and other children opens up opportunities to develop skills not as easily obtainable through other ways. Interactive computer software such as Arthur's Reading Race or Just Grandpa and Me (Learning Services) offers early literacy experiences, receptive and expressive language opportunities, and social friendship building. Another software resource is the *Children's Software Revue* (www2.childrenssoftware.com). This online newsletter provides reviews of the latest children's software and provides recommendations for its use. Whether implementing use of the computer to generate developmental skill improvement, to increase social interactions, or to better assess a child's abilities, it can make a world of difference for the child.

Concluding Thoughts

Assistive technology, whether used as a tool for moving, speaking, or learning or as a service for children who qualify for it in early intervention or special education programs, can help young children become more independent throughout their daily lives in all of their environments. The use of AT can create situations where children who did not or could not participate before can become active participants. It can lead to improvement in a child's personal efficacy, new friendships, new knowledge and skills, and even provide a way for a child to demonstrate to others what they may have known all along, but did not have a way of showing. Assistive technology is more than integrating computers into learning environments. It is a device, a tool, that is brought into a child's life that facilitates learning and functioning in new and more effective ways.

References

Bowser, G., & Reed, P. (1998). *Education tech points*. Winchester, OR: Author.

Children's Software Revue. (2002). [Online]. Available: www2.childrenssoftware.com

Hutinger, P. L., & Johanson, J. (2000). Implementing and maintaining an effective early childhood comprehensive technology system. *Topics in Early Childhood Special Education, 20*(3), 159–173.

Individuals with Disabilities Education Act Amendments of 1997, Public Law 105–117.

Learning Services. (2002). *Learning services spring 2002 multimedia technology showcase catalog.* Eugene, OR: Author.

Learning Services. (2002). *Living Books* [Online]. Available: www.learningservicesinc.com

National Center to Improve Practice in Special Education Through Technology, Media, and Materials. (1998). [Online]. Available: www2.edc.org/NCIP/default.htm

National Information Center for Children and Youth with Disabilities. (1989). Assistive technology: Becoming an informed consumer. *News Digest, 13* [Online]. Available: www.nichcy.org/pubs1.htm

Quality Indicators for Assistive Technology (QIAT) Consortium. (n.d.). *Quality indicators for assistive technology* [Online]. Available: http://sweb.uky.edu/~jszaba0/QIAT.html

Rehabilitation Engineering and Assistive Technology Society of North America (RESNA). (2002). *Technical assistance project: State contact list* [Online]. Available: www.resna.org/taproject/at/statecontacts.html

Simmons, S. (2001, November). *Assistive technology strategies for early childhood educators.* Paper presented at the Midwest Faculty Symposium, Kansas City, MO.

Stremel, K. (2000). Recommended practices in technology applications. In S. Sandall, M. E. McLean, & Smith, B. J. (Eds.), *DEC recommended practices in early intervention/early childhood special education.* Longmont, CO: Sopris West.

chapter 4

M. G. (PEGGY) KELLY

Assessing Early Learners

How do you know whether your students are learning? The way teachers assess student learning is continuing to receive considerable attention from researchers, parents, administrators, and government. Chapter 4 focuses on three topics important to the issue of assessment as it relates to the material in this book. Teachers need to know how to assess learning, how to assess the way technology is facilitating learning, and how to assess students' overall understanding of the content in the units provided in section 2.

Assessing Learning

Assessment in early childhood education has been a consistent topic of scholarly investigation and debate. The term assessment has many definitions. This discussion concentrates on the following definitions:

"Assessment is the process of observing, recording, and otherwise documenting the work children do and how they do it, as a basis for a variety of educational decisions that affect the child. Assessment is integral to curriculum and instruction." (National Association for the Education of Young Children [NAEYC] & National Association of Early Childhood Specialists in State Departments of Education, 1990)

"Assessment is the process of gathering information about children in order to make decisions about their education. Teachers obtain useful information about children's knowledge, skills, and progress by observing, documenting, and reviewing children's work over time. Ongoing assessment that occurs in the context of classroom activities can provide an accurate, fair, and representative picture of children's abilities and progress." (Dodge, Jablon, & Bickart, 1994, p. 181)

"Assessment involves the multiple steps of collecting data on a child's development and learning, determining its significance in light of the program goals and objectives, incorporating the information into planning for individuals and programs, and communicating the findings to parents and other involved parties." (Hills, 1992, p. 43)

A combination of the above definitions provides a holistic view of the complex process of assessment in the early childhood classroom and how easily it can be misused and abused. In discussing technology use in the early learning classroom, we would be remiss if issues of accountability, standardized testing, and performance-based assessment were not considered.

ACCOUNTABILITY MOVEMENT

With the passage of the No Child Left Behind legislation and the Enhancing Education through Technology Act of 2001, students in eighth grade will now be assessed on their technology competence. In an effort to make educators accountable for students' performance, benchmark assessments have become part of the funding mechanism by Congress as well as mandated by state legislatures. Although the eighth grade seems far from the realm of the early childhood educator, the foundation for meeting those content and technology competencies begins in the early childhood classroom. Developmentally appropriate experiences throughout a child's education can make what seem to be onerous assessment benchmarks more attainable. It is the definition of "developmentally appropriate" that makes creating curriculum for the early childhood classroom a difficult task in an atmosphere of accountability and "high stakes" testing.

As educators, we know that stakeholders in the education process have high demands for accountability for their tax dollars and the learning of students in public schools. The pressure for "high stakes" assessment has spawned movements in some districts to ban all subjects except for the basic skills of reading and mathematics. Although requiring accountability for the judicious expenditure of tax dollars and having expectations of student learning are appropriate, the manner in which these have played out in some settings has had an enormous effect on teaching and learning in the classroom to the detriment of long-term student outcomes. Early childhood teaching requires a multidisciplinary approach to learning. It is the context for the learning, such as science, social studies, art, and music, that provides the schema for children to understand their world. Consequently, the mandate to focus on only literacy and mathematics has made compliance difficult in supporting the learning of young children. With this understanding in mind, the authors of this book created units with activities in many disciplines to support student learning.

STANDARDIZED TESTING

The NAEYC position statement on standardized testing makes it very clear that for children under the age of 8, the detrimental and often misused results of standardized tests should cause educators to question the financial expenditure and time spent conducting them. Although the intended school use of such measures is to provide a common frame of reference for student performance, the results for young children are very suspect because of their rapid intellectual growth and highly influenced social and emotional nature. The NAEYC position statement focuses on the "utility criterion," as follows:

"The purpose of testing must be to improve service for children and ensure that children benefit from their educational experiences. Decisions about testing and assessment instruments must be based on the usefulness of the assessment procedure for improving services to children and improving outcomes for children." (NAEYC, 1987, p. 2)

The utility criterion can be applied to any type of assessment intended for young children. Whether it is observational instruments, rubrics, or other performance indicators, a beneficial purpose of the assessment and a clear definition of its use in improving instruction and outcomes for children should be the guiding principles.

PERFORMANCE ASSESSMENT

Examining student performance has become a well-recognized form of assessment for all children. Early childhood educators have always used performance assessment, as young children are not able to perform on the traditional pencil/paper style of assessment. The early learning classroom is replete with opportunities to observe children and their actions. Checklists and observational tools abound in early childhood, often provided by school districts and states as ways to monitor student progress.

Performance assessment results are often presented in the form of a portfolio. As a purposeful collection of student work, a portfolio can be used to show how a student meets a specific set of standards or how the student has grown over time. Rather than a random collection of all student work, the portfolio contains evidence of growth in specific areas with well-articulated criteria.

A portfolio can contain digital files of student work as well as video and audio clips. Increasingly, school districts are examining digital means for retaining student portfolios as a way to document student achievement over time. Saving student work in digital format allows teachers to retain high-quality evidence of student performance as well as to pass that evidence on to families. As opposed to a paper-based portfolio that has only one high-quality copy, a digital portfolio can be shared with others in many ways.

FROM ARTIFACTS TO EVIDENCE When observing children in the classroom, the project, drawing, printout, and so forth are considered artifacts that can be used to show how a student is progressing. Artifacts become evidence of student achievement when a rationale or context is attached to the evidence. Those artifacts not already in a digital format can be scanned, photographed, or taped to become part of a digital portfolio. Early writing and drawings can be scanned and filed along with pictures, videos, and slideshows created in Kid Pix or other productivity software. Digital video documenting fine and gross motor skills, singing, playing with others, and reciting poetry all find their way into the digital portfolio. All of these artifacts can be dated and transferred to a CD or DVD and kept to document the steps and progression of development. Many teachers attach sticky notes (even digital stickies) to artifacts to capture the student's thoughts on how a particular artifact exemplifies meeting a goal or standard. It is important to make decisions early in the year about which artifacts are important to collect, while being open to collecting others that happen to be good examples.

OBSERVATION   Because young children are so active and exhibit many behaviors that are being monitored in the early years, checklists and observational tools are important and readily available for most milestones from birth to 8 years of age, as a quick Internet search on "developmental milestones" or "ages and stages" will show. Increasingly, student checklists and observational tools are being loaded into personal digital assistants (PDAs) as an easy way to maintain records. Imagine a skills checklist such as the Learning Accomplishment Profile, available from the Chapel Hill Training-Outreach Project, Inc., in booklets (**www.chtop.com/assprod. htm**) or in HTML or pdf formats (**www.unc.edu/~cory/autism-info/lapinfo.html**), or the Brigance Inventory of Early Development (Curriculum Associates, **www. curricassoc.com/order/**) loaded for each child onto the teacher's PDA. The PDA can be carried in the teacher's pocket and used whenever appropriate to access a database of each student's individual record. Upon return to the room or office, the data can be downloaded into the computer and synchronized with other data kept on students. When used appropriately, the information entered in a PDA can provide valuable information for teachers to examine their own practices as well as to monitor the progress of their students.

RUBRICS   With the recognition of performance-based assessment, the use of rubrics has increased markedly. Different from a checklist, a rubric provides a guideline for assessing student performance or work based on specified criteria and levels of quality. Rubrics come in three, four, or five levels, and can be organized by specific criteria or collapsed into a holistic form. Well-done rubrics are difficult to write and yet can be easy to use. Electronic banks of rubrics are available that can be used as a starting point. One source is Rubistar (**http://rubistar.4teachers.org**). The rubrics at this site are developed by teachers and are available for sharing. The user can edit the rubrics provided or develop new ones using some of the criteria suggested.

Rubrics have been effectively used in assessing the work of emerging readers and writers. For example, Northwest Regional Educational Lab has developed a rubric, Six Traits Assessment for Beginning Writers, that enables teachers to examine student work in the dimensions of ideas, organization, voice, word choice, sentence fluency, and conventions (**www.nwrel.org/assessment/pdfGeneral/BWC.pdf**). The work is rated as experimenting, emerging, developing, capable, or experienced. It is assessment tools such as these that enable teachers and parents to monitor the growth of a child's learning in ways that easily communicate accomplishments and expectations.

Assessment Using Technology

Assessment in the area of technology takes two forms: (1) assessment of the learning that takes places as a result of the use of technology in the learning process and (2) assessment of student technology competence while learning content. Each is important, as meeting both the content-area standards and the NETS for Students happens simultaneously when technology has been integrated into classroom practice. However, the purpose of the various assessment checklists and rubrics should not be confused. Students and parents should be clearly informed about the purpose of the unit of instruction, the intended outcomes for both content and technology competence, and the assessment criteria. Clear articulation of the purpose of a project and the assessment procedure helps students and parents focus their attention on what the teacher feels is important.

ASSESSMENT OF TECHNOLOGY-RICH LEARNING

The use of technology for learning may be examined in two ways: (1) using technology as a tool for learning content in deeper and more meaningful ways and (2) using technology as an assessment tool to obtain information about learning. Assessment of learning in the technology-rich early childhood classroom is no different than assessment of learning in any other classroom. In these situations, content standards and a holistic look at the development of the child are taken into account. What can be different are the manner in which the assessment takes place and the artifacts that are collected.

The use of technology in the learning process can provide access to information and tools for clarifying thinking. As stated earlier, the selection of the tools and resources is paramount to making the learning situation meaningful. For example, young children's interaction with a Web site that contains interesting and relevant information provides many opportunities for incidental learning in which the children are in control of the direction of inquiries as interests are pursued and discussion takes place. "When used in appropriate ways (and this cannot be overemphasized), computers not only support and enhance young children's creativity, self-esteem, and cooperative learning, but they also help them develop a fearless, joyful attitude toward all learning" (Thouvenelle, n.d.). Therefore, although observation checklists and rubrics are created to focus on the intended learning, it is important to maintain a narrative component that enables the teacher to record the incidental learning that is observed and to take reflective time to record teaching and learning outcomes—adjusting the assessment instruments for future use.

In addition to using technology as a resource, young students may use technology to demonstrate their understanding of concepts in ways that traditional pencil and paper or even the ever-necessary teacher observation cannot capture. When students' performance is videotaped, when student artifacts are produced on the computer using the powerful tools available for young children, and when students are able to respond to questions or record data using PDAs, technology can provide more complex information than a traditional means of assessment. The technology becomes a tool of assessment in addition to a tool for learning.

In each of these situations, the technology itself needs to be assessed in terms of its contribution to the learning or ability to capture student performance. The underlying reason for assessing the use of technology is to determine whether the technology is a contributor, neutral, or a detriment to learning. After removing the typical time it takes to introduce and become comfortable with the new tool, does the technology provide positive outcomes for teaching and learning? Can those outcomes be identified? The ability to answer these questions will provide data for justifying or increasing the expense and time to use the technology. Keeping good records that include observations, student artifacts, and assessment rubrics will help when those data are required.

ASSESSMENT OF TECHNOLOGY USE

As discussed in the Introduction, achieving the ISTE NETS for Students requires young learners to have experiences using technology in their learning environment. As students actively participate in the experiences described in the themes and units, assessment of how they are developing in meeting the ISTE NETS should be recorded.

Within every theme of this book, opportunities exist for students to demonstrate meeting each of the PK–2 performance indicators in a developmentally appropriate manner. A checklist can be created for the profile and attached to the content assessment for each theme or unit. The degree to which students are able to perform each task is dependent on their developmental level and the resources available. A modified checklist in the form of a rubric is provided in Table 3 using examples from the unit **Things That Go on Land** in the **On the Go** theme. This checklist was created for a kindergarten or first-grade classroom for autumn completion. A checklist or rubric is highly individual to the setting. This one is provided only as a sample.

Technology Rubric

TABLE 3

NOTE: This technology rubric is for unit **Things that Go on Land** in the **On the Go** theme. It is designed for kindergarten or first grade.

PERFORMANCE INDICATOR	APPROACHES TARGET	MEETS TARGET	EXCEEDS TARGET
1—Student uses input devices and output devices to successfully operate computers, VCRs, audiotapes, and other technologies.		• Uses Kid Pix • Operates Roamer Robot • Operates Museum of Buses slideshow	
2—Student uses a variety of media and technology resources for directed and independent learning activities.		• Uses buttoned Web resources	
3—Student communicates about technology using developmentally appropriate and accurate terminology.		• Participates in discussions throughout unit • Provides directions to Roamer Robot	
4—Student uses developmentally appropriate multimedia resources to support learning.		• Operates student-created slideshows • Listens to Web-played music	
5—Student works cooperatively and collaboratively with peers, family members, and others when using technology in the classroom.		• Demonstrates cooperative and collaborative behavior at computer center	

continued on next page

Technology Rubric

TABLE 3
continued

PERFORMANCE INDICATOR	APPROACHES TARGET	MEETS TARGET	EXCEEDS TARGET
6—Student demonstrates positive social and ethical behaviors when using technology.		• Shows positive social and ethical behavior in large and small group situations	
7—Student practices responsible use of technology systems and software.		• Behaves responsibly at computer center • Takes turn shutting computer down and storing computer software and peripherals	
8—Student creates developmentally appropriate multimedia products with support from teachers, family members, or student partners.		• Contributes to class slideshows • Creates slideshow pages on vehicles—includes writing on pages	
9—Student uses technology resources for problem solving, communication, and illustration of thoughts, ideas, and stories.		• Creates Web dictionary • Visits buttoned Web sites, recording essential learning • Uses graphing program to record results of Lego car run down inclined plane. Makes generalizations from results • Creates Kid Pix safety poster	
10—Student gathers information and communicates with others using telecommunications, with support from teachers, family members, or student partners.		• No opportunity in this unit	

Notice that as the unit is written, there is no opportunity to use telecommunications embedded in the activities of the unit. Several first-grade teachers added telecommunications opportunities to the unit naturally, as some of the parents had e-mail addresses. Students in the classroom sent their slideshows to their parents and grandparents as another way to share their experiences. As stated earlier, the units act only as a starting point for embedding the technology in learning.

Assessment in Units

The themes and supporting units have been designed to include many opportunities for teachers to assess student performance. As a result of the multidisciplinary and activity-based approach to conveying key concepts in the units, teachers are able to collect student artifacts, observe students working, and obtain performance-based information to assess student comprehension.

FORMATIVE ASSESSMENT

To meet formative assessment needs, each unit contains many opportunities for observing students at work. As an example, examine the **My Life** unit. Opportunities for general and concept-based observation are present in the following ways:

ART
Facial awareness (developing awareness of facial features and location)
Fine motor skills (multiple opportunities for drawing)
Verbal communication (recording description)
Language development (describing family event)
Computer skills (using mouse in drawing)

GROSS MOTOR
Gross motor skills (going through obstacle course)
Right/left orientation (following the directions in movement and dance)
Awareness of body part (playing Simon Says, "head," etc.)

MUSIC
Auditory processing of music and language (participating in sing-along)
Self-image (discussing Marsupial Sue)

LANGUAGE ARTS AND READING
Writing and related skills (creating autobiography)
Fine motor skills (writing autobiography)
Spelling and writing of name (doing acrostic poem and other activities)
Knowing address (writing a letter to self)

Many situations in the units provide opportunities for observation. The checklist used for these observations is determined by the grade level, time of year, and district and state developmental guidelines. No matter what the checklist consists of, it is important that teachers be aware that students at this age level learn and change quickly. The moment at which the observation takes place is merely a snapshot of the performance at that time.

END OF UNIT ASSESSMENT

At the conclusion of every unit is an assessment activity with associated rubrics. The assessment activity is designed to be used for both observation and collection of artifacts that show student progress. Like an observation, the assessment activity is a snapshot of the performance at the time it is given. Other forms of assessment, such as the formative observations and activity artifacts, should also be taken into consideration when examining student learning at the conclusion of the unit.

Two rubrics have been developed for each unit. One is designed specifically for younger learners and one is designed for more able learners. Younger learners may be preschool, kindergarten, or, in general, students who have not yet mastered reading and writing. The data obtained in marking the rubric are generally acquired through observations. The rubric designed for more able learners is for students who are able to read and write independently. The data obtained for marking this rubric focus more on the artifacts produced but may require some observation.

RUBRIC FOR YOUNGER LEARNERS

NOTE: This is the rubric for the **My Life** unit in the **All About Me** theme.

Because this rubric is designed for observations, the rubric column headings require the teacher to assess how the student is approaching the task and what is apparent at the conclusion of the task. Here is an example:

CRITERIA	NOT INTERESTED	TRYING IT	WORKING ON IT	GOT IT!	HELPING OTHERS
Selected three important ways he or she has grown and learned					
Each growth is sequenced					
Labels are provided throughout the picture					

The rubric scale assesses developmental competence with any concept, using these five categories:

NOT INTERESTED Student makes no attempt to complete the criteria, indicating that the concept is not understood. If the lack of interest can be attributed to a lack of motivation, the activity should be adjusted to increase motivation for a more accurate assessment. However, sometimes the lack of interest is evident when the student does not have the prerequisite skills to be successful even when trying.

TRYING IT There is evidence that the child attempted to show what was asked but it is not clear if there is understanding. The task requires more experience or instruction.

WORKING ON IT The child understands the directions and is still trying to effectively demonstrate what has been asked. There may be some confusion in the child's mind. Task completion may simply require more time.

GOT IT! It is clear that the child understands and is able to act on the understanding.

HELPING OTHERS The child is confident in his or her understanding to the point of wanting to help others. With a friend, the child may use the phrases "Let me help you" or "Let me show you how." Note that children who are often in this situation need to be coached on how not to do the work for others.

RUBRIC FOR MORE
ABLE LEARNERS

The assessment activity and associated rubric can typically be used for first- and second-grade students who have reading and writing skills. The rubric column headings are descriptive of the levels of achievement—approaches target, meets target, and exceeds target. Note that there is no heading for "none" or "no evidence demonstrated." It is a philosophical decision not to have a negative assessment column. When children do not demonstrate the criteria in any form, the teacher needs to determine the appropriateness of the activity for the student and, if it is appropriate, may need to remind the student that there was no evidence presented—and to try again. Questions to clarify their thinking may urge them forward. However, the activity may require significantly more instruction, thus providing another opportunity for success.

Unlike the rubrics designed for younger learners, the rubrics for this developmental level are descriptive for each criterion and level. Here is an example:

NOTE: This is the rubric for the **Changes in My Neighborhood** unit in the **Communities** theme.

CRITERIA	APPROACHES TARGET	MEETS TARGET	EXCEEDS TARGET
Change needed	Is not related to an area discussed in class or does not make sense for the community	Is clearly identified with extensive	Is clearly identified and a rationale is provided from a variety of perspectives
Plan to make the change	Is provided but is not clearly related to the problem or does not make sense	Is provided and makes sense	Is provided in great detail and/or has unique and creative solutions
Results	Are identified but may not be reasonable or make a positive contribution to the community	Are identified, reasonable, and make a positive contribution to the community	Are clearly identified, take a unique and creative perspective on the problem, are reasonable, and make a positive contribution to the community
Pictures or labels	Are distracting or not related to the proposed results	Make a positive contribution to understanding the issue	Extend and further clarify the understanding of the issue

References

Chapel Hill Training-Outreach Project, Inc. (n.d.). *Learning accomplishment profile* [Online]. Available: www.chtop.com/assprod.htm and www.unc.edu/~cory/autism-info/lapinfo.html

Curriculum Associates. (n.d.). [Online]. Available: www.curricassoc.com/order/

Dodge, D. T., Jablon, J. R., & Bickart, T. S. (1994). *Constructing curriculum for the primary grades*. Washington, DC: Teaching Strategies.

Hills, T. W. (1992). Reaching potentials through appropriate assessment. In S. Bredekamp & T. Rosegrant (Eds.), *Reaching potentials: Appropriate curriculum and assessment for young children* (Vol. 1, pp. 43–63). Washington, DC: National Association for the Education of Young Children.

National Association for the Education of Young Children (NAEYC). (1987). *Standardized testing of young children 3 through 8 years of age* [Online]. Available: www.naeyc.org/resources/position_statements/pstestin.htm

National Association for the Education of Young Children & National Association of Early Childhood Specialists in State Departments of Education. (1990). *Guidelines for appropriate curriculum content and assessment in programs serving children ages 3 through 8* [Online]. Available: www.naeyc.org/resources/position_statements/pscuras.htm

Northwest Regional Educational Lab. (n.d.). *Beginning writers' continuum* [Online]. Available: www.nwrel.org/assessment/pdfGeneral/BWC.pdf

Rubistar. (2002). [Online]. Available: http://rubistar.4teachers.org/

Thouvenelle, S. (n.d.). *Do computers belong in early childhood settings?* [Online]. Available: www.earlychildhood.com/Articles/index.cfm?FuseAction=Articles&A=23

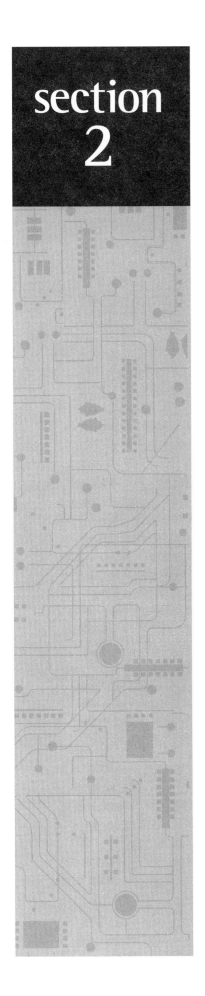

section 2

Resource Units

"Life is what happens
to you while you are
busy making plans."
—John Lennon
(1940–1980)

All About Me

The **All About Me** theme takes children from studying about themselves in the context of their friends and family, noticing similarities and differences, to looking at their role in the home and school. The purpose of this unit is to raise self-esteem and awareness of the diversity of the people we interact with every day. The activities in the unit build on notions of cooperation, helping others, and the interdependence of all the other people at home and at school.

The following standards-based curriculum units enable students to explore the concepts of interdependence by focusing on themselves as they take part in the following activities. Students:

- Use multiple technologies to create self-portraits that contribute to a class slideshow.
- Investigate the meaning of their own name and why their parents selected the name.
- Interview their parents to learn more about family traditions.
- Make a map of their own house, then explore the White House over the Internet.
- View and contribute to the school Web site.
- Make a map of the school.

Unit Tools

SPOTLIGHT ON
TECHNOLOGY

Productivity Software: A children's writing and drawing program allows students to create a class slideshow with drawings, photos, and sound. In other activities they take digital photos of their obstacle course and put the pictures in the right order in the slideshow.

E-mail: Students e-mail family members to gather information about themselves, their families, and the experiences of the family members when they were young.

Graphing: A children's graphing program is used extensively in this unit as a way to help students make generalizations about data and note the similarities and differences. Students compare information about physical characteristics, the number of people in the family, favorite things, attendance at school, and so forth. The electronic graphing program provides the opportunity to record and display the data quickly, and to translate the data in various graphical forms including a pie chart and bar graph. Students can be introduced to spreadsheets by first using an electronic graphing program to record data. The graphical display provides an opportunity to quickly change variables to engage in prediction and comparison. Children love to see their ideas recorded and contribute to an overall discussion.

WRITING ACROSS THE CURRICULUM

In every unit, children are given opportunities to write about what they see, experience, and imagine. Young children vary in their ability to express themselves in written form. While some are able to write words and stories with coherence, others are struggling to express themselves in pictorial form.

In the **My Life** unit, have students think about what they would tell a new baby coming to their house. Based on what they know about growing and changing, have the students write to a new baby to explain all the things the baby can expect and to offer some advice as they begin to grow.

In the **My Family** unit, children can write a letter to a relative who is not living at home. Letters can be written in the conventional form or sent as an e-mail. Children are highly motivated to write when someone is going to write back to them.

In the **My Home** unit, students can think about what the most ideal house would be. Using pictures cut out of magazines, they can put together a scrapbook of features they would like in their ideal house. As the pictures are collected, children classify and sort the pictures according to the type of room the picture applies to. Following the sorting and pasting, young children can begin writing sentences about what their ideal house would be like.

In the **My School** unit, find out how old your school is. Take a historical perspective on how your school has developed. Have the children find out whether any of their neighbors attended their school. Have the class interview older people who attended their school and find out what it was like. If the school is relatively new, have the students interview someone who attended another school in the area and talk about what was on the existing school property. Have the students write about what they heard.

TEACHER VOICES

About the My Life unit

"Many activities in this unit were highly motivating for my students. They loved learning about their name and looking it up on the Web. Many of them were surprised at what high expectations the name promised. I would say very few of my students knew why their parents selected their name. For most, that was a particularly interesting piece of information. One of my students is living with a grandparent while the parent is out of the country on an extended work assignment. Being connected by e-mail allowed me to help the child communicate with her father to find out about her name. So, I had an unintended outcome of being able to demonstrate how the technology can help with very quick communication. The child involved is now working very hard to be able to send her own e-mails to her dad."

About the My School unit

"I was initially reticent to get on the Internet to find a class to connect with. My students were so excited about having an exchange with another class across the country. Looking for where the class was located was their first motivated experience in examining the map. We had discussed the map and marked places that had come up in discussions and the news, but they wanted to know how to get there, how long it would take if you drove or took a plane, and whether the weather was really different. The corresponding teacher was wonderful. She shared information her class had collected. We compared data, exchanged digital pictures, and exchanged holiday gifts that were unique to our area. What a wonderful way to open the world to the kids!"

CHILDREN'S LITERATURE   Each unit of this theme includes an extensive list of children's literature related to growing up, families, houses and homes, and school. The books have been purposefully selected to match young children's interest and the topic of the unit. Choose ones available in your school, personal, or public library and be sure to search for new ones on the market. Your search can be at the local bookstore or online.

WEB RESOURCES   An extensive list of Web Resources accompanies every unit. All Web Resources listed in these units were current at the time of publishing. Because of the rapid growth of Internet use, sites can be expected to come and go. To keep the resources current, all software and online references are available online at www.edtech4teachers.com and will be updated frequently.

TEACHING TIPS   Like all curriculum organizational plans, variety is important. Vary your teaching strategies from whole group to small groups to individual activities. Many of the lessons in this theme are adaptable to whatever situation you want to employ: Your organizational strategy just depends on your purpose and desired outcome. Remember that keeping young children motivated and engaged will take care of many potential classroom management problems.

Consider team teaching with a partner in preparing the units in this theme. Sharing the responsibility for preparation reduces your workload in half if you find a way to trade classes for a period of time while instruction takes place. If you prepare two units and your partner prepares two units, then you each can teach the units twice, once to your own class and once to your partner's class. This way, you are also able to share resources, improve your own practice for better student outcomes, and learn about each other's class. Another set of professional ears and eyes is always good for peer dialog.

LESSON EXTENDERS

Focusing on houses from other climates could extend the **My Home** unit. Break students up into construction teams. Have one team build a replica of an igloo, while another builds a replica of a stilt house. Have one team build a flat roof home as another builds a hip roof home. Still other teams could build a mud or earthen house. The ability to touch and feel the different building materials, see the various shapes of the roof, and discuss why these are more effective than other designs creates a rich dialog and good hands-on experience.

The **My Family** unit could be extended to look at the various kinds of families that exist. Whether your class has mostly two-parent families or single-parent families, there are always children in a class who have neither or who have been adopted. It is comforting and helpful to talk about the family in a way that defines the support and nurturing that the adults bring to the children in the household. You will need to do some research on the structure of the families in your class before you introduce the topic. Adopted children need special consideration, as some adoptive parents may not have introduced the topic to their children yet.

THEME CULMINATING EVENT

In an All About Us celebration, have students share their slideshows, autobiographies, portraits, and other artifacts from studying the theme of All About Me. By this time, the children have learned a lot about each other, so have the children introduce each other at the event by telling unique characteristics of a partner. Create a Bingo game for parents and visitors in which they must find the child with a particular attribute. Have students give their parents a tour of the school on their way home from the open house. A complete plan for this activity is found at the end of the theme.

My Life

UNIT OVERVIEW

A key feature in the education of young children is to make them aware of similarities and differences in people, while at the same time helping them realize that when they are working on common tasks, the roles everyone plays are important. In this unit, students look to themselves to determine a developmental perspective on how all people live and grow. In addition, they explore how they are similar and different from the students in their class and those in a different part of the country or world. Finally, they work on projects where roles are differentiated, but a common goal guides the work.

UNIT OBJECTIVES

At the end of this unit, students will be able to:

- Tell about similarities and differences between themselves and others in their class.
- Explain about the similarities and differences between themselves and other similar-age children in books, videos, and other sources.
- Tell of the skills they have developed over time (physical—sitting, crawling, walking, running; academic—drawing, writing, reading, etc.).

STANDARDS ADDRESSED IN THIS UNIT

ISTE NETS for Students 1, 3, 4, 5
IRA/NCTE English/Language Arts Standards 1, 2, 3, 4, 5, 7, 8, 10
NCTM Math Standards 1, 4, 10
NAS/NSE Science Standards C1, C2, C3
NCSS Social Studies Standards 1a, 2b, 2c, 2d, 4

CHILDREN'S LITERATURE

All Kinds of Children, Norma Simon
Arthur's Eyes, Marc Brown
Arthur's Tooth, Marc Brown
Ask Mr. Bear, Marjorie Flack
Birthday Presents, Cynthia Rylant
Chrysanthemum, Kevin Henkes
Clifford Grows Up, Norman Birdwell
Different Just Like Me, Lori Mitchell
Faces, Jillian Cutting
The Foot Book, Dr. Seuss
Hands, Hands, Hands, Marcia Vaughan
Here We All Are, Tomie dePaola
Hooray for Me!, Remy Charlip & Lilian Moore
How Many Teeth, Paul Showers
I Can Do It by Myself, June Goldsborough
If You're Happy and You Know It, Jo Lodge
I Like Me, Nancy Carlson
I Love My Hair, Natasha Anastasia Tarplay

The Important Book, Margaret Wise Brown
In the Mirror, Joy Cowley
It's OK to Be Different, Todd Parr
Leo the Late Bloomer, Robert Kraus & Jose Aruego (Illustrator)
A Letter to Amy, Ezra Jack Keats
Marsupial Sue, John Lithgow
Mr. Rabbit and the Lovely Birthday Present, Charlotte Zolotow
The Secret Birthday Message, Eric Carle
Silly Sally, Audrey Wood
Stephanie's Ponytails, Robert Munsch & Michael Martchenko
Tacky the Penguin, Helen Lester
We Are All Alike—We Are All Different, Scholastic

WEB RESOURCES

Brush Your Teeth Online: www.bubblegum.com/activities/brushteeth/
Dental Care: http://education.wichita.edu/m3/tips/health/kdg/personal/brush/
    webqstfrm.htm
Dr. Seussville Games: www.randomhouse.com/seussville/games/
E-Pals: epals.com
Healthy Teeth Maze Craze: www.scholastic.com/magicschoolbus/games/colgate/
    mazecraze.htm
I Like Me!!: http://edtech.fc.peachnet.edu/~rdixon/webquest.htm
Johnson and Johnson Oral Health: www.mrreach.com/
Lithgow for Kids: www.lithgowforkids.com
Songs: www.niehs.nih.gov/kids/lyrics/littlecb.htm
Sparkle City: www.sparkle-city.com/index_flash.html
ToothAdventures: http://education.wichita.edu/m3/tips/health/second/personal/
    webqstfrm.htm

SOFTWARE

The Amazing Writing Machine, Broderbund
Arthur's Adventures with D.W., Broderbund (Living Books)
Arthur's Birthday (English, Spanish), Broderbund (Living Books)
The Graph Club, Tom Snyder Productions
Imagiprobe (includes both probe ware and software), ImagiWorks
Kid Pix (English, Spanish), Broderbund
Kid Pix Activity Kits, Volume 3, My Body, Broderbund
Kidspiration, Inspiration Software
The Magic School Bus Explores the Human Body, Scholastic
My Amazing Human Body, DK Interactive Learning
Sheila Rae the Brave, Broderbund (Living Books)
TimeLiner (English, Spanish), Tom Snyder Productions

teaching
the unit

Getting Started

In preparation for the unit, send a letter home to explain the purpose of the unit with an overview of the activities and expectations. Ask parents to work with their child at home to select four to eight photographs that depict the child's life—from infancy to the present. Ask parents to talk to the child about the photographs so the child is able to share the information with the class. Ask that the child's name and age be noted on the back of the photo. Be sure to let parents know that scanned or digital copies are welcome. (Be conscious of those children for whom photographs may not be available. Consider alternatives such as magazine cutouts or descriptions by family members.)

For this unit as well as later learning activities, consider scanning the original submissions and using the copies for student work. Consider returning the original photos at a parent-teacher conference to be sure they reach home.

Motivating Activity

Place all but one of each child's photographs on a bulletin board in a timeline fashion with the infancy photos in a group to the left and current photos to the right, clustering together photos of birth, sitting, first birthday, and so forth. For the first whole-group activity, use the saved photo of each child from the bulletin board. Of the photos you hold back, make sure you have a timeline of child growth among them, some infants, some toddlers, some younger children, some older.

Whole-Group Activities

Discuss how children are all alike and yet all different. Reinforce the concept by reading books that explain similarities and differences. Hold up photos of the children that you have saved from the bulletin board and have students guess who each might be. After identifying the picture, have the child whose photo it is get it from you, return to his or her place in the group, and place the photo down in front of him or her. After all children have had a chance to identify their picture, challenge the children to work to establish a human timeline. Start with the photo depicting earliest infancy and ending with the most current photo.

Multidisciplinary Activities

ART *Timeline:* Provide stacks of drawing paper 4 $\frac{1}{2}$" x 6" or 4 $\frac{1}{4}$" x 5 $\frac{1}{2}$" and art supplies at the art center (crayons, markers, paint, scissors, construction paper, glue, etc.). Have children draw several pictures depicting events during their lifetimes. When all the pictures are finished, have students construct a book including a cover and timeline or a scrapbook with annotations. If doing a timeline, provide students with long sheets of butcher paper (7" x 3') to complete the timeline.

Self-Portrait: Have students look in a mirror and draw themselves on a paper plate. Create a classroom bulletin board. (These faces can be used as the ending point of the timeline made in the prior activity.)

- As an added activity, give a drawing lesson on faces based on the Web site Learn How to Draw Lou Anne, the Pig (www.nancycarlson.com/newsletter/html/artist.html).
- Have students draw themselves using Kid Pix. Create a classroom slideshow. Have each student record him- or herself talking about something in the slideshow. Consider mounting the hand-drawn picture with the Kid Pix version side-by-side. The differences in the drawing techniques can foster interesting discussion of both the art techniques and the shapes.
- Scan the paper-plate pictures described above. Insert the pictures into a word processing program and let the students write a short biography of themselves.
- Have students use Kid Pix to draw a self-portrait and write an accompanying story describing an event in their life or about themselves. Gather the picture and the text slides for each student together in a class slideshow. Set the slideshow to show each slide for three to five seconds. Set up one computer during open house to allow the parents to get to know the other students in the class.
- Take digital photos of each of the students. After they have written their stories, allow them to record their name (first name only) and a few of their favorite things.
- Combine all the versions of self-portraits described above into a single slideshow. Have each child create a title slide with his or her first and last name and a few describing words. Follow the title slide with the various self-portraits—the plate, Kid Pix drawing, and digital photograph. Consider including some or all of the written work that originally accompanied each drawing.

Silhouette: Use an overhead projector to trace the profile of each child onto black construction paper. Have each child cut this out and mount it on lighter colored paper. Have the children write their name under this shadow picture.

Kinder Garden Slideshow: In Kid Pix have students draw the center of a flower and type their name. Save the file as theirname01.gif. Open that same file and add a petal to the center of the flower. Using the stamps, illustrate the petal with a stamp that tells something about the student. Save the file as theirname02.gif (the naming convention keeps the pictures in the right order). Continue this process until all of the petals have been drawn and illustrated. Then, create a slideshow that will show each student's flower blooming as petals are added. To do this, place each student's series of pictures in a folder labeled with his or her name. This enables Kid Pix to show all of the pictures in a single slideshow. You can make a whole class slideshow by placing the contents of each child's folder into a single folder.

GROSS MOTOR *Obstacle Course:* Students use indoor climbers, balance beams, jump ropes, Hula-Hoops, balance boards, and stairs to construct and complete an obstacle course.

- Draw an obstacle course using Kid Pix.

- Take digital photographs of students at each obstacle. Use the digital photos at a center where students practice sequencing for storytelling.

- Videotape students proceeding through the obstacle course. Digitize the videotape and post it to the class Web site

- Use the Imagiprobe device, which attaches to a handheld computer such as a Palm or Handspring, to show the heart rate. Transfer the data to a large screen monitor or print out the information. Use the data to help the children understand how the heart rate increases with increased exercise.

HEALTH *Fun Facts:* Have children draw a picture of themselves in the center of a large piece of paper. Cut pictures from magazines to show favorite foods and favorite physical activities. Cut numbers and words from magazines to indicate birth date, age, height, weight (omit this one if you feel it is necessary), eye color, and hair color.

- Read a book about exploring the senses. Use the Explore with Senses activity in Kidspiration to write about how the senses can be used to explore the world. Substitute a picture of a different place or a picture taken at night. Have students note which sense they use. At the conclusion, have students discuss how some senses are better developed than others for each person. Graphing the sense they feel they are best using can extend the activity.

- Finish the Health and Safety activity in Kidspiration. Have the students use symbols or record their voice telling how they keep themselves safe.

- Have students use Kid Pix to draw things that can be done with their hands. Create a classroom slideshow.

LANGUAGE ARTS AND READING *Autobiographies:* In a writing center, have students draw or write about their life, things they remember, and things that have been told to them by others about situations and experiences. The "stories" can be one to two sentences or one to two paragraphs. Each entry should include an approximate date of the event. When the children indicate they are finished, place all the entries into a book. Write the stories using Kid Pix and draw or insert pictures. Consider creating a slideshow of some of the pages.

Name Writing: Have students write an acrostic poem using their name in a vertical position. Have children work in groups to think of words to describe themselves using each letter of their name. Use Kid Pix alphabet stamps to find pictures that start with the letters in their name. After creating their name horizontally, have the children move the images to stamp their name vertically.

- Use the Initial Me activity in Kidspiration to have students find pictures that start with the first and last letters of their name.

- Use Kidspiration to make a ME mind map. Have students type their name in the middle and then link things they have learned to do as they've grown.
- Use the All About Me activity in Kidspiration to have students illustrate things about themselves at school and home, and their favorite things.

Send Mail: Have students use Amazing Writing Machine's Letter section to make an envelope addressed to themselves. The children can type their own name and address and create a stamp using the drawing tools. Print out these envelopes and use them to mail something to the students later in the year, such as a thank-you note, a Valentine, or just a note to say hello.

MATH

What's in a Name?: Project an overhead or show a screen in which every letter of the alphabet has a value assigned to it, such as A=1 cent. Assign a value to each letter of the alphabet based on the students' mathematical level and the basic skills you wish to reinforce. Consider giving vowels the lowest value. Have students add up the value of the letters in their name. Ask questions such as "Who has the most expensive name? The least expensive name? The name closest to _____?"

- Using Graph Club, make a class graph of the numbers of letters in the names. Find out how many letters are in all of the names together. Sort the names into categories, taking turns guessing how they have been sorted (by vowel sounds, number of letters, number of syllables, etc.).
- Make a personal timeline using TimeLiner as a sample for the students to view. Have each make a personal timeline. Attention to the dates and the sequence of events associated with the changing dates is important.
- Place all students' birthdays on a yearlong timeline using TimeLiner. Print and hang up in the classroom.

Graphing Me: Make a floor graph from a shower curtain or paint cloth by marking six-inch squares with masking tape. Use Graph Club to document the results of the following "real" graphs and print for display or later reference.

- *Eyes:* Select a book on eyes from your favorites or from the reading list to introduce the lesson on eyes. Use numbers on the vertical axis and eye color squares on the horizontal axis. Students may use a name marker of themselves to indicate eye color. The name mark may be a nametag or other identifying physical device. Formulate statements from the graph (i.e., More children have brown eyes. Only one has blue eyes.).
- *Hair:* Select a book on hair from your favorites or from the reading list to introduce the lesson on hair. Use numbers on the vertical axis and hair color squares on the horizontal axis. Students may use a name marker of themselves to indicate hair color. Formulate statements from the graph (i.e., The same number of children have brown hair and black hair.).
- *Teeth:* Select a book on teeth from your favorites or from the reading list to introduce the lesson on teeth. Use numbers on both the vertical and horizontal axis of the graph. Count the number of teeth each child has lost. Use a name marker in a square to indicate how many teeth have been lost. Formulate

statements from the graph (such as, Five children have lost two teeth and five have lost three teeth.).

- *Favorite Stuffed Animal:* Have children bring their favorite stuffed animal from home (have some extras at school). Select a story about stuffed animals to begin the activity. Use numbers on the horizontal axis and animal pictures on the vertical axis. Have each child place his or her animal in a square that tells what type of animal is their favorite. Formulate statements from the graph (i.e., More children have a favorite teddy bear than a favorite whale.).

MUSIC

Hokey Pokey: Sing and do the "Hokey Pokey" with the children, reinforcing right and left, and body parts (www.niehs.nih.gov/kids/lyrics/hokey.htm).

Simon Says: Play Simon Says to reinforce body parts, following directions, and body and spatial awareness (right/left, over/under, on/next to).

Head and Shoulders, Knees, and Toes: While singing, touch both hands to the head, then the shoulders, then the knees, and then the toes, in time with the words. Then on the second verse, omit the word "head," but still do the actions. On the third verse, omit the word "shoulders," and so on. Finish with all the words back in, but singing as fast as possible (www.niehs.nih.gov/kids/lyrics/headsh.htm).

It's Not Easy Being Green: Although none of your students are green, each may have a unique trait that makes him or her feel different. Have students discuss their differences after singing "It's Not Easy Being Green" (www.niehs.nih.gov/kids/lyrics/green.htm).

Farkle and Friends: Listen and sing along to the John Lithgow CD of Farkle and Friends. You can download a sample of John Lithgow performing "Marsupial Sue" (www.lithgowforkids.com). Click on Music and then Downloads.

SCIENCE

Study About Teeth: The primary years are typically the time in which children lose most of their baby teeth. However, this happens at different rates for each child. There are many places on the Internet where resources and activities have been developed to support dental education. Several of the sites below are linked to one site for second grade:

Tooth Adventures: http://education.wichita.edu/m3/tips/health/second/personal/webqstfrm.htm

Others Web sites for young children are linked to:

Brush Your Teeth Online: www.bubblegum.com/activities/brushteeth/
Dental Care: http://education.wichita.edu/m3/tips/health/kdg/personal/brush/webqstfrm.htm
Healthy Teeth Maze Craze: www.scholastic.com/magicschoolbus/games/colgate/-mazecraze.htm
Johnson and Johnson Oral Health: www.mrreach.com/
SparkleCity: www.sparkle-city.com/index_flash.html

Counting Teeth: Record information in a an electronic table with the name of the student on the left axis and the words "baby teeth," "adult teeth," and "total teeth" across the top. Complete the cells of the table with the students' numbers.

SOCIAL STUDIES

Celebrating Diversity: Diversity can be defined in many ways. One of the ways that is often overlooked with young children is discussing individuals with unique challenges.

- Learn about people with disabilities. Get a Braille menu from McDonald's, use Amazing Writing Machine to create a Braille letter, or find a book to read and then talk about being different. Have children brainstorm things they can do to help someone with a disability.

- Use the Kidspiration activity Lend a Helping Hand to illustrate how they can help others.

- Log on to **epals.com** and e-mail with other classes to find out how they are different or the same as your class. There are many dimensions you may want to use to ask about the differences. These include gender, physical appearance, size of families, and so on.

Family Interviews: Ask children to interview others in their homes about their year in kindergarten, first grade, or second grade. Have family members write stories. The story collection could become a family kindergarten, first grade, or second grade book.

The Meaning of Names: Look up the meaning of each student's name in a baby book. Have students illustrate themselves as the meaning of their name describes them. Does this meaning fit their personality? Have students ask their parents if they were named after someone or how and why their name was chosen.

- Have students e-mail family members to get the desired information.

- Using Kidspiration, create an All About Me mind map. Have each student type his or her name in the middle and then add links to all of the different roles that he or she plays in the family and the community. Is he or she a sister, niece, cousin, granddaughter, soccer player, dancer, or something else?

- Use Kidspiration to create a family tree. Use the people symbol library to create and illustrate the family tree.

Assessment

FOR YOUNGER LEARNERS

As a performance assessment task, ask children to make a story timeline of how they have grown and changed since they were infants. Fold or divide sheets of paper into at least three panels. Label the panels: Me as a Baby, Me as a Toddler, and Me Now. Have the students pick three important ways they have grown, learned, and changed since they were a baby. Remind them to be sure to label the important parts of the pictures.

NOTE: This performance task addresses only one of the objectives. The other objectives can be observed during the unit.

NOTE: For a description of the values "Not Interested," "Trying It," "Working on It," "Got it!," and "Helping Others," see chapter 4.

CRITERIA	NOT INTERESTED	TRYING IT	WORKING ON IT	GOT IT!	HELPING OTHERS
Student selected three important ways he or she has grown and learned.					
Each growth is sequenced.					
Labels are provided throughout the picture.					

FOR MORE ABLE LEARNERS

Have students make a Venn diagram comparing themselves to another member of the class. Have the students use small pieces of paper to write down words describing themselves. Have them make pieces of paper that are describing words about their friend. Place the describing words that are the same in the intersection of the two circles. Then record the results on a paper Venn diagram.

Have students repeat the exercise, comparing themselves to a character in a favorite book. Also record the results on a Venn diagram.

Have the students describe themselves beginning with the sentence stem: "I am unique because..."

NOTE: This assessment can be done individually using Kidspiration or Kid Pix if children have independent computer skills in using the program.

CRITERIA	APPROACHES TARGET	MEETS TARGET	EXCEEDS TARGET
Descriptive words about self	Descriptive words are accurate but limited to three or fewer.	Reasonably accurate characterization of physical traits and talents	Reasonably accurate characterization of many aspects of self including physical characteristics, talents, relationships, etc.
Descriptive words about friend	Descriptive words are accurate but limited to three or fewer.	Reasonably accurate characterization of physical traits and talents	Reasonably accurate characterization of many aspects of friend, including physical characteristics, talents, relationships, etc.
Comparison between self and friend	Comparison is limited to a few physical traits.	Demonstrates understanding of things that are the same and things that are different	Accurately notes similarities and differences using descriptive words that include many aspects of both individuals
Descriptive words about character	Descriptive words are accurate but limited to three or fewer.	Reasonably accurate characterization of physical traits and talents	Reasonably accurate characterization of many aspects of character including physical characteristics, talents, relationships, etc.
Comparison between self and character	Comparison is limited to a few physical traits.	Demonstrates understanding of things that are the same and things that are different. Notes fictional nature of character	Notes fictional nature of character in the context of comparing self with character on many dimensions
Description of uniqueness	Recognizes only one or two qualities	Provides a list that is reasonably accurate and demonstrates understanding of own special qualities	Perceptive response that goes beyond the obvious physical characteristics and academic talents

Assessment of technology use depends on the level of student use permitted, the technology available, and the age of the students. See chapter 4 for additional information on assessing technology use.

Additional criteria should be added focusing on writing. The criteria used for the rubric should reflect the objectives and expectations for the students.

My Family

UNIT OVERVIEW

Each student comes from a family and home situation that is unique. Adults in the home may be relatives (adult siblings, moms, dads, foster parents, aunts, uncles, grandparents, great grandparents) and friends (girlfriends, boyfriends, or acquaintances, temporary or permanent). Children in the home may be relatives or foster brothers and sisters including twins, triplets, and quadruplets. They may be younger or older, natural or adopted. They may include cousins, children of friends, and children in a family day care home. The cultures of the people living in the home may be the same or different. The ethnicity as well both in and between families may be the same or different.

Regardless of the combinations, each child in the classroom has a different family situation. Even when the numbers are the same, the dynamics are different. In this unit each student examines his or her own family first—the people, the work they do outside the home, and the contributions each makes inside the home. Each student listens and learns about others' families in a caring, accepting environment.

UNIT OBJECTIVES

At the end of this unit, students will be able to:

- Recognize similarities and differences between their families and others in their class.
- Explain the roles each family member plays within the family.
- Explain the differences in holiday traditions in various families.
- Tell about or write about the importance of each member of the family.

STANDARDS ADDRESSED IN THIS UNIT

ISTE NETS for Students 1, 3, 4, 6
IRA/NCTE English/Language Arts Standards 1, 3, 5, 8
NCTM Math Standards 1, 4, 6
NAS/NSE Science Standards C1, C2, C3
NCSS Social Studies Standards 1, 2, 3, 4, 5, 6

CHILDREN'S LITERATURE

Adoption, Fred Rogers
Are You My Mother?, P. D. Eastman
Arthur's Clean Your Room, Marc Brown
The Berenstain Bears and Baby Makes Five, Jan & Stan Berenstain
The Berenstain Bears and Mama's New Job, Jan & Stan Berenstain
Clifford's Family, Norman Birdwell
The Color of Us, Karen Katz
Divorce, Fred Rogers
Families, Ann Morris
Grandma Mix-up, Emily McCully
The Grandpa Book (The World's Family), Ann Morris
Grandpa's Slippers, Joy Watson

Have You Seen My Brother?, Elizabeth Guilfoile
Houses, Ann Morris
Houses and Homes, Ann Morris
Just Grandpa and Me, Mercer Mayer
Just Like Dad, Kim Watson
Just Me and My Dad, Mercer Mayer
Just Me and My Mom, Mercer Mayer
Just Shopping With Mom, Mercer Meyer
Light the Candle, Bang the Drum: A Book of Holidays Around the World, Ann Morris
Love You Forever, Robert Munsch
Mama, Do You Love Me?, Barbara M. Joosse & Barbara Lavallee (Illustrator)
My Family and Friends, Lisa Lenthall
My Grandma Is Wonderful, Nick Butterworth
My Grandpa Is Amazing, Nick Butterworth
My Mom Is Excellent, Nick Butterworth
My Mother Is Weird, Rachna Gilmore
The New Baby, Fred Rogers
The Relatives Came, Cynthia Rylant
Shoes, Shoes, Shoes, Ann Morris
Spot's Baby Sister, Eric Hill
Step Families, Fred Rogers
There Was an Old Woman Who Lived in a Shoe, nursery rhyme
What Was It Like, Grandma? series, Ann Morris
Work, Ann Morris

WEB RESOURCES
The Berenstain Bears Official Web Site: www.berenstainbears.com
Grandmother and Me Project by Kidlink: www.kidlink.org/KIDPROJ/grandmother/
How Can You Help Your Family? (parents are guided to have children help with chores in the family): http://pbskids.org/rogers/R_house/object9.htm
My Family and Me: www.atozteacherstuff.com/lessons/MyFamilyandMe.shtml
Songs: www.niehs.nih.gov/kids/lyrics/littlecb.htm
Who Am I? A program by Kidlink (online collaborative learning modules for students): www.kidlink.org/kie/nls/index.html
Who Is in Your Family?, Sesame Street: http://home.nc.rr.com/muppetsongs/

SOFTWARE
The Amazing Writing Machine, Broderbund
The Berenstain Bears Get in a Fight (English, Spanish), Broderbund (Living Books)
The Graph Club, Tom Snyder Productions
Just Grandma and Me (English, German, French, Spanish), Broderbund (Living Books)
Kid Pix Studio Deluxe (English, Spanish), Broderbund
Kidspiration, Inspiration Software
Tabletop Jr., Broderbund
TimeLiner (English, Spanish), Tom Snyder Productions

teaching the unit

Getting Started

In preparation for the unit, send a letter home to explain the purpose of the unit with an overview of the activities and expectations. Depending on the activities selected to teach this unit, ask parents to provide (1) a copy of a recent family picture, (2) information about birth dates of grandparents, parents, and children in the family, and (3) the celebrations that are most important to the family.

Motivating Activity

Prepare a slideshow that shows your own family—your grandparents, parents, and present family. Include information in the slideshow about birth dates, the number of children in the families, and the celebrations that are most important to your family. The personal information helps the children understand that everyone has some kind of family. Save the slideshow for open house and show it as you introduce yourself to your students' families.

Multidisciplinary Activities

ART   *Family Pictures:* Have children draw and color a picture of each member of their family including themselves on pieces of card stock paper. Cut them out and use them for several activities within this unit.

- Scan pictures and insert them into a word processing program.
- Have children draw a picture of their families using Kid Pix. Ask the students to draw the people in their family in proportion to how big they are.
- Put each student's family picture into a Kid Pix slideshow. Have students record themselves introducing their own family by saying their names and who they are. Share this slideshow with the class.

Hand Rainbow: Using Kid Pix, have student pairs take turns holding their hands up to the monitor as the partner draws around the hand using the draw tool and the mouse. Go to the crayon box or the color wheel. Have the students pick the color closest to their skin color to use with the fill bucket to color in the hand. Talk about the differences in skin colors, shapes, and sizes of hands. Ask the students to look at the hands in their family as homework. They can draw around the hands of each family member, order the hands according to size, and color in the hands.

- Put all the students' electronic hand pictures together into a slideshow. Use the clapping sound effect as the transition between slides.

GROSS MOTOR   *Crawl, Walk, Run:* Examine the way different people in the family move. Babies roll, scoot, crawl, walk unsteadily, and then walk. Toddlers begin to run. Young children jump, hop on one foot, and hop on the other foot. Older grandparents might walk stooped, with a cane, or wobbly. What are some of the ways that the children in your class can move? Play Follow the Leader using the sequential motor skills just mentioned and then shifting into more difficult movements, doing each movement five times so that the sequence becomes an aerobics exercise.

- Record the aerobic exercise on videotape for later sharing. Record a few students narrating the tape.
- Use iMovie or a movie-editing program to create a composite tape of several aerobic exercise combinations created and narrated by the students. This exercise tape can become a gift for the parents or a promotional for keeping fit.

HEALTH   *Our Lost Teeth:* Use an electronic graphing program to make a graph of how many teeth the class has lost.

Vaccinations: Use TimeLiner to create a timeline of children's vaccinations, regular check-ups, and dental visits. Discuss how many times a year students might see the doctor or dentist even if they are well.

LANGUAGE ARTS AND READING   Grandparents Remember Book: Read several of the books in Ann Morris's What Was it Like, Grandma? series. Help children develop a list of questions they would like to know from their grandparents or an elderly person in the neighborhood. Send (mail or e-mail) the list of questions to the grandparents. Make the questions and answers into a Grandma/Grandpa Remembers book for children.

- Join the online Grandmother and Me project by Kidlink by adding a page to the collaborative online story. Read what others have written about their grandmothers: www.kidlink.org/KIDPROJ/grandmother/
- Have students write a My Family and Me book. Download templates here: www.atozteacherstuff.com/lessons/MyFamilyandMe.shtml
- View and participate in several of the Mercer Mayer software stories, the Just Me and... series. Have students, in groups or individually, create a Just Me and My Mom or Just Me and My Dad slideshow using Kid Pix.

MATH   *The Size of Shoes:* Read *Shoes, Shoes, Shoes* (by Ann Morris). Send home enough paper for each child to trace around one shoe of each family member including his or her own. At school, have the children color each shoe, cut it out, and label it on the back with the family member's name and role in the family (mom, dad, older/younger brother, older/younger sister, etc.). Measure each shoe and record the number of inches on the back of the shoe. In a long part of the room or building, organize the shoe tracings in one line by size.

- Use an electronic graphing program to record the number of shoes that are the same size. Ask analysis questions from the results of the graph.

People in the Family: Make a floor graph from a shower curtain or paint cloth, marking squares with masking tape. The following activities can be displayed on the graphing plastic with real objects then transferred to an electronic graph using a graphing program. Place numbers on both the vertical and horizontal axis. The bottom row shows the number of people in the family. Students place a picture marker of themselves (from the art activity) in a square above the correct number. The numerals on the vertical axis will indicate how many children have each number of people in their families. Formulate statements from the graph (such as, More people have four people in their family than any other number.).

- Use an electronic graphing program to make a graph of the total number of brothers, sisters, mothers, fathers, and so on that the entire class has living in their families. Make a bar graph, pie graph, and line graph. Compare the way each graph represents the numbers.

- Have students use Kidspiration's people symbol library to make a graph of their family. The x-axis will represent each category of person they have in their family—sisters, brothers, mother, father, and so forth. Duplicate the people symbols to show the amount along the y-axis.

MUSIC   *Who Is in Your Family?* After singing "Five People in My Family" (Sesame Street, visit **http://home.nc.rr.com/muppetsongs/** for song lyrics), have students describe the oldest, youngest, tallest, smartest, and fastest people in their family.

SCIENCE   *Beginning Genetics:* Have students take an inventory of their physical characteristics: What colors are their eyes and hair, how tall are they, and so on. Use a graphing program to analyze and compare the classroom data. Ask students to take this same inventory of their family. Ask: "Are we similar to our parents and our siblings? How many are like our parents and how many are different?" Use a graphing program to depict and analyze this data.

Ant Families: Study an ant farm and how the ants work together as a "family" unit or colony. What kinds of roles do ants have? How are these roles important to the ant colony?

- Use a Web cam to take time-lapse photos of the ant farm. What are the changes that take place over time?

- Use TimeLiner to mark the changes over time in the ant farm by inserting the photos and writing notes about each one.

SOCIAL STUDIES   *Family Tradition:* Read one of the birthday or holiday books from the reading list. Select a holiday that is close or students' birthdays. Ask parents to share holiday recipes or traditions by sending them in print or electronic form. Print the recipes and traditions on a half sheet of paper, leaving the other half for the individual student illustrations or explanatory narrative. Bind copies to share with all families.

Family Jobs: Read to the children books about family responsibilities or view Mr. Rogers' Web page on family laundry (**http://pbskids.org/rogers/R_house/ object9.htm**). Provide students with a template of eight tags or tickets on which to record, in handwriting or with a word processor, ways they help or can help at home.

- Create a blank job chart using a word processor. Print a copy for each child. Have children draw pictures to fill out the jobs they do at home. Have students fill in the job chart for a week at home. The following week, discuss and compare the different types of work students do at home to help their families.

- Using an electronic graphing program, create a graph of the types of jobs that members of the class do at home. Print a bar, pie, and line graph. Point out how the numbers are represented using each kind of picture. Discuss the similarities and differences in the various jobs each child does at home.

- Have students use Kid Pix to make a certificate for their mom or dad for one extra chore, backrub, or something else that they think would be helpful to their parents. Have students make another certificate for another family member.

Assessment

FOR YOUNGER LEARNERS

Ask children to draw a My Family portrait or create a My Family slideshow that contains information about the people in their family, the roles they play, and other significant facts. Remind the children about all the aspects of their family that they have studied. Use the following scoring rubric to assess student work.

NOTE: For a description of the values "Not Interested," "Trying It," "Working on It," "Got it!," and "Helping Others," see chapter 4.

CRITERIA	NOT INTERESTED	TRYING IT	WORKING ON IT	GOT IT!	HELPING OTHERS
Family members are evident.					
Roles and jobs of family members are depicted and/or explained.					
The importance of family members is noted.					
Labels are provided throughout the picture.					

FOR MORE ABLE LEARNERS Ask children to write a My Family story that includes a family portrait or create a My Family slideshow that contains information about the people in their family, the roles they play, and other significant facts. Remind the children about all the aspect of their family that they have studied. Use the following scoring rubric to assess student work.

CRITERIA	APPROACHES TARGET	MEETS TARGET	EXCEEDS TARGET
Family members	Are not all evident	Are all evident	Are all evident and described in detail
Roles and jobs of family members	Only focuses on parents or is otherwise incomplete	Are depicted and/or explained	Are depicted and/or explained in a way that demonstrates understanding of the relationships and interdependence of members of the family
Importance of family members	Is limited to one member (if applicable)	Importance of various family members is noted	Includes information on how family members contribute to the family as a whole both inside and outside the home
Labels	Are insufficient, limiting assessment of student understanding	Are provided throughout the picture that contribute to understanding	(Not applicable)

Assessment of technology use depends on the level of student use permitted, the technology available, and the age of the students. See chapter 4 for additional information on assessing technology use.

Additional criteria should be added focusing on writing. The criteria used for the rubric should reflect the objectives and expectations for the students.

My Home

UNIT OVERVIEW
Each student lives in a home. The homes vary in many ways: size, shape, location, color, building materials, type of yard, and so forth. Homes include permanent single-family dwellings through multifamily, multiple story apartment houses. Homes can be located on the ground or under the ground, can be built on land or sea, in the desert and on mountains, in cold and warm climates. Homes can be permanent, movable, or temporary, foster homes, group homes, and orphanages. In addition, some children are homeless, living on the streets, in cars or in shelters.

Regardless of the home situation, most provide shelter from the elements. The geography and climate of the area influence the types of homes that are built. The culture also determines the types of houses built and occupied.

In this unit each student examines his or her own home first—the location, the structure, the inside, and the outside. Each student listens and learns about others' homes within a caring and accepting environment.

UNIT OBJECTIVES
At the end of this unit, students will be able to:

- Describe several different types of houses.
- Describe the purposes of different parts of a house.
- Explain how climate and geography influence the types of houses.
- Tell of home safety issues.

STANDARDS
ADDRESSED
IN THIS UNIT
ISTE NETS for Students 3, 4, 5
IRA/NCTE English/Language Arts Standards 1, 3
NCTM Math Standards 1, 4, 8, 10
NAS/NSE Science Standards A1, C3
NCSS Social Studies Standards 1, 3, 4, 5, 6

CHILDREN'S
LITERATURE
Houses and Homes—General
Anna Then, Anna Now, Josette Blanco & Claude d'Ham
Building a House, Byron Barton
Castles, Caves, and Honeycombs, Linda Ashman
Come Home With Us, Annie Kubler
Ésta Es Mi Casa, Arthur Dorros
Floating Home, David Getz
Homes and Houses: Then and Now, Alastair Smith
Homes (Around the World), Margaret C. Hall
Homes Around the World, Mike Jackson & Jenny Mumford
Homes on Water, Alan James
The Homes We Live In (Have You Noticed), Sally Hewitt & Jane Rowe
The House Book, Keith Duquette

A House Is a House for Me, Mary Ann Hoberman
Houses and Homes, Ann Morris
Just Me and My Dad, Mercer Mayer
Just Me and My Mom, Mercer Mayer
Let's Go Home: The Wonderful Things About a House, Cynthia Rylant & Wendy Anderson
My Home (My World), Tammy J. Schlepp & Alvin Granowsky
My Little Island, Frane Lessac
Old MacDonald Had an Apartment House, Judi Barrett & Ron Barrett
Our Home Is the Sea, Riki Levinson
Rehema's Journey: A Visit in Tanzania, Barbara A. Margolies
Stephen Then, Stephen Now, Josette Blanco & Claude d'Ham
Uptown, Bryan Collier
The Village of Round and Square Houses, Ann Grifalconi
When Africa Was Home, Karen L. Williams
When I Was Young in the Mountains, Cynthia Rylant

Nursing Homes
Let's Talk About When Someone You Love Is in a Nursing Home, Diana Star Helmer
Mr. K and Yudi, Karen Stanton
Sunshine Home, Eve Bunting

Homeless
Fly Away Home, Eve Bunting

Orphan Homes
Train to Somewhere, Eve Bunting

Moving from Mexico
Going Home, Eve Bunting
Just Like Home/Como En Mi Tierra, Elizabeth I. Miller & Mira Reisberg

Miscellaneous
Home Safety, Pati Myers Gross & Tom Gibson
Making My Room Special, Emilie Barnes & Ann Buchanan
A Safe Place Called Home, Eileen Spinelli
Tool Book, Gail Gibbons
Tools, Ann Morris

Stories and Nursery Rhymes
There Was an Old Woman Who Lived in a Shoe
The Three Little Pigs

WEB RESOURCES

House Pictures
The Peace Gallery: www.peacegallery.org
Where People Live ThinkQuest: http://library.thinkquest.org/3140/

Houses of Famous People
Anne Frank House: www.pbs.org/wnet/1900house/
Clara Barton House: www.nps.gov/clba/
Louisa May Alcott's House: www.louisamayalcott.org
Mark Twain's House: www.marktwainhouse.org
Mary Todd Lincoln House: www.uky.edu/LCC/HIS/sites/todd.html
Noah Webster's House: www.noahwebsterhouse.org
Stonewall Jackson House: www.stonewalljackson.org
Susan B. Anthony's House: www.susanbanthonyhouse.org

The White House
Barney's White House ABCs: www.whitehouse.gov/kids/abc/
Biography of First Lady: www.whitehouse.gov/kids/firstlady/
Biography of President: www.whitehouse.gov/kids/president/
Spotty's White House Tour: www.whitehouse.gov/kids/tour/
WhitehouseKids.gov: www.whitehouse.gov/kids/index2.html

House Safety
How Safe Is Your Backyard?: www-ed.fnal.gov/ntep/f98/projects/pppl/
backyard/student1scenario.html
Learn About Chemicals in Your House: www.epa.gov/opptintr/kids/hometour/

Houses and Homes—General
The 1900 House: www.pbs.org/wnet/1900house/
Cowboy Life: www.cowboylife.com/features/index.htm
Garden and Yard: www.pdictionary.com
Gingerbread House: http://dinnercoop.cs.cmu.edu/dinnercoop/Recipes/karen/
GingerbreadHouse.html
Homes and Communities: www.hud.gov/groups/students.cfm
Houses and Homes: www.schools.ash.org.au/elanorah/homes.htm
Kidd Safety House: www.cpsc.gov/kids/kidsafety/memory/index.html
KidsFarm: www.kidsfarm.com
MapQuest: www.mapquest.com
Mr. Rogers' House: http://pbskids.org/rogers/R_house/
The Oldest House (in the U.S.): www.oldcity.com/oldhouse/
Ronald McDonald House: www.rmh.org.au/
Songs: www.niehs.nih.gov/kids/lyrics/littlecb.htm
Teachers and Parents, Houses and Homes: www.bbc.co.uk/scotland/education/
whatwherewhenwhy/houses_and_homes/teachers.shtml
What? Where? When? Why?: www.bbc.co.uk/scotland/education/
whatwherewhenwhy/

SOFTWARE

The Amazing Writing Machine, Broderbund
The Graph Club, Tom Snyder Productions, or Tabletop Jr., Broderbund
Kid Pix Studio Deluxe (English, Spanish), Broderbund
Kidspiration, Inspiration Software
TimeLiner (English, Spanish), Tom Snyder Productions

teaching
the unit

Getting Started

In preparation for the unit, create a parent letter and a house survey to send home. The letter should explain the purpose of the unit with an overview of the activities and expectations. The survey should explain the purpose of collecting the information and contain a place for the child's name, four to six open-ended questions, and a thank you (with the school or room phone number for questions).

Motivating Activity

Read the story *The Three Little Pigs*. Provide several different types of materials for children to build their own houses including straw, wood, Legos, Duplos, clay, and dirt/mud. As they work, encourage the children to think about and talk about the materials that their own houses and others are made of.

Multidisciplinary Activities

ART *Building and Drawing Model Homes:* Provide drawing, coloring, and painting materials along with building materials, sculpting materials, and boxes out of which children can make models of houses and rooms. Make a mural for the flat drawings or layout (using a 4' x 8' piece of plywood) of all of the houses, leaving room for recreation areas, schools, businesses, industry, roads, and so forth. Consider limiting the size of the boxes used in the sculptures to keep the proportions of the created houses within similar dimensions.

Ask children to draw pictures of their house. Make labels for the various types of homes (apartment, trailer, one-family house, one-story, multistory, duplex, etc.). After the drawings are complete, have students sort their houses according to the labels.

- Draw a picture of your home using Kid Pix. Use a text box to add the address numbers. Draw a street sign close by. Use a text box to put in the street name.
- Scan the pictures and insert them into a work processing program. Have students add descriptive language or stories about their house.

GROSS MOTOR *Sidewalk Typewriter:* As a skill-building exercise, have students practice typing the words from the Language Arts and Reading section into Kid Pix or a children's word processing program. Then draw a large computer keyboard outside using sidewalk chalk. Hand each student a card with one of the words from the Language Arts and Reading activity written on it. Have students jump to spell the words on the sidewalk computer keyboard.

LANGUAGE ARTS AND READING *Describe Your House:* Have students list as many words (or pictures) as they can that describe their house. Each word or picture should be written on a 2" x 3" piece of paper. Have each student put his or her name or initials on the back of each slip of paper. Using a piece of posterboard, make a house shape. Use the house as the frame for a word bank. Have one student read one of his or her words. Each student who has that word turns the word card in. Record the word on the house word bank. Continue around the class. Save the word cards for making a bar graph that represents how common the various features of students' houses are.

In My House Book: Have students cut out several pieces of house-shaped pages, preferably the shape of their own house. Staple them together to make a book. On each page, describe one room by its function and on the opposite page, draw a picture of the room.

- Use the Amazing Writing Machine to create a house book. Change the page layout with the house pattern and use the home stamp set. Print as a folded book.

MATH   *What Type of House?:* Have students draw a picture of their own house (or use pictures provided by parents). Read books from the Children's Literature list, including books about people living in nursing homes, homes on the water, and the homeless. Or, do a Web search for pictures of other types of houses. In a large open place, sort children's house pictures into the various types.

- Use the Graph Club to graph the information. Print the graph in poster size and put on the bulletin board, adding the pictures beside the graph. Formulate statements from the graph (such as, More children live in apartments than in trailers.).
- Scan your house drawings and e-mail them to post in the Home Gallery of the What? Where? When? Why? Web site.

Describe Your House: Graph the word cards from the Describe Your House Language Arts and Reading activity.

How Many?: The White House has 6 floors, 132 rooms, 35 bathrooms, 147 windows, 412 doors, 12 chimneys, 8 staircases, and 3 elevators. How many of each does your house have? Use the Graph Club to graph this information and compare.

Our Ages: Create a timeline showing the birth dates of those living in your home.

MUSIC   *Home on the Range:* Have students sing "Home on the Range," and ask if they know what the song means. Provide guidance to help them discover the ways and lives of cowboys (Cowboy Life: **www.cowboylife.com/features/index.htm**; KidsFarm: **www.kidsfarm.com**). Discuss the difference between what cowboys of old called home and how people live now.

SAFETY　　*How Safe Is Your Backyard?:* Have children tell about their backyards. Examine information at two Web sites. Have children write a note to their parents about what they have learned and ask the parents to take a tour with their children around the backyard and make needed changes to make it more safe.

> Garden and Yard: www.pdictionary.com
> How Safe Is Your Backyard?: www-ed.fnal.gov/ntep/f98/projects/pppl/ backyard/student1scenario.html
> Learn About Chemicals in Your House: www.epa.gov/opptintr/kids/hometour/ backyard.htm#view

Fire Safety: As homework, have students map out a safety plan in case of fire. Follow the safety guidelines provided by the local fire department. Ask students who live in multistory buildings to learn how to get from their apartment to the ground floor.

SCIENCE　　*Effects of Weather on House Design:* Look at homes around the world. Learn about different types of houses, where they are located, and why they are made that way. Why do some people live in houses on stilts? Why do people live in houses with flat roofs? Use the Peace Gallery Web site listed in Web Resources to see examples.

Animal Houses: Learn about animal homes. Have children look at many animal picture books to get a sense of the various kinds of houses animals live in.

- Play the Where matching game at the Kid's Home section of the What? Where? When? Why? Web site.

- Use the Kidspiration activity What Lives Here to group animals in the climate that they live. If the place is unknown, use the online or CD encyclopedia.

- Edit the Kidspiration activity Effect of Event by replacing the event "volcanoes" with climate or culture. Save as a new activity. Have students use this activity to describe how climate or culture affects people, animals, and cities.

SOCIAL STUDIES　　*Being Helpful:* Read a book on family responsibilities related to clean rooms, helping the family, or doing work around the house, or view the Web site Mr. Rogers' House (http://pbskids.org/rogers/R_house/). Provide students a template of eight tags or tickets on which to record in handwriting or with a word processor ways they help or can help at home. The tags or tickets can be used as gifts for others in the house as a way to help out by doing those helpful chores.

Where Do You Live?: Enlarge a map of the school neighborhood or city. Place a map pin on the location of each student's house.

- Use the Kidspiration activity Welcome to My Town to design your own town. Use the activity My Community to describe and write about your town.

- Use the Internet site www.mapquest.com to find your own home or school on a map. Use the zoom function to show more or less of the surrounding area.

Mapping Your House: Have children draw a picture that shows all the rooms and/or places in their house or their room and all the things in it.

- Have students use the Kidspiration activity My Place to create your favorite room. Record your voice describing what makes this room your favorite.

- How did we live long ago? What did we do before electricity, telephones, microwaves, cars, and TV? Show students pictures and books depicting homes and household objects of long ago. Bring in some of your own artifacts. Have students draw pictures or find pictures on the Internet. Read *Little House in the Big Woods,* by Laura Ingalls Wilder. Use TimeLiner to put these pictures into perspective. Put milestone inventions in your timeline. How did they change homes and home life?

- Use the Kidspiration activity How People Live or Now and Long Ago to show how people lived long ago and now. Adapt the activity to your classroom level and save as a new activity if necessary.

- Have students play the Home game in the Kid's section of the What? Where? When? Why? Web site.

The White House Web Activity: Type the list of questions below in a word processing document that will allow hyperlinks and make the document a template. Ask students to work in pairs or small groups to search the links provided to find the answers.

Search these Web sites to find the answers to the questions below:

Barney's White House ABCs: www.whitehouse.gov/kids/abc/
Spotty's White House Tour: www.whitehouse.gov/kids/tour/
WhitehouseKids.gov: www.whitehouse.gov/kids/index2.html

1. List and describe as many rooms in the White House as you can.

2. Who lives in the White House now? What are their favorite things to eat? To do?

3. How many? ___elevators, ___ floors, ___ rooms, ___bathrooms, ___ windows, ___ doors, ___ chimneys, ___ staircases

4. What is the largest room in the White House?

5. What pets live in the White House?

6. Who was the first president to live in the White House?

7. How many people can eat in the State Dining Room?

Visit the following Web sites and read the biographies of the president and first lady. Then answer the questions listed at the bottom of the Web site.

Biography of First Lady: www.whitehouse.gov/kids/firstlady/
Biography of President: www.whitehouse.gov/kids/president/

Assessment

FOR YOUNGER
LEARNERS

In the teacher function of Kidspiration, create a picture library of houses collected during this unit. In the Picture mode, design and save an activity that asks students to sort a collection of houses into single-family dwellings and multifamily dwellings. At the bottom of the Kidspiration screen, ask two to three questions critical to the information your students learned.

NOTE: For a description of the values "Not Interested," "Trying It," "Working on It," "Got it!," and "Helping Others," see chapter 4.

CRITERIA	NOT INTERESTED	TRYING IT	WORKING ON IT	GOT IT!	HELPING OTHERS
Houses sorted correctly					
Question 1					
Question 2					
Question 3					

FOR MORE ABLE LEARNERS

Have students design a house. The design must be accompanied by a drawing that can either be a floor plan or a picture. The description of the house must include a rationale for the roof style, a discussion of safety features, and a description of basic home areas including a living room, eating/cooking area, sleeping location, and bathroom. The home is to be designed with safety features in mind.

CRITERIA	APPROACHES TARGET	MEETS TARGET	EXCEEDS TARGET
Drawing	Is incomplete and does not clarify description	Illustrates description	Is very detailed. Provides considerably more information to support description
Reason for exterior design	Indicates misconception of design concerning issues of weather and climate	Is connected to weather and climate	Is very carefully designed to meet the climate and weather conditions. Considers aspects not covered in class
Description of basic home areas	Is not complete, lacking one or more areas	Is complete, including the function of each area	Goes beyond basic areas, providing additional space that is justified by those who will reside in it
Safety features	Includes an inadequate fire safety plan	Are evident and appropriate including a fire plan	Includes an elaborate fire safety plan as well as backyard safety

Assessment of technology use depends on the level of student use permitted, the technology available, and the age of the students. See chapter 4 for additional information on assessing technology use.

Additional criteria should be added focusing on writing. The criteria used for the rubric should reflect the objectives and expectations for the students.

My School

UNIT OVERVIEW

Schools take many forms. In your community children might be aware that there are preschools and elementary schools mostly because they have been or are presently in them. They might be aware of the middle schools, high schools, community colleges, universities, medical schools, and law schools as well. This is especially true if the students have older siblings or friends who go to those schools or if your community is small enough that many functions take place in these school buildings. But there are many other types of schools as well: public, private, parochial; schools for kids and schools for grown ups; schools for pets; and schools to learn to drive, to sew, to work on cars, to be a nurse, doctor, or dentist. And some children are aware that there are other children who are schooled in their homes.

UNIT OBJECTIVES

At the end of this unit, students will be able to:

- Name the people who work in their schools and the jobs they do.
- Describe the inside of the school building and the classrooms.
- Describe the grounds surrounding the school and its vegetation.
- Compare their school to other schools.
- Describe the physical activities that happen each day at school.

STANDARDS
ADDRESSED
IN THIS UNIT

ISTE NETS for Students 3, 4, 5
IRA/NCTE English/Language Arts Standards 1, 2, 3, 4, 5, 8, 12
NCTM Math Standards 1, 4
NAS/NSE Science Standards D1, D3, F1, F3, F4, F5
NCSS Social Studies Standards 3, 4, 5, 6

CHILDREN'S
LITERATURE

Arthur's Teacher Trouble, Marc Brown
The Berenstain Bears and the Bully, Stan Berenstain & Jan Berenstain (Contributor)
The Berenstain Bears and the Dress Code, Stan & Jan Berenstain
The Berenstain Bears and the Drug Free Zone, Stan & Jan Berenstain
The Berenstain Bears and the Excuse Note, Stan & Jan Berenstain
The Berenstain Bears and the Homework Hassle, Stan Berenstain & Jan Berenstain (Contributor)
The Berenstain Bears and the New Girl in Town, Stan Berenstain & Jan Berenstain (Contributor)
The Berenstain Bears and the School Scandal Sheet, Stan Berenstain & Jan Berenstain (Contributor)
The Berenstain Bears and the Trouble With Friends, Stan Berenstain & Jan Berenstain (Contributor)
The Berenstain Bears and Too Much Teasing, Stan & Jan Berenstain
The Berenstain Bears' Trouble at School, Stan & Jan Berenstain

Clifford's First School Day, Norman Bridwell
Curious George Goes to School, Margaret & H. A. Rey
Fluffy's School Bus Adventure, Kate McMullar
Friends With Special Needs, Fred Rogers
Miss Nelson Has a Field Day, Harry Allard
Miss Nelson Is Back, Harry Allard
Miss Nelson Is Missing, Harry Allard
Spot Goes to School, Eric Hall

WEB RESOURCES   Animals in Our Backyard: www2.lhric.org/pocantico/trail/trail.htm
Backyard Wildlife: Create a Habitat: www.nwf.org/backyardwildlifehabitat/
createhabitat.cfm
Elmer the Safety Elephant: School Bus Safety: www.elmer.ca/english/thinksafe/
school/index.htm
Find Your School: http://nces.ed.gov/nceskids/school.asp
K–12 Online: http://seamonkey.ed.asu.edu/~cdowns/
Medco School First Aid: www.medco-school.com
RedCrossShop.org: www.redcross.quinstreet.com/storefront/kits_school.jsp
School Gardens: http://aggie-horticulture.tamu.edu/kindergarden/Child/school/
sgintro.htm
Schoolyard: www.k12science.org/curriculum/squareproj/index.html
Songs: www.niehs.nih.gov/kids/music.htm
Starting a School Garden slideshow: http://tarranttaex.tamu.edu/hort_slideshow/
start.html
Student's Classroom: http://nces.ed.gov/nceskids/
Web66: International School Web Site: http://web66.coled.umn.edu/schools.html

SOFTWARE   The Amazing Writing Machine, Broderbund
Arthur's Teacher Trouble (English, Spanish), Broderbund (Living Books)
The Graph Club, Tom Snyder Productions, or Tabletop Jr., Broderbund
HyperStudio
iMovie
Kid Pix (English, Spanish), Broderbund
Kidspiration, Inspiration Software
Let's Pretend! Many Lands, Many Playgrounds, Mind Magic
Let's Pretend! Our World Is a Playground, Mind Magic
Little Bear Preschool, Broderbund
Little Monster at School, Broderbund (Living Books)
Madeline Preschool and Kindergarten, Creative Wonders!

teaching the unit

Getting Started

The exploration of school is something that happens at the beginning of each school year to initially familiarize students with the school or to make them aware of the changes of surroundings from the previous year. These activities provide a focus for that exploration and lead to a presentation for open house or the construction of (or an addition to) a school Web site.

A Note about Acceptable Use Policies: Before starting this unit, make sure that you have checked on the district and school acceptable use policies (AUPs). Ensure that safety issues have been addressed and policies are in place for young children to be online. When setting up communication with other schools or individuals, investigate their AUP by viewing their Web sites or obtaining a copy of the policy to be sure that there is alignment with the expectations of your school. At this age level, children can participate in a whole-group activity by looking at their school Web site, and then can explore it further on their own. If adults are available to be with small groups, further investigation of other schools' sites can be undertaken.

Motivating Activity

Set up a computer and a projection device in your classroom to show your school Web site. Explore the Web site with the students, allowing them to tell you the story of what is on the pages. The two sites located below will allow you to register your school Web site and view other schools' Web sites. Check out each to see whether your school is registered. After checking with your administrator, consider adding your school if it is not listed. After checking to see whether your site is registered, click on the area or state you are most familiar with and attempt to find another school close by. Regardless of whether you can find another close by, visit several sites (preselect some you find most interesting).

> Web66: International School Web Site: **http://web66.coled.umn.edu/schools.html**
> K–12 Online: **http://seamonkey.ed.asu.edu/~cdowns/**
> Find Your School: **http://nces.ed.gov/nceskids/school.asp**

Search for schools inside the U.S. (there are more than 6,000) and in foreign countries (there are more than 3,000) at **www.yahoo.com**. Use this search term: K–12 schools. Click on Elementary Schools, then click on By Regions.

Whole-Group Activities

After taking a tour of the school, use Kidspiration to brainstorm the facilities and activities found at your school, especially those that would tell others about your school. Plan to use this information for an open house or for placing on the school Web site. Use the school pictures as the focus for the brainstorming web. Let the children control the development of the web, but guide them to include the building (a description that includes the number of stories, the number and purpose of the classrooms, the gym, the lunchroom, etc.), areas outside the building (the playground, the grounds, the views from each direction), the classroom (layout, equipment, materials, supplies), and the class (the children, the teacher, the aides, the parent volunteers).

Multidisciplinary Activities

ART *Self-Portraits:* Ask students to draw self-portraits that tell as much about them as they want others to know. Discuss how different children make up the group that is called a "class" in a school.

- Scan pictures and insert them into a word processing program. Have students write a short biography of themselves, using only their first name to identify themselves.

- Have students use Kid Pix to draw their pictures and write their stories. Provide each student with only one slide. Save the whole class to a slideshow, setting the timer at five seconds. Set up one computer during open house to allow the parents to get to know the other students in the class. Precede the class slideshow with a group picture of the class. Put the same picture at the end of the slideshow to further illustrate how individuals compose a class.

- Take digital photos of each of the students. After they have written their stories, allow them to record their names (first name only) and a few of their favorite things.

GROSS MOTOR *Activity Quilt:* Make a list of all the physical activities that take place in school, in physical education classes and outdoors on the playground. Include walking or biking to and from school. Assign one student to each of the activities. The children's responsibility is to make a 6" x 6" labeled picture that depicts their assigned physical activity. Post all pictures together to make a school activity quilt. Posting the activity quilt in the classroom creates an excellent reminder of all the physical activities that can be done in school. When students can't seem to think of any activity to do, refer them to the activity quilt for ideas.

- Scan the 6" x 6" pictures into a Kid Pix slideshow. Select five activities that can be done in the classroom as "wiggle removers." Record into the slideshow a recording of active music the children recognize. Set the slideshow to 10 to 30 seconds per slide depending on the attention level of the group. Replay the slideshow each time you need a little "wiggle removal." Periodically reorganize the slides, adding or deleting activities to keep it interesting and novel.

HEALTH *First-Aid Kits:* Examine the different kinds of first-aid kits that are available from the American Red Cross for schools at RedCrossShop.org (**www.redcross.quinstreet. com/storefront/kits_school.jsp**). Click on (1) Student Disaster Kit, (2) Fanny First-Aid Kit, (3) Child Care Kit, and (4) Field Trip First-Aid Emergency Kit to find out what is in each kit. Keep another list that shows what is in a portable first-aid kit.

Nurse's Office: Send three or four students at a time to the nurse's office for an observation activity. Limit the time in the nurse's area to 10–15 minutes, either with an adult or with the school nurse. Ask students to inventory as much as they can while they are in the room. (For an idea of what they might find, visit Medco School First Aid: www.medco-school.com.) When each group returns to the room, have them pass along the list to the next set of students to ensure that items are not double-counted. Keep one list that includes what is in the room.

LANGUAGE ARTS AND READING

Biographies: Ask students to write a short biography (in pictures or words) of themselves, focusing on their life as a student (name, grade, previous schooling, favorite subjects, most memorable time in school).

- Take digital photos of the students. Load the pictures into a Kid Pix slideshow. Have the students type their stories or record a narration. Use the Read or Listen button to let them listen to each other's story.

- Set up a TV interview desk. Decorate the backdrop. Let each student interview another, asking a prescribed set of questions that are based on the writing assignment above. Videotape the interviews to show at open house. Select clips from each student to digitize and post to the Web.

MATH

Attendance: Construct a large graph that lists the days of the week across the top and the names of the teachers down the side. By the teacher's name, record the number of student enrolled in his or her class. Ask other teachers to participate in this activity by counting the number of students in attendance each day and recording the number on a square of paper (which you provide—the size is equal to the size of the squares on the graph, and the teacher's name is at the bottom of the square). Send one pair of students to each class to gather the squares each morning (send an adult along if necessary). Allow the student pair to place the attendance squares in the correct cell.

- Use a calculator to determine how many total students are at school each day.

- Set up a spreadsheet in which students can record the number in attendance each day for the classes. Click the graph button and print out the attendance graph for each day.

Take attendance of all the critters and plants that live in your classroom or school. Make a graph of the things that live in your school that are not people. In which classrooms do they live? What do they eat? Who takes care of them? What do they do all day?

MUSIC

Class Chant: Write a class chant or song that identifies things the class thinks are important.

- Record the class chant or song in a Kid Pix slideshow with the class picture as the visual. Retain this clip for later insertion in class slideshows.

SCIENCE
Backyard Animals: Explore a Web site that tells of one class's study, entitled Animals in Our Backyard (www2.lhric.org/pocantico/trail/trail.htm). Examine all the different types of living things around your school. Take digital photos of each. Use print and nonprint resources to identify each. Ask a local horticulturalist for help with the more difficult ones—either by taking the photos to them or by e-mailing them.

- Insert the photos into a word processing document, label them, and write about each. Photos can also be inserted into a Kid Pix document for writing.
- Using HyperStudio or a similar program, insert a large photo of the schoolyard and label the living things so that when the user moves the mouse pointer over the area, a hidden pop-up window shows the name of the animal.

School Garden: View the Starting a School Garden slideshow, which explains how to start a school garden (http://tarranttaex.tamu.edu/hort_slideshow/start.html). Ask the assistance of the parent group and a couple of parents in the classroom.

Identify a plot of land that could be used as a garden of some type (fruit, vegetable, flower, greenery, rock). Have children sketch the area while sitting outside using lapboards, paper and pencil, or laptops. Have children work in teams of three to draw a "bird's eye view" of their design. Direct students to decide what they would put into the space. When they have decided what to put in their garden, have students "plant" the area (with markers, paints, etc.).

- Have students scan pictures from seed packets and horticulture magazines to arrange and "plant" on their pictures.

SOCIAL STUDIES
Roles Children Play in School: Examine the roles that children play in school. What is their "job" at school? Include learning, listening, following the rules, asking questions, and so on.

Roles Adults Play in School: Examine the roles of all people in the school building. Include people who are specific to your school: principal (or director), assistant principal, secretary, teacher (including substitute teacher), aide, school nurse, custodian, cook, volunteer. Tape an interview with them individually, asking their names, their jobs, and what they do in their jobs.

- Take digital pictures of each person at school. Have students write or record comments about what the person does at school. This information can be transferred to print media to create a booklet.
- Edit the tape to the essential portions for replaying by the children. Or have older children use iMovie to edit the tape to include comments by the younger children on how the person identified has helped them in school.
- Freeze a picture from each of these interviews that shows the person at work. Make a set of thumbnails. Insert a voice recording in which they tell their names, jobs, and what they do in their jobs.

Map the Classroom: Provide students with large sheets of paper and have them draw a picture of their classroom. Younger children could cut items from school catalogs and glue them onto their pictures. Older children can use $1/2$" grid paper, cut the shape of the room, allowing $1/2$" per foot. Have children measure the bases of objects in the room and cut objects of those measurements to place on the grid. Pencil in the doors, cabinets, windows, and so on.

- As a group activity, use a drawing program to make a grid. As the class identifies an object and provides the measurement, fill in squares with various colors to indicate objects in the room. Code the colors to a legend or map key that identifies the various objects.

Have students write a set of directions using right and left commands that tells others how to get from one point to another in the classroom. Record the directions on cards for the students to take with them as they test the directions.

Friendship: Read a book on making friends. Discuss what makes a person a friend. Role play how to approach someone to become a friend. Role play behaviors that are inappropriate for friends.

- One of the aspects of being a friend is communicating and keeping in touch even when you are far away. E-mail a friend of yours and ask for a return e-mail to show how friends keep in touch.

Classroom Survey: Have children in the room fill out a survey that asks them for some demographic information and favorites. Calculate the results. Have the class draw generalizations out of the survey. Ask questions that compare the results of your class with the results of all the classes that have taken the survey. What did they learn about themselves? Draw on the learnings from the first unit on individual uniqueness. What makes the class unique?

Assessment

FOR YOUNGER
LEARNERS

Have each student draw two pictures of the school, one of the outside and one of the inside. Make each picture an active picture that shows as much about the school as the student can think of. Remind them to illustrate what it looks like, what is happening, who is there, and any safety signs. Be sure to have them label as much as they can.

NOTE: For a description of the values "Not Interested," "Trying It," "Working on It," "Got it!," and "Helping Others," see chapter 4.

CRITERIA	NOT INTERESTED	TRYING IT	WORKING ON IT	GOT IT!	HELPING OTHERS
The outside of the school is somewhat accurately drawn.					
The inside of the school is somewhat accurately drawn.					
Appropriate activities are depicted in pictures.					
Pictures appropriately depict school personnel and classmates.					
Safety procedures or signs are depicted.					
Labels were attached to important items on pictures.					

FOR MORE ABLE LEARNERS — Ask students to draw pictures of both the inside and the outside of the school on 9" x 12" paper. Mount each drawing on a 12" x 18" piece of paper. Give each student Post-its to write narrative explanations of parts of the school, activities taking place, and safety signs, and to label and provide other explanatory information. Instruct children to place the Post-its on the border around the drawing with arrows pointing to what is being referred to.

CRITERIA	APPROACHES TARGET	MEETS TARGET	EXCEEDS TARGET
Drawing of outside of school	Was attempted but is missing major elements	Reasonably resembles exterior of school	Is accurate and has considerable detail
Drawing of inside of school	Was attempted but is missing major portions of either the room or the general area	Reasonably resembles interior of school room or general area	Is accurate and has considerable detail
Activities	Are limited in number and too sketchy in detail to ensure understanding	Are appropriate for drawing and described adequately	Are depicted appropriately with additional explanatory information that demonstrates a deep understanding
School personnel	Personnel are inadequately described or some important individuals are missing	Are depicted in the appropriate place with description of activity	Are depicted accurately including some personnel who are not often seen by students
Safety signs	Are present only for either interior or exterior drawing and/or not explained	Are present, including traffic signs, exit signs, and fire safety signs	Are all present with additional detail explaining their purpose and the procedure used

Assessment of technology use depends on the level of student use permitted, the technology available, and the age of the students. See chapter 4 for additional information on assessing technology use.

Additional criteria should be added focusing on writing. The criteria used for the rubric should reflect the objectives and expectations for the students.

theme culminating **event**

All About Us

Work with the children to prepare an All About Us celebration. Set a date on the calendar. Create an invitation to send to the groups that are to be invited. Consider posting the invitation on the class Web page or sending the invitations by e-mail with an e-mail RSVP. Encourage each child to write and illustrate invitations to the people they choose to invite.

PLAN THE EVENT

Checklist: Create a checklist for what will happen during the All About Us celebration using a table format with the activities listed in one column, materials needed in another, and people responsible in a third. Include the following activities, other activities from the units, or activities generated by the students.

- All About Me slideshows
- Autobiographies
- Timelines
- Self-portraits and family portraits
- Videos of children participating in the activities

STAGE THE EVENT

Introductions: Have children introduce each other by telling unique characteristics of a partner and explaining the artifact that best describes the partner.

Audience Participation: Create a Bingo game for parents and visitors in which they must find the child with a particular attribute. Have students give their parents a tour of the school on their way home.

- Have the children and the audience join in a game of Hokey Pokey or Simon Says.

My First School Program: Have the audience members write an "I Remember When" entry to a My First School Program book, providing the event, approximate grade and year, and their name. Illustrate with photos or hand-drawn illustrations and publish.

ARCHIVE THE EVENT

Videotape the Event: Videos can be transferred to VHS format to send home to parents to play on their VCRs. They may be burned on CDs. CDs can then be played back on CD drives in computers. These videos could also be burned on DVDs to be shown using a DVD player or a DVD drive in a computer. Other devices such as the Sony Play Station II also have the capability of showing DVDs.

"Variety is the spice of life. That's what gives it flavor."
—William Cowper
(1731-1800)

Communities

The notion of community as a larger area beyond the neighborhood encompasses ideas of unique places, jobs, and vitality in the form of constant change. This theme explores various aspect of community in an effort to expand young children's view of themselves and the world around them.

The goals of this theme include having children become aware of what goes on in the neighborhood and in the community, who works in the community, and the changing nature of the community.

The following standards-based curriculum units enable students to explore the concepts of community as they take part in the following activities. Students:

- Take several walks around the neighborhood, each with targeted observations.
- Take an oral history of their community from an elderly person.
- Plan a field trip within the community.
- Create a multimedia slideshow of what their parents do for work and one that depicts what the children want to do when they grow up.
- Create a Welcome book for someone coming into the class and a Remembrance book for someone moving away.
- Study issues of recycling trash in the community.

Unit Tools

SPOTLIGHT ON
TECHNOLOGY

Kid Pix: Kid Pix is used to create slideshows to display student ideas. As an example, students create a Kid Pix illustration of what a parent or relative does for work and create another slide of what their favorite job is. Using the software tools allows students to explore how the tools are used in the context of demonstrating their understanding of employment. Envisioning themselves in the world of work helps young children conceptualize their place in the world. The class slideshow is a way to share their ideas and see the ideas of others. Students love to replay the slideshow at the computer center as well as share it with parents and friends at open house.

Mapping and Construction Software: Mapping and construction software allows students to create replicas of their neighborhoods and to create new ones.

Kidspiration: Kidspiration has numerous pictures in a picture gallery for students to use in a number of community activities. However, it also allows pictures to be collected into a photo gallery that students can then use to complete or create activities.

WRITING ACROSS THE CURRICULUM

In every unit, children are given opportunities to write about what they see, experience, and imagine. Very young children vary in their ability to express themselves in written form. While some are able to write words and stories with coherence, others are struggling to express themselves in pictorial form.

In the **My Neighborhood** unit, students could write a summary of the observations made during their walks around the neighborhood. After looking at the slideshows, ABC books, and results of other activities, the class can discuss things that neighborhoods have in common. Students could write about the aspect of the neighborhood that is most important to them.

In the **Community Places** unit, students look at places for spending leisure time with their friends and family. They can create a proposal ("I think our community should have a . . .") for something that the community doesn't have available that they think would benefit most people in the community. They would have to think about those who are elderly as well as those who are very young.

In the **What Do Workers Do?** unit, children learn about the concept of a job and the responsibilities of some jobs. As an extension, students can write job descriptions for the jobs in the classroom. Working in collaborative groups, students can create a job description that encompasses all the tasks that a person who does the job would engage in. The collaborative writing and the brainstorming of responsibilities should enable them to better understand the expectations of the jobs and to use the results of their writing for later reference.

In the **Changes in My Neighborhood** unit, students could write to a government official, sharing plans for change (as documented in the assessment task). The letter could request that the official write back about plans related to the issues at hand.

TEACHER VOICES

About the Community Places unit

"I discovered that many of my students have been very sheltered in their experiences beyond the local neighborhood. They have been to some of the places that are popular but not to local parks, playgrounds, and community centers. I expanded the unit to look at places that are free to go to, as the families have limited resources. Rather than staying at home when they couldn't go to an expensive theme park or children's restaurant with a play yard, parents were delighted that their children wanted to go to local city parks and small discovery centers around town. The unit was as much of an eye opener to the parents as it was to the children."

About the Changes in My Neighborhood unit

"The **Changes in My Neighborhood** unit put our class in a position of being proactive about one of the greatest problems of our school–so many kids move in and out of the school during the year. It never occurred to anyone to make a Welcome book for the new kids from a kid's point of view. We have welcome packets for the parents to orient them to the expectations of the school and the community, but nothing that is warm and friendly.

"My kids worked very hard in making the Welcome book. Since so many of them had moved already in their short school careers, they very well knew what it felt like and what they would have liked to have known as soon as they came. The booklet has created a real sense of community in the classroom. Our school is now working on Welcome books for each grade level. The kids love them!"

CHILDREN'S LITERATURE — Each unit includes an extensive list of children's literature related to neighborhoods, places in communities, workers, and change. The books have been purposefully selected to match young children's interest and the topic of the unit. Choose ones available in your school, personal, or public library and be sure to search for new ones on the market. Your search can be at the local bookstore or online.

WEB RESOURCES — An extensive list of Web Resources accompanies every unit. All Web Resources listed in these units were current at the time of publishing. Because of the rapid growth of Internet use, sites can be expected to come and go. To keep the resources current, all software and online references are available online at **www.edtech4teachers.com** and will be updated frequently.

TEACHING TIPS — Teaching very young children requires a balance between holding discussions to clarify thinking and practice oral language skills and having students take part in hands-on activities to keep them exploring and engaged. The unit activities can be used as either center or whole-class lessons depending on the class and the amount of help available in the classroom.

Keep in mind that the units were written to give you a series of multidisciplinary ideas from which to choose. As part of the selection process, think about how much time you are willing to devote to the unit, how long you keep centers up, what your rotation time frame is, and how you are building a sense of independence and responsibility in your students.

As the computer activities are woven into the centers, make sure that your students have had instruction on expectations for completing the task. If you have students who are new to your class or seem to forget what the task and standards are when they get to the computer station, be sure to pair those up with students who are good coaches. Because very young students do not naturally coach others, you will want to do a lesson on how to help someone without giving answers or doing the work for them. Young children are very responsive to being helpers.

LESSON EXTENDERS

The **My Neighborhood** unit could be extended by creating an additional version of a neighborhood that mirrored the students'. Give student groups a one-time-use camera to take pictures of every building on their block. Take the groups' cameras to be processed and ask to have the pictures put on a CD. This is becoming cheaper than prints. Print out the pictures from the CD and place them on a bulletin board that has a large map of the community with all the neighborhood streets already drawn. Have the students place the pictures in the order that the buildings appear. It is interesting to listen to the conversations students have about the sequence of the buildings or homes on their block. (The large map can be made by taking a map from MapQuest, showing it on the wall through a projector, and drawing the streets onto bulletin board paper. Or a copy of the map can be taken to a copy shop or district media center to be enlarged in segments. Once the map is completed, it can be used in succeeding years. The digital pictures can be used as a sorting activity in succeeding years.)

The **What Do Workers Do?** unit could be extended by having students engage in a Shadow a Parent Day. Some schools have days set aside for professional development for teachers in which the students stay home. Ask parents to make that a learning experience in which the child accompanies the parent to the job for a portion of the day. Have students keep notes or draw pictures of what their parent does while at work. Tie the experience in with reading the time on a digital clock so that the time can be recorded with each task that is done. Students can then share the activities by making a timeline of the day using TimeLiner. Have students (and parents) compare this with the unit beginning activity that asked students to record their impressions of what their parent did at work.

THEME CULMINATING EVENT

Host a neighborhood block party. Invite workers the children come in contact with (store clerk, recreation leader, bus driver, crossing guard, etc.), parents, and city officials. Have students' neighborhood replicas, writing samples, and digital slideshows available in addition to displaying Web sites the children have used. Have the class sing some of the songs that they have learned in the unit, share what they would like to do when they grow up, and present their plans for changes in the community. Make the event a celebration of the character and features of the community. A complete plan for this activity is found at the end of the theme.

My Neighborhood

UNIT OVERVIEW

Outside the confines of their own home, young children should become familiar with their immediate surroundings and neighborhood. In this unit, students explore two neighborhoods, around their home and around their school. Supplemented with numerous resources, children look at their backyard and their schoolyard (which they also visited as parts of **My Home** and **My School** in the **All About Me** theme), as well as the blocks immediately surrounding their home, comparing and contrasting that information with others in their class. Upon completion of the unit, students recognize that a series of houses make up a neighborhood, and that a series of neighborhoods make up a community.

UNIT OBJECTIVES

At the end of this unit, students will be able to:

- Demonstrate their understanding of the safety rules for the neighborhood.
- Describe the area or block surrounding their school as part of the school neighborhood.
- Describe the area or block surrounding their home as part of their home neighborhood.
- Categorize and classify items in the school and home neighborhoods.
- Compare and contrast items in their neighborhood with other neighborhoods.
- Describe the areas of the neighborhood as residential, business, industry, recreational, school, and related to transportation.

STANDARDS
ADDRESSED
IN THIS UNIT

ISTE NETS for Students 3, 4, 5
IRA/NCTE English/Language Arts Standards 1, 2, 4, 5, 7, 8
NCTM Math Standards 1, 3, 4, 8, 10
NAS/NSE Science Standards A1, A2, B1, C3, D1, E3, F3, F4
NCSS Social Studies Standards 1d, 2c, 2d, 3a, 3b, 3g, 3h, 5d, 6a, 6d, 8a, 10b, 10c

CHILDREN'S
LITERATURE

Alphabet City, Stephen T. Johnson
Bus Route to Boston, Maryann Cocca-Leffler
Cassie's Word Quilt, Faith Ringgold
Curious George in the Big City, Margaret & H. A. Rey
I Went Walking, Sue Williams
Living in a Desert, Jan Kottke
Living in a Rainforest, Joanne Winne
Living Near a River, Joanne Winne
Living on a Mountain, Joanne Winne
Living on an Island, Joanne Winne
Living on a Plain, Joanne Winne
Madlenka, Madlenka's Dog, Peter Sis
My Town, William Wegman

Night City, Monica Wellington
One Afternoon, Yumi Heo
On the Town: A Community Adventure, Judith Caseley
Rory's Random Walk Down Wall Street, Amy Doherty
Uptown, Bryan Collier
Where I Live, Frances Wolfe

WEB RESOURCES

Barnyard Friends, A Visit to the Farm: www.plainfield.k12.in.us/hschool/webq/webq43/shannon.htm
Buckle Up Baby (songs): www.state.oh.us/odps/kids/html/songs.html
Elmer's Look Both Ways: www.safety-council.org/info/child/pedest.htm
Elmer's Seven Traffic Safety Rules: www.safety-council.org/info/child/elmer/7rules.html
Elmer the Safety Elephant: www.safety-council.org/info/child/elmer/elmerthe.htm
Great Games From the Ohio Department of Safety: www.state.oh.us/odps/kids/html/safety.html
Journey With Care (several countries): www.careusa.org/vft/bolivia/
Lizzy Visits the Sculpture Garden: www.nga.gov/kids/lizzy/lizzy.html
Road Safety (bike, walk, bus, car): www.roadsafety.net/KIDS/HTML/licence.html
Search for garbage and recycling sites: http://yahooligans.com
Sidewalk Safety: www.state.oh.us/odps/kids/html/safety.html
Songs: www.niehs.nih.gov/kids/music.htm
Who Are the People in My Neighborhood?: http://home.nc.rr.com/muppetsongs/songs/people_in_your_neighborhood).

Dictionaries
  Internet Picture Dictionary: www.pdictionary.com
  Little Explorers Picture Dictionary: www.enchantedlearning.com/Dictionary.html
  Merriam-Webster's Word Central: www.wordcentral.com

SOFTWARE

The Amazing Writing Machine, Broderbund
Choices, Choices: Kids and the Environment, Tom Snyder Productions
Choices, Choices: On the Playground, Tom Snyder Productions
Community Construction Kit, Tom Snyder Productions
Diorama Designer, Tom Snyder Productions
The Graph Club, Tom Snyder Productions, or Tabletop Jr., Broderbund
HyperStudio
Kid Pix Studio Deluxe (English, Spanish), Broderbund
Kidspiration, Inspiration Software
Let's Pretend! Many Lands, Many Playgrounds, Mind Magic
Let's Pretend! Our World Is a Playground, Mind Magic
Neighborhood Map Machine, Tom Snyder Productions
Reader Rabbit, Preschool Sparkle Star Rescue, The Learning Company
Roamer Robot, TerrapinLogo

teaching the unit

Getting Started

On the Friday before beginning the unit, send a note to parents explaining the purposes and desired outcomes of the unit. Ask parents to take a walk with their child over the weekend around their neighborhood block. Instruct parents to point out various areas and types of buildings close to their homes. Suggest they point out homes and yards, streets and sidewalks, fenced and unfenced areas, safe and unsafe places, traffic and street signs, addresses and mailboxes. Have parents make a list of the things their children seem to find most interesting and return the list to the teacher in a note or by e-mail. Alternatively, on Monday, children can draw pictures of the things they found most interesting on their walk.

Motivating Activity

Read a book about exploring the neighborhood or city such as *One Afternoon, Night City, Where I Live,* or *On the Town: A Community Adventure.*

Whole-Group Activity

Referring to the walk they took at home, have children briefly share what they saw. Record the important points on a chart or on an overhead displayed word processor. Prepare students for a walk in the school neighborhood by explaining the safety rules children need to follow (holding hands; staying on the sidewalks; walking, not running; stopping at the corners; not crossing the street without an adult). Based on information about things they found in their neighborhoods, have students generate a list of things they think they will see or questions they might want to find answers for. Use the Kidspiration activity Rules Rule! to write about or discuss rules for taking a walking trip in the neighborhood.

Take digital cameras, clipboards, or PDAs for the children. Capture the sequence of your walk on camera as you proceed. Plan your walk by staying on the side of the street the school is on. This allows you to walk with the class around the block without crossing a street. Whether in the middle of downtown Washington, D.C., or on an isolated plain in Kansas, examine as many things as you can in this neighborhood. Describe what is seen in terms of businesses that sell things, industries that make things, recreational areas to have fun in, residential or places to live, schools, places that facilitate travel, and utilities or community services. In addition, decide whether things are living or nonliving. Discuss rights of landowners and respecting the rights of occupants and workers. Point out measures taken for security. Point out all the street, safety, and traffic signs and signals.

Multidisciplinary Activities

ART *My Neighborhood:* Have children draw picture maps of their own neighborhoods, encouraging them to place pictures on their maps of items they remember from their walk with their parents. Compare the similarities and the differences in the areas around the homes including landscaping and personal preferences in design.

- Have children design a new safety sign or street sign using Kid Pix.
- Insert the digital pictures that were taken on your neighborhood walk into Kid Pix and make a slideshow to review what was seen. Have students use Kid Pix to draw the signs, houses, buildings, trees, and other things that were seen on the walk and add those to the slideshow.

Build a Neighborhood, Outside: If there is a large sand area close by, have children build a neighborhood in the sand. Inside, create a large grid that simulates the neighborhood. Have students place buildings or labels where things are located on the grid.

- Use Community Construction Kit to build a city.
- Use the Kidspiration activity Welcome to My Town to design a neighborhood.
- Import a black line outline of a house into Kid Pix or have children draw one. Have children experiment with color combinations by painting the house, trim, doors, and so on with the paint can. What are common colors for houses? Why are there not very many purple or pink houses?

Sculpture Garden: View the Web site Lizzy Visits the Sculpture Garden, provided by the National Gallery of Art (**www.nga.gov/kids/lizzy/lizzy.html**).

- Take pictures of various pieces of artwork in the community and set up a digital trip of the sculptures.

GROSS MOTOR   *How Many Steps?:* Put pedometers on a couple of the children and a couple of adults to wear on the walk around the block. Record the number of steps it takes for each person on the walk. Discuss why there might be differences.

- Program the TerrapinLogo Roamer Robot to use different units of measure. Program it for an adult and a child. Simulate with the Roamer the difference between the two steps.

Follow the Leader: Take a second tour around the block, going single file and playing Follow the Leader using baby steps, hopping on one foot, jumping, walking, and skipping (no running).

HEALTH   *Where Does the Trash Go?:* Have students find out the answers to the following questions: How is the trash and other waste taken care of? Does the neighborhood have a community recycling program? Where do you dispose of paint, batteries, and other hazardous wastes? Why can't you throw them in the trash can? If you don't already have one in your class or school, create a recycling bin for paper; find out where to take it or have it picked up. If the school already has a recycling program, create posters to encourage recycling and discuss why it is necessary.

■ Have students conduct a search using Yahooligans.com to find background information on garbage and recycling.

LANGUAGE ARTS AND READING

My Neighborhood: Have children create a written or picture story of their neighborhood.

■ Have students use Kid Pix to design a travel brochure that tells others about the neighborhood.

■ Use the Kidspiration activity My Neighborhood to list symbols seen in the neighborhood and write about what each means.

My Own Neighborhood of Old: An Oral History: Generate a list of questions children can ask of an older person in their neighborhood to determine what the neighborhood used to be like and how it developed. Have parents accompany their children on a visit with an older person in the neighborhood to get the answers to the questions. Have children fold a piece of paper in half to record what their neighborhood looked like a long time ago and what it looks like now.

■ Use the Kidspiration teacher activity How People Live to record information.

■ Ask parents to videotape the interview, if possible, to be used later to document how the community as a whole developed.

■ If older citizens are willing, borrow old pictures of the community to scan. Take similar pictures of the location from the same vantage point as the original photograph. Show students both pictures and ask about what has happened since the original picture. Be sure to discuss what happens to buildings and landscaping with the passage of time.

Our School Neighborhood: Repeat the activities above focusing on the school neighborhood. Use a Venn diagram to look at the similarities and differences of students' own neighborhoods and their school neighborhood.

■ Use Kidspiration to create the Venn diagram as the discussion takes place.

Our Neighborhood Word Quilt: Read an alphabet book or a quilt book. Create a word quilt or an ABC book using words that describe the school neighborhood.

From School to Home and Back: Have children create a written or picture story of how they get to school each day.

■ Compile the stories of how students get to and from school into a book or a Kid Pix slideshow. Document one child's trip and caption the photos. Use online children's dictionaries or picture dictionaries to help with the words. Insert the photos into a slideshow or create a Web page.

■ Use Kidspiration to create a web of the various ways children get to school. Provide each child with a 4" x 4" piece of paper on which to draw a picture of and label how they get to school (by foot, bike, car, bus, subway, train, etc.). Use online children's dictionaries or picture dictionaries to help with the words. Graph the ways they get to school. (If all are bussed, put the bus numbers on each bus and record how many students are on each bus.)

MATH   *Getting Around:* Generate a list of ways to get around in the city to the neighborhood. Set up a traffic-recording sheet by placing each type of vehicle brainstormed at the left-hand side of the line, leaving plenty of room to make tally marks as vehicles pass by. Enlist the help of three other adults. Divide the class into four groups, placing each group in the middle of a block about 20 feet back from the street. Spend 30 minutes tabulating the number of different vehicles that pass by. Back in the classroom, discuss the results.

- Use a spreadsheet to graph the results and make pie charts, bar graphs, and line graphs. Discuss how the different graphs represent the same information.

How Far Around the Block?: Measure pieces of string that are in 48, 24, 12, 6, 3, and 1 foot lengths. Place a piece of tape around each to note the length. Using the combination of measurement devices, measure the perimeter of the block. Have students tally each time they use one of the measuring lengths. Have students use a calculator to sum up all the measurements to determine the perimeter of the block. Alternatively, use a trundle wheel to measure the perimeter of the block. If students are adept at using the trundle wheel, have students who live close to each other take the trundle wheel home and measure the perimeter of their own block. Create a chart and compare the results. Have students discuss why the measurements of blocks might be very different.

How Far to School? How Far to Home?: Use Yahoo! Maps to determine the directions and distance between each child's home and school. Each child will need his or her address and the school address to determine this information. (This is a meaningful way to have children memorize their addresses if they don't already know them.) Yahoo! Maps provides a map and a reverse map. See how far away each child lives from school. Are the distances the same or different? Why might they be the same? Why might they be different?

Using the grid created in the Art section, label the streets as you would a coordinate grid using the school as the zero point. Although a real map will probably not work for the location of houses relative to the school, have students find specific locations on the grid-map by giving coordinate directions. For example: "Draw a route that follows the order of the following points (0,1), (3,1), (3,5), (5, 5). Where are you?"

- Use Kid Pix or a word processing program to have students make "Where are you?" riddles that use coordinate pairs. Keep the riddles in a book for use by other classes.
- Create a simulated neighborhood with tape on the floor marking landmarks in the neighborhood. Program the TerrapinLogo Roamer Robot to complete a journey.

MUSIC   *Who Are the People in My Neighborhood?:* Students can sing this famous Sesame Street song and then have a discussion about the people who live in their neighborhood (http://home.nc.rr.com/muppetsongs/songs/people_in_your_neighborhood).

SAFETY *Neighborhood Safety:* The study of neighborhoods is a good time to discuss walking safety, bike safety, skateboard safety, stranger danger, car safety, and sidewalk safety. View several of the safety sites available at Elmer the Safety Elephant (www.safety-council.org/info/child/elmer/elmerthe.htm).

- Create a step-by-step book or slideshow highlighting one area of safety (sidewalk, bike, car, traffic). Take photos of each step, and create a captioned photo gallery to post online.

Computer Station: Set up several of the safety sites listed below to reinforce safety rules.

Buckle Up Baby (songs): www.state.oh.us/odps/kids/html/songs.html
Elmer's Look Both Ways: www.safety-council.org/info/child/pedest.htm
Elmer's Seven Traffic Safety Rules: www.safety-council.org/info/child/elmer/7rules.html
Elmer the Safety Elephant: www.safety-council.org/info/child/elmer/elmerthe.htm
Road Safety (bike, walk, bus, car): www.roadsafety.net/KIDS/HTML/licence.html
Sidewalk Safety: www.state.oh.us/odps/kids/html/safety.html

Street and Traffic Safety: Draw pictures of all the street and traffic signs you see on the walk around the school neighborhood. Write a brief description of what each tells you to do.

- Using the templates, stamps, or characters in Kid Pix, have students create the street sign they see most often. Have the signs labeled with the meaning of the sign described.

- Have students contribute to making a safety slideshow in Kid Pix that includes the signs made by the class, safety tips discussed in class, directions to common places, and cautions for young children.

SCIENCE *Living and Nonliving Things in My Neighborhood:* Have children sort the objects they see in their neighborhood into living and nonliving things. Create a teacher activity in Kidspiration using two super groupers, one labeled Living and the other labeled Nonliving. Stamp a series of symbols and have students drag symbols to the appropriate group.

Tree Types: Take pictures of all the different types of trees during the walk in the school neighborhood. Post the pictures in the classroom. Provide online tree resources and tree books to help children identify each tree. Take a picture of the full tree and take a close up of the leaves, berries, or other features. Print out cards so that students may play a matching game.

- Allow students to take digital pictures of trees around school from far away and close up. Complete the same activity as above. (Allowing young students to use the digital camera will help them learn how to appropriately use the equipment.)

Flat, Hilly, Smooth, Rough: Read one or more of the Winnie the Pooh books about living in a rainforest, near a river, or on a mountain, plain, or island, or read a different book about places to live. What is the terrain around the school? As the students walk around the school block, talk about the earth formations around the block that are visible from each spot.

My Home, Your Home: Study habitats in the neighborhood—those for animals and for people. Document the habitats (without being obtrusive) using a digital camera.

- Create a HyperStudio stack or Kid Pix slideshow of the essential parts of the habitat for humans and for animals.

SOCIAL STUDIES   *Where Do You Live?:* Enlarge a map of the city or the portion that shows your school and all the addresses of the children. Use a map pin to locate each student's home and places that children know. Post the map on the north side of the room so that up is north, left is west, right is east, and down is south. Play 20 Questions with the children using houses, places, and directions to zero in on the place you have selected.

- Create the map in Neighborhood Map Machine. Let the children add the details: signs, trees, cars, and so on.

Our Neighborhood: Tape two pieces of butcher paper together to make a 4' x 8' piece. Tape it to a piece of plywood and place the plywood on a set of desks or a table. Create the school neighborhood on the board. Use different colors to label the different uses of the property: business, industry, residential, travel, recreation, school, and so forth.

- Use a Word newsletter template to design a travel brochure that tells others about your school neighborhood.
- Use Community Construction Kit to create the houses, buildings, cars, trees, and other features. Place them on the board to create a miniature neighborhood.

Assessment

FOR YOUNGER LEARNERS

Ask children to draw a My Neighborhood picture that includes residential, school, business, industry, recreation, travel, and safety elements. Ask students to label elements of their picture. Adjust the rubric to fit the topics covered in the unit.

NOTE: For a description of the values "Not Interested," "Trying It," "Working on It," "Got it!," and "Helping Others," see chapter 4.

NOTE: Adjust this list to make it appropriate for your students' neighborhoods.

CRITERIA	NOT INTERESTED	TRYING IT	WORKING ON IT	GOT IT!	HELPING OTHERS
Drawing the picture					
Labeling elements in the picture					
Picture includes homes					
Picture includes school					
Picture includes businesses					
Picture includes industry					
Picture includes recreation					
Picture includes ways to travel					
Picture includes safety elements					

FOR MORE ABLE LEARNERS

Ask children to write a My Neighborhood story with an illustration or create a My Neighborhood slideshow. Either should include information about residential, school, business, industry, recreation, travel, and safety elements. Adjust the rubric to fit the topics covered in the unit.

NOTE: Adjust this list to make it appropriate for your students' neighborhoods.

CRITERIA	APPROACHES TARGET	MEETS TARGET	EXCEEDS TARGET
Picture includes homes	One home is present.	More than one home is present and in approximately the correct place in the neighborhood.	More than one home is present, located correctly, and described accurately. The owner's name may be included.
Picture includes school	The school is present but in the wrong location.	The school is present and in approximately the correct place in the neighborhood.	The school is present with descriptive information.
Picture includes businesses	Only one business is present. It may be inaccurately positioned or described.	More than one business is present and in approximately the correct place in the neighborhood.	More than one business is present, located correctly, with a description of the business included.
Picture includes industry	Industry is included. It may be inaccurately positioned or described.	An industry is included and in approximately the correct place in the neighborhood.	Local industry is included with a description of what is produced.
Picture includes recreation	Picture includes one recreation facility such as a park or playground but it is not located in correct proximity to other buildings.	Recreation facilities are included and located somewhat correctly in the neighborhood.	Recreation facilities are included, located correctly, and described in detail.
Picture includes ways to travel	Some ways to travel are included such as a street or subway. They may be inaccurately positioned or described.	Streets and rail lines (if applicable) are included and positioned or described accurately.	Streets and rail lines (if applicable) are included, positioned accurately, and have cars or trains on them heading the right direction with reference to where they might be going.
Picture includes safety elements	Few safety elements are included such as traffic signs or crosswalks.	Traffic signs, crosswalks, fences, and other safety elements are present.	Traffic signs, crosswalks, fences, and other obvious and hidden safety elements are present and described.

Assessment of technology use depends on the level of student use permitted, the technology available, and the age of the students. See chapter 4 for additional information on assessing technology use.

Additional criteria should be added focusing on writing. The criteria used for the rubric should reflect the objectives and expectations for the students.

Community Places

UNIT OVERVIEW

A community is defined as a body of individuals with common interests or a group linked by common interests or policies. A study of the community is a natural extension following the study of the home and school neighborhoods. In some parts of the country the community is defined as a section of the city. In other places, the community is the city itself. In this unit, children examine their community by looking at fun places (recreational areas), businesses (stores), and travel paths (ways to get places).

UNIT OBJECTIVES

At the end of this unit, students will be able to:

- Identify and sort places in their community and the various functions they serve such as businesses, industries, schools, recreation areas, travel stations and routes, residential areas, government offices, and medical facilities.
- Describe one place in the community by its function.
- Describe the jobs and responsibilities of those who provide merchandise or services.
- Label the different pathways for travel (paths, sidewalks, bike paths, streets, highways, interstate highways, monorails, dual rails, waterways [rivers, lakes, seas, oceans, canals]) and the mode of transportation appropriate for each.

STANDARDS
ADDRESSED
IN THIS UNIT

ISTE NETS for Students 3, 4, 5
IRA/NCTE English/Language Arts Standards 1, 2, 3, 4, 5, 7, 8
NCTM Math Standards 1, 4, 6
NAS/NSE Science Standards C3, E3, F3, F4
NCSS Social Studies Standards 2c, 2d, 2e, 3g, 3h, 3k, 6e, 7c, 7d, 7e, 7g, 8a, 8b, 10c

CHILDREN'S
LITERATURE

At the Post Office, Carol Greene
At the Trucking Company, Carol Greene
Behind the Scenes at the Shopping Mall, Marilyn Miller
Buying a Pet From Ms. Chavez, Alice K. Flanagan
Flea Market Fleas From A to Z, Thelma Kerns
Grandpa's Corner Store, Dyanne Disalvo-Ryan
Life on a Pig Farm, Judy Wolfman
A Visit to the Gravesens' Farm, Alice K. Flanagan & Christine Osinski (Illustrator)
Working at a Museum, Arthur John L'Hommedieu
Working at a TV Station, Gary Davis
The Zieglers and Their Apple Orchard, Alice K. Flanagan
Zoo Keepers, Tami Deedrick

WEB RESOURCES

Bike Safety: www.nhtsa.dot.gov/kids/biketour/index.html
Buckle Up Baby (songs): www.state.oh.us/odps/kids/html/songs.html

Children's Section of Art Expression: www.artexpression.com/child.htm
Road Safety (bike, walk, bus, car): www.roadsafety.net/KIDS/HTML/licence.html
Sidewalk Safety: www.state.oh.us/odps/kids/html/safety.html
Songs: www.niehs.nih.gov/kids/music.htm
Virtual Fire Station Field Trip: http://education.wichita.edu/twitherspo/
    firestation_vft/index.htm
Yahoo! Maps: http://maps.yahoo.com

Dictionaries
    Internet Picture Dictionary: www.pdictionary.com
    Little Explorers Picture Dictionary: www.enchantedlearning.com/Dictionary.html
    Merriam-Webster's Word Central: www.wordcentral.com

SOFTWARE Community Construction Kit, Tom Snyder Productions
    The Graph Club, Tom Synder Productions, or Tabletop Jr., Broderbund
    Kid Pix (English, Spanish), Broderbund
    Kid Pix Studio Deluxe (English, Spanish), Broderbund
    Kidspiration, Inspiration Software
    Neighborhood Map Machine, Tom Snyder Productions
    Roamer Robot, TerrapinLogo
    TimeLiner (English, Spanish), Tom Snyder Productions

**teaching
the unit**

Getting Started

In a letter sent to parents before the unit, ask for their assistance in helping students find a way to work to earn money to go on a field trip. Also, ask them to determine any jobs the children can do around the house to earn the money. Even if the families are not required to pay for the trips, ask parents to work with their children to earn a reasonable predetermined amount of money. In addition, ask parents open-ended questions that help you understand what the families do for fun. For example: What do you and your family enjoy doing together for fun? What are the favorite places in our community that you and your family like to go? If your child could choose one place to go for his or her birthday, what would that place be? For the purpose of surveying shopping habits, ask parents to save the sacks from the stores where they shop and send a set of them to school each week for a month.

Motivating Activity

As a whole class, take a virtual field trip to a place where most of the children have never been. Discuss what it takes to go to the place you visit. Encourage students to think through the process of going on a trip to visit the community in which the virtual field trip site is located. Discuss the effect on the community of having a destination for tourists, particularly if you select a virtual tour of a major tourist attraction.

Plan a field trip with the students to a high-interest location in the community. The children's role will be to (1) select a place to go that most everyone will enjoy, (2) identify what will be needed to take on the trip, (3) work at home and at school to earn money as well as the right to go, and (4) collaboratively write the request to order the buses.

Multidisciplinary Activities

ART   *Recreation Collage:* Examine the newspapers and local magazines for pictures of places to go for fun. Make a class collage of the pictures. Write a sentence on a cloud shape describing each location, and place the shapes around the edge of the collage. Use pins to fasten the clouds to their locations.

   ■ Use online children's dictionaries or picture dictionaries to help with the words.

   ■ Have students search the local community or state Web site for pictures of their favorite locations in the community. Teach the students how to save the pictures to the desktop of the computer for later use. Insert the pictures into Kid Pix for students to label and describe.

Create other collages of stores or other businesses, local industry or manufacturing areas, schools and colleges, and medical facilities.

Classroom Mall: Construct a mall in the block area. Design signs for the stores in the art area and tape them to the blocks.

- Use Community Construction Kit to create and print out buildings in the community: a bank, post office, grocery store, church, school, and so on.
- Program the TerrapinLogo Roamer Robot to take a trip through the community. What is the shortest way to get from one place to another?

Digital Postcards: (Reprinted from *National Educational Technology Standards for Students—Connecting Curriculum and Technology,* Eugene, OR: ISTE, 2000, p. 225.)

- Have students take pictures of highlights in the neighborhood and/or community. As a class, discuss each location; create a caption for each picture that describes it adequately to someone who does not live in the community. Use online children's dictionaries or picture dictionaries to help with the words. Print or save the postcards digitally. Have students send the postcards by mail or attach to an e-mail to family, friends, or e-pals.

Fun in Paintings: Examine artist master paintings in which people appear to be having fun (www.artexpression.com/child.html). Note the date of the paintings. Post the results in a timeline using TimeLiner.

GROSS MOTOR
Charades: Have students act out what they would be doing at the places they have listed as possible field trip sites.

- Video the students as they act out the motions. Be sure to time the students so that their acting lasts at least one minute. Have them repeat the action over and over to ensure that you capture at least one minute of action. Create a guessing game of what the location is by viewing the video clips. Replay the video and have everyone mimic the actions in the video as a physical exercise. If the video clips are saved digitally and as individual clips, periodically re-order the clips to keep the students guessing and watching the video carefully.

HEALTH
In Case of Emergency: Use the phone book to look up hospitals, health departments, doctors' offices, dentists' offices, the Red Cross, and other medical facilities. Locate each place on maps. Use Yahoo! Maps to determine how far each is from the school.

LANGUAGE ARTS AND READING
Let's Go!: Make a book of fun places to go in the community. Have each child make an entry of his or her favorite place. Include the name and address of the place and a story about being there. Post the list of fun places.

- Search the Web for fun places in the vicinity.
- Use the Kidspiration teacher activity My Community to record information about the community.
- Use Kid Pix to create a slideshow of the places to visit in the community.

Sack Reading: Do at least one week of the Math Sack Sort activity first. Ask parents to save the sacks and bags from the various stores as they purchase merchandise for the entire length the unit. (See Getting Started.) Put the entire sack or a portion of the sack on each page of a scrapbook. Have students write a simple sentence under each, using a consistent language pattern. For example: We buy groceries at [Kroger's]. We buy food at [McDonald's]. We buy clothes at [Macy's]. Locate ads in the newspapers that coincide with the sacks. Glue the pictures onto cards. Ask children to match the cards to the sacks.

- Search for the stores online. What is the logo? Use the capturing pictures skill taught in Art to have students save the logos to the desktop of the computer. Print the logos out to add to the scrapbook.

MATH   *What's the Cost?:* Make a list of fun places to go in the community and an accompanying table of the costs. Determine how much it would cost for one person to go, for two people to go, for each child's family to go, and to go as a whole class. Compare and contrast costs for all fun places.

- Create an electronic graph of the data. Point out to the children that as the number of people increases, the cost goes up. This is illustrazted by the slope of the line (The relationship of variables is an important algebraic principle.)

Earning Money: Determine with families the various ways the children can earn money to go on a field trip. Make a list of all of the things the students can do. Have students discuss how much money they can make by working. (Be sure to discuss how the quality of the work completed is a criterion for earning money.) Share with students the actual cost of the field trip. Have students discuss what their contribution pays for.

- Create a budget for the field trip. Use a spreadsheet to show how the money for the trip is acquired and spent.

What Does Everyone Like to Do?: Use the list of fun places generated in the Language Arts and Reading activity. Ask each child to vote by secret ballot on the top three places they consider to be the most fun. Tally, post, and analyze the results. (Be sure to list only those places the class is really able to go. Use the results to determine where the class will go on a field trip.)

Sack Sort: To find out a rough estimate of the volume of goods the families purchase during the period of this unit, have students bring the saved sacks to school once a week. Create a sorting activity in which student sort the sacks and count the number of each kind of sack. Create a table to show the results of the sorting from each week. Create interpretive questions about the results of the sorting. Sum the results and discuss what the data show.

- Use Graph Club to record the results. Consider preassigning the sack sorting to groups of students. Have the students record the results in the electronic table.

MUSIC   *Let's Go to a Concert:* Visit local theaters or concerts appropriate for children. Replay the music from the play or concert at the music center. Link the play or concert with the location of the theater on the community map. If available, locate the music on the Internet for students to replay on their own.

SCIENCE

What Makes It Work?: Examine the fun places to go in the community, such as roller coasters, water parks, indoor and outdoor playgrounds. Before you go, ask children to draw pictures or write stories that tell what makes each work. After a trip, ask the children to again draw pictures or write stories to tell what makes the things work. Compare their results and ask them why their pictures or stories changed. Use Kid Pix to generate the before and after pictures. Add all to a class slideshow.

SOCIAL STUDIES

At the Movies: Create a movie theater in the classroom by lining the chairs up in a row, setting up a ticket booth and a ticket taker stand, designing a concession stand, and selecting a good movie. Have children work in school to get (fake) money to attend the movie and buy concessions. Have students help with the process by making sure that they clean up after themselves. Discuss the jobs that are needed to run the movie theater. Include a discussion of appropriate behavior in the movie. Consider showing some of the slideshows made in class as part of the movie experience.

Where Are the Fun Places?: Use the fun places identified in the Language Arts and Reading activity in which children made a book of all the activities in the community. Find the addresses of each in the phone book.

■ Use Yahoo! Maps to locate directions from school to the places. On a city map, pin each place with a unique map pin color. Have students use colored markers to show the route to each place following the directions from Yahoo! Maps.

Business Stories: Read a book that tells about buying things at stores or the jobs that people at these places do. What are all the different stores you go to? Why do you go to them? What goods do these places sell? What services do they provide? Make a list of the names of the stores and the products or services they sell. Compare and contrast these. Categorize the stores. Make one page for each store and construct a slideshow or Big Book.

Industry: Have students locate the places in their community where goods are manufactured. If there are no industries in the community, discuss industry in general. Look at the state and largest city Web sites. Discuss the industries that are highlighted on the Web sites.

Way to Go!: Take a walk outside the school on the sidewalk. Examine the sidewalk as a way to get from one place to another by walking. Ask the children the names of other ways to get from one place to another by walking. (A path is one.) Ask them if the street is a way to get from one place to another. Is it by walking. No, it's by car. See how many different ways of getting from one place to another they can suggest. Make a table to show the path (sidewalk, rail, street, highway) and the method of transportation (by foot, car, truck, subway, train, monorail, air, boat).

Waterways: What are the waterways in the local community? Are there lakes, rivers, streams, or canals? How are each used for transportation, recreation, or business? Locate each on a map. Interview two or three adults in the community about how they use the waterways. Compile the information in stories to post on a class Web site.

Who's in Charge?: What are the government buildings in your community, those owned and run by the local, state, and federal government? Include in this list the fire stations, police stations, hospitals (if appropriate), city hall, county court houses, capitol buildings, and so on. What happens in these buildings? What are the jobs and roles people play? Take a virtual field trip to the Fire Station Web site (http://education.wichita.edu/twitherspo/firestation_vft/index.htm).

Design a Virtual Field Trip: For use this year and with future classes, design a trip to another building or station or take the class along. Document the visit on film or video. Be sure to note the tools and technology used in these places, who works there, what their job is, the function of the building, and so on.

- Document the trip with digital photographs.
- Make a scrapbook or slideshow using the photographs. Have children record stories about each picture.

Assessment

FOR YOUNGER
LEARNERS

Ask children to complete a two-column table of community places. In the first column, they will record at least one place in the areas they have studied (businesses, industries, schools, recreation areas, modes of travel, residential areas, government offices). In the second column, they will tell the importance or a notable fact about each one. Have nonreaders use pictures from the lessons to convey meaning. For responses, have parent helpers or others record the child's thinking.

NOTE: For a description of the values "Not Interested," "Trying It," "Working on It," "Got it!," and "Helping Others," see chapter 4.

NOTE: If desired, list items for the criteria as separate areas on the rubric.

CRITERIA	NOT INTERESTED	TRYING IT	WORKING ON IT	GOT IT!	HELPING OTHERS
Businesses, industries, schools, recreation areas, moves of travel, residential areas, government offices, and medical facilities are noted.					
Clear reasons as to the need for each are noted.					

FOR MORE ABLE
LEARNERS

Ask children to complete a two-column table of community places containing relevant areas that they have studied (businesses, industries, schools, recreation areas, modes of travel, residential areas, government offices). In the second column, ask them to tell the importance of or a notable fact about each one. The rubric below is designed to be a checklist. Each entry is judged by the degree to which the student described or provided notable facts about that area of the community.

CRITERIA	ATTEMPTS TO DESCRIBE BUT SHOWS SOME MISCONCEPTIONS	DESCRIBES THE AREA ACCURATELY	PROVIDES CONSIDERABLE DETAIL IN MAKING ACCURATE DESCRIPTIONS
School			
Business			
Industry			
Recreation			
Modes of travel			

Assessment of technology use depends on the level of student use permitted, the technology available, and the age of the students. See chapter 4 for additional information on assessing technology use.

Additional criteria should be added focusing on writing. The criteria used for the rubric should reflect the objectives and expectations for the students.

What Do Workers Do?

UNIT OVERVIEW   Most young children express a desire to have a certain vocation when they grow up. Sometimes these initial aspirations reflect the jobs their parents or siblings have. Sometimes they reflect their heroes. Regardless of their choices at an early age— doctors, clowns, ball players, dancers, or geniuses—an exploration of those jobs will provide students with some clear expectations related to the work people do.

UNIT OBJECTIVES   At the end of this unit, students will be able to:

- Identify several jobs in the community and the tasks associated with those roles.
- See their work as schoolwork and the chores they have at home and school.
- Describe the various roles played by the many workers in one place (store, business, recreation area, school, fire station, etc.)

STANDARDS ADDRESSED IN THIS UNIT
ISTE NETS for Students 3, 4, 5
IRA/NCTE English/Language Arts Standards 1, 2, 3, 4, 5, 7, 8
NCTM Math Standards 1, 4, 5, 6, 8, 10
NAS/NSE Science Standards C3, G1
NCSS Social Studies Standards 7a-j, 8a, 9a

CHILDREN'S LITERATURE
Work—General
All About Things People Do, Melanie Rice
Busy Careers, Diane Muldrow
Career Day, Anne F. Rockwell
Community Helpers From A to Z, Bobbie Kalman & Niki Walker
I'm Gonna Be (Afro-Bets Kids Series), Wade Hudson
Jobs People Do, Christopher Maynard
Mommy Works, Daddy Works, Marika Pederson & Mikele Hall
What Do You Want to Be?, Kate Davis
Work, Ann Morris

Individual Jobs
A Day in Court With Mrs. Trinh, Alice K. Flanagan
A Day in the Life of a Builder, Linda Hayward
A Day in the Life of a Dancer, Linda Hayward
A Day With a Bricklayer, Mark Thomas
A Day With a Carpenter, Joanne Winne
A Day With Air Traffic Controllers, Joanne Winne
A Day With an Electrician, Mark Thomas
A Day With a Plumber, Mark Thomas
Astronauts Work in Space, Carol Greene

Bank Tellers, Katie Bagley

Call Mr. Vasquez, He'll Fix It!, Alice K. Flanagan

Carpenter, Angela McHaney Brown

Cashiers, Katie Bagley

Coaches, Katie Bagley

Computer Engineer, Melissa Maupin

Consultant, Phillip A. Laplante & Melissa Maupin

Farmers, Dee Ready

Flying an Agricultural Plane With Mr. Miller, Alice K. Flanagan

Garbage Collectors, Paulette Bourgeois

Garbage Collectors, Tami Deedrick

I Am an Artist, Pat Lowery Collins

Jobs People Do—A Day in a Life of a TV Reporter, Linda Hayward

Learning About Bees From Mr. Krebs, Alice K. Flanagan

Librarians Help Us Find Information, Carol Greene

Mayors, Alice K. Flanagan

Meet Rory Hohenstein, a Professional Dancer, Jill D. Duvall

Mr. Duvall Reports the News, Jill D. Duvall

Mr. Paul and Mr. Lueke Build Communities, Alice K. Flanagan

Mr. Santizo's Tasty Treats, Alice Flanagan

Mrs. Scott's Beautiful Art, Alice K. Flanagan

Ms. Moja Makes Beautiful Clothes, Jill D. Duvall

The Night Worker, Kate Banks

The Paperboy, Dav Pilkey

Pharmacists, Karen Bush Gibson

Pilots Fly Planes, Fay Robinson

Raising Cows on the Koebels' Farm, Alice K. Flanagan

Recreation Director, Kathleen Ermitage

Riding the Ferry With Captain Cruz, Alice K. Flanagan

Trashy Town, Andrea Griffing Zimmerman, David Clemesha

TV Reporters, Tracey Boraas

What Do Authors Do?, Eileen Christelow

What Do Illustrators Do?, Eileen Christelow

Who Keeps the Water Clean? Ms. Schindler!, Jill D. Duvall

Willie & Sam, Jr., William R. Tonsgar

The Wilsons, a House-Painting Team, Alice K. Flanagan

Yippee-Yay, Gail Gibbons

WEB RESOURCES

Amazon.com: **www.amazon.com**

Barnes and Noble: **www.barnesandnoble.com**

Bureau of Labor Statistics Career Information: **http://stats.bls.gov/k12/html/ edu_over.htm**

Careers, You Are Going to Be a . . . : **http://projects.edtech.sandi.net/chavez/ careers/top.htm**

Community Club: **http://teacher.scholastic.com/commclub/index.htm**

Mizzou Magic: **www.mizzoumagic.missouri.edu/2001_2/index.lasso**

Role Model Project for Girls: **www.womenswork.org/girls/careers.html**

Role Models on the Web: www.rolemodel.net/
Songs: www.niehs.nih.gov/kids/music.htm

Dictionaries
Internet Picture Dictionary: www.pdictionary.com
Little Explorers Picture Dictionary: www.enchantedlearning.com/Dictionary.html
Merriam-Webster's Word Central: www.wordcentral.com

SOFTWARE AND VIDEOS

Software

The Amazing Writing Machine, Broderbund

The Graph Club, Tom Snyder Productions, or Tabletop Jr., Broderbund

I Can Be an Animal Doctor, MacMillan Digital Publishing

I Can Be a Dinosaur Finder, MacMillan Digital Publishing

Kid Pix (English, Spanish), Broderbund

Kidspiration, Inspiration Software

Videos

A Community at Work, Clearvue/eau

Economics in Our Age: Goods and Services, Clearvue/eau

Economics in Our Age: Supply and Demand, Clearvue/eau

teaching the unit

Getting Started

Before the unit begins, send a letter to parents explaining the purpose of the unit. Ask parents to discuss the work they do inside and outside the home and tell their child what technology is used in their jobs. For the beginning activity, ask parents to send an item to school with their child that tells something about what they do (a briefcase, a picture of a computer, an empty grade book, etc.) and the name and address of their place of business.

Motivating Activity

On a Friday before the unit, work with students to develop a list of questions they might want to have answered as they learn about the jobs people do. Read and discuss a biography of someone whose name they recognize, emphasizing the similarities of the celebrity as a child with the students, and the responsibilities and tasks the celebrity assumed as he or she grew up. (Search an online bookstore [see Web Resources earlier in this unit] for a variety of biographies available for children ages 4–8). Encourage the children to talk with their parents about growing up and making the decision to do the jobs they are doing today.

On Monday ask children to begin sharing information about the jobs of their parents.

- Use a computer with a projection device to record the various jobs in a table or spreadsheet.

- Discuss the jobs in terms of type (business, industry, school, recreation, travel, residential, government, medical), and two to three skills needed. Use Kidspiration to create an organizer around the types of jobs and skills needed. Be sure to record the child's parent's name on the diagram with each description.

- View the video *A Community at Work* (published by Clearvue/eau) to learn about community jobs.

Eventually, ask each child to select a different career to focus on for this unit. Record their choices on a chart. Group the careers using the same organizing pattern as their parents' jobs. Post information about all careers in the room or online.

Multidisciplinary Activities

ART *All Kinds of Jobs:* Cut photographs from newspapers and magazines to make a job collage. Scan the pictures the students cut from magazines of people at work.

- Take digital photos of students. Use photo-editing software to replace the face in the scanned picture with a student's face. Print and add to the job collage.

- Using Kid Pix, have students draw themselves in their dream job. Create a classroom slideshow.

GROSS MOTOR

Work Bench: Introduce the construction trades. Have a parent who is in the construction trades or a local handyman visit the class. Show the tools used in construction. Emphasize how much energy it takes to build something. Place child-size construction tools on a workbench with lumber scraps obtained from a local builder's supply. Have a parent supervise students hammering building materials together.

LANGUAGE ARTS AND READING

ABCs of Jobs People Do: Read or create a book about jobs people do. Have children brainstorm a list of all the jobs in the community. Spend one day each on workers involved in rescues, stores, medical professions, schools, recreation, the travel industry, government, and others. After completing the overview of workers, assign each child one of the workers to draw a picture of, write a paragraph or short story about, or record information about the work they do. Alphabetize them into a big book called The ABCs of Jobs People Do. Use bookmaker software to type the students' stories into a single book. As an alternative, have children each make a page in a personal book on each worker.

- Have students use Kid Pix to draw and illustrate their information to create a slideshow.
- Take a virtual tour of a hospital or fire station on the Internet and find out more about jobs. (Search online for "virtual tours.")

On the Job: Select a book that describes work children might want to do when they grow up. Interview or have guests from a variety of vocations speak to the class. Ask questions through an interviewer or provide a list to the guest.

- Work with the class in advance to decide on a list of questions to ask people about the jobs they do. Use Kidspiration to brainstorm the questions to ask and to organize the questions for a smooth interview.
- Videotape the interviews. Digitize the video clips to post with pictures and short job descriptions on the class Web site.
- Enter the answers to the questions in a spreadsheet or database so that you can sort them later to see whether any are alike or different.

In the Ads: Have students write a classified ad looking for a worker by listing the qualifications and job conditions. Type these and print them out in newspaper form. Have students interview classmates interested in those jobs, using some of the same questions that were used to interview the guests.

Highlights of Mom's/Dad's Life: Ask children to work with a parent or caregiver to record or draw on paper or in Kid Pix about one part of the adult's life. Title the books/slideshows, Highlights of [Mom's/Dad's/Caregiver's] Life, inserting the adult's name in lieu of "Mom/Dad/etc." if they choose. Have these biographies available at open house or conference time to keep one set of parents busy while you are talking to another. Ask parents while they are there to record a short (15 to 30 second) piece about their work to use as a sound file for the Kid Pix slides.

A Teacher's Life: Create a slideshow about yourself and your job as a teacher. Use this as an example for the students and to introduce you to parents at open house.

Reading About Jobs: Select a book that describes a job from the Children's Literature section, or view an online source to see what people do in their jobs, such as Community Club (**http://teacher.scholastic.com/commclub/index.htm**). Prepare a short book report (oral or visual) about the book to entice other students to want to read the book.

MATH

Math in Jobs Information: Use a screen reader to review information about the various skills (focusing on math for this activity) needed for different occupations. The Bureau of Labor Statistics Career Information is a good source (**http://stats.bls.gov/k12/html/edu_over.htm**). Write or e-mail people in chosen professions to ask them what math skills are needed for their jobs.

What Our Parents Do: Examine the data collected from the parents to determine the types of jobs, the number of people in each job, and the skills required.

- Use Kidspiration to have students create a concept map of the types of equipment or tools that would be needed for their selected career.
- Share in circle time the types of technology, tools, or equipment students anticipate using. Are there any jobs that don't use technology? If so, what are they? Electronically create a list of the types of technology students will need to know how to use in their jobs and post it beside the job collage.

Follow the Market: Identify several businesses in the community that have stocks for sale through one of the stock exchanges. Simple businesses that are in every community are fast food restaurants and store chains. Examine the stock daily and record the ups and downs for several weeks. Make projections for purchase.

- Record stocks on an electronic spreadsheet. Because stock prices are listed in fractions, be prepared to explain the meaning of the fractions found.

How Far?: Use a city map or Yahoo! Maps to determine how far it is from the child's home to his or her parent's place of work.

- Create a table to analyze distances. Record the name of the parent in one column, the place of work in the second column, and the number of miles to work in the third. Sort by places of work to see whether there are duplicates in the classroom. Sort by number of miles to work to see whose work is closer and farther.

MUSIC

This Is the Way: Sung to the tune of "Here We Go Round the Mulberry Bush," create phrases appropriate to the workers that include hand and body motions such as: This is the way we pump the gas, pump the gas, pump the gas . . .

SCIENCE

Science in Jobs Information: As in the math activity, use a screen reader to review information about the various skills (focusing on science for this activity) needed for different occupations (using the Bureau of Labor Statistics Career Information Web site, http://stats.bls.gov/k12/html/edu_over.htm. Write or e-mail people in chosen professions to ask them about the science skills needed for their jobs.

Animal Jobs: Examine some of the jobs related to animals described on Mizzou Magic (www.mizzoumagic.missouri.edu/2001_2/index.lasso). Write a brief description of skills and responsibilities.

Plant Jobs: Do a Web search to identify jobs related to plants. Describe the skills needed for the job and the job's responsibilities.

SOCIAL STUDIES

Mommy Works, Daddy Works: Read some of the stories about what moms and dads do at work. Create stories about parents and family members on jobs. Collect the stories into books using word processing programs. Write and illustrate the books using Kid Pix. Compile all of the stories into a slideshow. Post the slideshow on the Web for families to view.

Chores—Online: Create a Web page that shows the helpers for the day. E-mail the children to tell them what their responsibilities are or to provide them the link on the e-mail.

Health and Safety Jobs: Use a screen reader to review information about the various skills needed for health and safety occupations (Bureau of Labor Statistics Career Information: http://stats.bls.gov/k12/html/edu_over.htm). Write to people in chosen professions to ask them about the skills needed for their jobs.

Assessment

FOR YOUNGER LEARNERS

Using the theme On the Job, ask students to write a story, draw a picture, or create a slideshow about a job and the skills and responsibilities associated with it. For the picture, have students label the important parts to help everyone understand it. (Compare their first work on what they wanted to be with the final work.) For the story, nonwriters may share theirs orally.

NOTE: For a description of the values "Not Interested," "Trying It," "Working on It," "Got it!," and "Helping Others," see chapter 4.

CRITERIA	NOT INTERESTED	TRYING IT	WORKING ON IT	GOT IT!	HELPING OTHERS
The job is clearly identified.					
The job responsibilities are described or depicted in a picture.					
The job is shown in the context of the community.					
Labels are provided throughout the picture.					

FOR MORE ABLE LEARNERS

Ask students to write an On the Job story in which they explain their favorite job and how responsibilities are carried out. Compare this description with what was written at the beginning of the unit. Note in the individual assessment whether students' job choices changed. If so, ask students to explain why.

CRITERIA	APPROACHES TARGET	MEETS TARGET	EXCEEDS TARGET
Job	Description of job is incomplete or shows confusion.	Job is clearly described.	Job is clearly defined with many details indicating depth of understanding.
Responsibilities of job	Responsibilities are described in a limited way, indicating the student lacks a clear idea of what the job entails.	Responsibilities of the job are clearly described.	Job responsibilities are clearly described with examples of how the job is done, what is liked about the job, or other relevant ideas.
Relationship of job to community	No relationship with the community is included.	Description of the job includes relating to others in the community.	Description of the job includes detailed situations and interactions with others in the community as well as co-workers.

Assessment of technology use depends on the level of student use permitted, the technology available, and the age of the students. See chapter 4 for additional information on assessing technology use.

Additional criteria should be added focusing on writing. The criteria used for the rubric should reflect the objectives and expectations for the students.

Changes in My Neighborhood

UNIT OVERVIEW   When children move from one place to another they are often concerned about how different things will be. An examination of the changes that are continually taking place in their family and school neighborhoods as people build, tear down, plant, clean up, paint, landscape, and move helps children see that change is going on everywhere; life is filled with adjustments to those changes. The activities in this unit focus on three areas of change that are most recognizable for young children: (1) changing old ways of doing things to learning to take care of the earth, (2) moving from one place to another, and (3) helping others.

UNIT OBJECTIVES   At the end of this unit, students will be able to:

- Explain how the neighborhood changes.
- Describe ways to take care of the earth including recycling, reusing, reducing, and repairing.
- Understand the aspects of change that cause those moving and those left behind to be fearful.
- Identify ways to be neighborly and help others.

STANDARDS ADDRESSED IN THIS UNIT
ISTE NETS for Students 3, 4, 5, 6
IRA/NCTE English/Language Arts Standards 1, 2, 3, 4, 5, 7, 8
NCTM Math Standards 1, 4, 10
NAS/NSE Science Standards A1, B1, C3, E3, F3, F4
NCSS Social Studies Standards 1a, 1b, 1d, 1e, 2b, 2c, 2d, 3c, 3d, 3f, 3g, 3h, 3i, 3j, 3k

CHILDREN'S LITERATURE
What Goes On in the Neighborhood
And to Think That I Saw It on Mulberry Street, Dr. Seuss
Something's Happening on Calabash Street, Judith R. Enderle & Stephanie J. Gordon
What Zeesie Saw on Delancey Street, Elsa Okon Rael

Earth Day
Earth Day, David F. Marx
Earth Day: Keeping Our Planet Clean, Elaine Landau
Let's Celebrate Earth Day, Connie Roop
The Lorax, Dr. Seuss

Moving and Changes
The Berenstain Bears' Moving Day, Stan & Jan Berenstain
City Green, Dyanne Disalvo-Ryan
Everybody Brings Noodles, Norah Dooley
Flat Stanley, Jeff Brown
The Garden of Happiness, Erika Tamar

Ira Says Goodbye, Bernard Waber
The Last Dragon, Chris K. Soentpiet (Illustrator) & Susan Miho Nunes
Light Your Candle, Carl Sommer
The Lot at the End of My Block, Kevin Lewis
Moving, Janine Amos
Moving Is Hard, Joan Singleton Prestine
A Pig Is Moving In, Claudia Fries
Robobots, Matt Novak
Somebody Loves You, Mr. Hatch, Eileen Spinelli
Special Deliveries, Alexandra Day (Illustrator) & Cooper Edens
We Just Moved, Stephen Krensky
Who Will Be My Friends?, Syd Hoff

WEB RESOURCES

American Red Cross: www.redcross.org
Celebrate Earth Day With The Lorax: www.randomhouse.com/seussville/titles/lorax/
Earth Day Energy Fast: www.earthdayenergyfast.org
Earth Day Groceries Project: www.earthdaybags.org
Earth Day in Your Neighborhood: www.allspecies.org/neigh/blocka.htm
Earth Day Network: www.earthday.net/
EcoKids: www.allspecies.org/ecokids/index.htm
Flat Stanley Project: http://flatstanley.enoreo.on.ca/
Helpful Hints for Planet Earth: www2.lhric.org/pocantico/earthday/earthday.htm
Kid's Domain Earth Day: www.kidsdomain.com/holiday/earthday/
Let's Learn to Precycle: www.planetpals.com/precycle.html
The Official Site of International Earth Day: www.earthsite.org/
Recycle City: www.epa.gov/recyclecity/
Songs: www.niehs.nih.gov/kids/music.htm
The Weather Channel: www.weather.com

Dictionaries
   Internet Picture Dictionary: www.pdictionary.com
   Little Explorers Picture Dictionary: www.enchantedlearning.com/Dictionary.html
   Merriam-Webster's Word Central: www.wordcentral.com

SOFTWARE AND VIDEOS

Software
The Amazing Writing Machine, Broderbund
Excel
The Graph Club, Tom Snyder Productions, or Tabletop Jr., Broderbund
iMovie
Kid Pix (English, Spanish), Broderbund
Kidspiration, Inspiration Software
Neighborhood Map Maker, Tom Snyder Productions
Printshop Deluxe, Broderbund

Videos
Economics in Our Age: Factors of Production and Economic Systems, Clearvue/eav
This Is Your Government: Good Citizen, Clearvue/eav

Getting Started

In a letter to parents, explain the purpose of the unit. Ask parents (1) to review with their child the recycling processes they use in their family and how the family reduces use, reuses, and repairs items; (2) to take time with their child to help a needy or elderly neighbor or relative–bringing food, doing yard work, shoveling show, sweeping decks, waxing floors; (3) to keep track of the leftovers that occur at dinner time for a week including what was left over, how much, and what was done with the leftover food; and (4) to share information and experience with a child if the child has recently moved, plans to move, or knows someone who is or has recently moved.

Motivating Activity

In a previous unit, **My Neighborhood**, it was suggested that students take a walk in their neighborhood, write and draw pictures of what they saw, and interview older people to see how things used to be. To begin this unit, revisit the alphabet books they made, the word quilts they created, and the stories they wrote. Read *And to Think That I Saw It on Mulberry Street, Something's Happening on Calabash Street,* or *What Zeesie Saw on Delancey Street* as an introduction to the next walk in the neighborhood. The focus for the walk is to examine things that have changed since the last walk. Additionally, have students look around for things that should change or need changing to make the neighborhood better or safer.

Set up recycling bins in the classroom for items that can be reused, recycled, reduced, or repaired.

Multidisciplinary Activities

ART   *Reusing:* Have students bring items from home that can be reused or repurposed. Place appropriate items in a bin in the art area, where children can think of creative ways to reuse the materials. Discuss sculpture and free-form development of objects with a purpose.

- As students complete a sculpture, have them use Kid Pix or another word processing program to write about their sculpture using descriptive words that include the shape, texture, and color. Have students write what the sculpture means or resembles as well as the materials or objects they used in their creation.
- Take digital pictures of the sculptures and insert them into the children's word-processed description. Some young children can learn to do this skill and teach others as they are ready.

Recycling Poster: Ask each child to create a recycling poster and post them throughout the school, encouraging other students and families to recycle.

- Have the students use a drawing program such as Kid Pix to create the posters.

- As a remembrance of the posters, insert miniature versions of the posters into a single document using Printshop Deluxe. Consider using the option of making a collage of the posters or placing them in rows like stamps on a single poster.
- Have students create three slides in Kid Pix to show the process of recycling, reusing, and reducing. Have students illustrate each slide and create a slideshow.

Moving Day: If a child in the room is going to move and go to a different school, ask each child in the room to draw a picture of him- or herself and write a note wishing the student well. Package these together with digital pictures of the school and the class to send along.

- Exchange e-mail addresses with the student and parents so that they can keep in touch with the class. Very young children often have no concept that the child leaving can still be communicated with once gone from the class. E-mail is a good way to exchange pictures and stories about the move and the new school. The class the child goes into is a potential e-pal exchange class.
- Have students read the book *Flat Stanley.* Join the Flat Stanley Project online. Have students create Flat Stanleys to send to people who are going places or live outside the area. Post the Flat Stanleys you receive on a map on a bulletin board.

Helping Hands: Ask each child to trace around his or her hand. Have a discussion with students about the difference between working at a job and being a good citizen or friend by helping without expecting to be paid. Interview each to determine how they might help in their neighborhood, at home, or in their school neighborhood. Post the hands in a circle on the bulletin board.

- Have students use Kidspiration to brainstorm the ways they could be helpful to others at school or at home. Categorize the ways of helping.
- Use Kidspiration to brainstorm a list of jobs that are done as the season changes such as raking, shoveling snow, planting flowers, and so on. Categorize the jobs as outside or inside, by weather, or by seasonal sequence.

GROSS MOTOR *Musical Houses:* Have students play Musical Chairs. Explain that sometimes people move into houses that were owned by someone they already know. Sometimes people move to larger homes in the same neighborhood because their family has grown. In a reference to Musical Chairs, people jokingly refer to moving to different houses in the same community or neighborhood as "musical houses."

HEALTH *Leftover Food:* Discuss what happens to leftover food at home. If children are served family style at the table, remind children to take only the food that they think they are able to eat. Ask students to keep track of the leftovers from dinner for a week. They should note what was left over, how much (the quantity), and what was done with the leftovers (thrown away, served for another meal, left in the fridge to be thrown away later). Have students bring the data back to class for discussion.

- Use Graph Club or Tabletop Jr. to record data. Make generalizations based on the data. Have students suggest alternative ways for reducing or using leftover food.
- Bring some leftovers from home or use a sample of leftover food to show why food should be refrigerated. Leave food out for one day. Use the digital microscope to look at the growth of mold on the food. Leave the food out for several days, watching the mold and unusual cells grow on the food. Have students observe and record their findings electronically as digital pictures are taken to follow the process. Help students come to the conclusion that food changes over time and becomes unhealthy when not handled properly.

Environmental Health: Read *The Lorax* to the children. Ask them to tell about the environmental changes that happen in the book. Lead a discussion on the relationship between the issues in the book and environmental issues in the community.

- Access the Celebrate Earth Day With The Lorax Web site (**www.randomhouse. com/seussville/titles/lorax/**). Create a list of ways to save the earth.

Adjusting to Moving: Read one of the books about moving or try *Ira Says Goodbye, Moving, Who Will Be My Friend?,* or *Moving Is Hard.* Examine all the feelings that accompany moving represented in the stories. Create a two-column poster on which students can put their fears on one side and answers on the other. For example: I will miss my friends. I will make new friends.

- Use the Amazing Writing Machine to create a book for children who are moving. Have the class contribute their fears and solutions to the book. Run off enough copies of the book to give to students in the school who are about to move.

Safety in the Neighborhood: Read *Light Your Candle,* a book that tells of a child's move to make a neighborhood safe. As appropriate, talk with children and families about ways to keep neighborhoods safe through the use of flyers designed by the children and organized efforts with the local officials.

- Have students make their flyers using Kid Pix.
- Create a poster using Printshop Deluxe that includes miniatures of all the children's flyers in a collage or in a patchwork quilt form.

LANGUAGE ARTS AND READING

And to Think That I Saw It on Our Street: In a pattern similar to the Dr. Suess book read as part of the motivating activity, *And to Think That I Saw It on Mulberry Street,* have students create a page for a book entitled And to Think That I Saw It on _____ Street. Use online children's dictionaries or picture dictionaries to help with the words.

I'll Be Missing Many Things: Read one of the books on moving from the Children's Literature list at the beginning of this unit such as *The Berenstain Bears' Moving Day, Ira Says Goodbye, Moving,* or *Moving Is Hard.* Create an I'll Be Missing Many Things book that allows children to tell what they would miss the most if they were going to be moving away. Ask students who have moved into the area to add additional pages to say what they miss from their prior residence and what they enjoy most about where they live now. Emphasize how each place is unique and has different positive attributes.

- Have students use the Amazing Writing Machine to create a book of what they would miss.
- Have students use Kid Pix to create a slideshow illustrating what they would miss most. Be sure to add an additional slide of those who have moved into the area that tells about what they appreciate most about living in the community.

Address Books: For children who will be moving away, ask the rest of the class to fill in an address book entry. Ask the child who is moving to share the new address. Staple the address book entry sheets together as a going-away gift. This also works well at the end of the year as children move to the next grade or school. Be sure to get parental permission for sharing contact information.

- Use a database to create the address book. Conduct a lesson with students on what a database is and how it is useful in organizing information and sorting to find specific information. Create a list of questions that can be asked by sorting the address book information such as: Who lives on ____ street? How many students are in our class? If a list is made of the students in backwards alphabetical order, who would be first, second, and so on?

Nursing Home Visit: Select a book similar to or read *Somebody Loves You, Mr. Hatch, Special Deliveries,* or *Everybody Brings Noodles.* These are stories in which people reach out to others and good things happen. Plan a visit to a nursing home where the older citizens can read to the children and the children can provide them pictures and crafts to brighten up their rooms. Discuss with the class what it must have been like for the residents to move from their homes into the nursing home.

- Over several visits, video- or audiotape the children interviewing the residents. (More able students can take notes.) Have the students ask questions such as: How has the community changed since you began living there? What is the biggest change you have seen? What was ___ grade like when you were in school?
- Have the children make Kid Pix slides on their visits that include pictures and stories about what they learned.
- Use the sound from the audiotape as background to the slideshow.
- Use iMovie to edit the videotape and create a videotape collage of the visits.

MATH

NOTE: At some point in the graphing of the trash, the amount should level off and become constant. It is that data that you want to use to predict how much will be saved.

The Weight of Trash: Weigh the empty trash can. Record the weight. For one to three weeks, weigh the trash can at the end of each day. Afterward, set up recycling bins and weigh the amounts in each of the bins each day. Record, graph, and post the results daily. Have students analyze reasons and the effect of the reduction in the weight of the trash. By how much have students reduced the weight of the trash that actually gets thrown away? If the data have some abnormal entries, have students justify why the data for the given day are not fitting into a pattern.

- Use Graph Club or Tabletop Jr. to enter and display data in a graph. Continue to update data daily.
- Create an additional chart on Graph Club or Tabletop Jr. that makes a prediction on how much weight would be saved over a month, two months, a year, and so on if the trash was recycled.

The Volume of Trash: Redo the above activity focusing on the volume of trash rather than the weight. Discuss how the volume of trash affects the size of landfills. Predict how much space would be saved if recycling took place. For very young children, equivalence will have to be illustrated using something they are familiar with. For example, the volume of their family's trash barrel or enough trash to fill up their bedroom could be used as the measuring shape. Ask: How many bedrooms full of trash will be saved if we . . .

How Far Away?: If a child in the room is moving away, determine how far away he or she will be.

- Use Yahoo! Maps to determine how far away the child will be.
- If no children are moving away, find out how far away children moved from to be in the community. Make a table using Graph Club or Tabletop Jr. graphing the distance from closest to farthest away by looking at the total mileage on the map.
- Have students go to Yahoo! Maps to find a location where a relative lives or a place they would like to go to examine how far away it is. The Web site gives an approximate time it takes to drive to the location. Arrange the results in terms of amount of time from shortest to longest. Develop analytical questions based on the results of the table.

MUSIC

This Is the Way: Sing to the tune of "Here We Go Round the Mulberry Bush": This is the way we pick up the trash, plant our gardens, clean up our yards, mow our lawns, pack our clothes, move our furniture.

SCIENCE

Clean Up Day: Select one day as Clean Up Day to clean up the schoolyard or the school neighborhood. Encourage parents to have a Clean Up Day at home around the same time. Discuss with students the type of trash they are allowed and not allowed to pick up. Divide students into small groups with an adult supervisor. Provide rubber gloves and a set of trash bags for each group. Have students designate one bag for recycleable items and one for trash items. Sort the recycleable items into the designations provided by the school or community recycling program.

Examine the rest of the trash and make suggestions on how the items might have gotten to where they were and what the people might have done with them instead of dropping them in the area.

- Document the process using a digital camera. Post the captioned pictures on the class Web site or use them for a slideshow or bulletin board display.

- Have students write a journal entry or recommendations about how to get people to put their discards in the right place.

- Use Graph Club or Tabletop Jr. to record data on the type of trash picked up. Have students analyze the data to make recommendations about how to avoid depositing the quantity of trash found.

Making Something of Nothing: Select a story similar to or read *City Green, The Garden of Happiness,* or *The Lot at the End of My Block.* Each story tells of a way people cleaned up and improved an area and the happiness that comes to those who help—and to others, too. Identify an empty area around the neighborhood and start a project to beautify the area or a way to put the empty area to productive use. Conduct a debate about cleaning up the area. Place students in opposing groups to discuss the pros and cons of changing this area. Once a decision is made to progress, enlist the help of parents and community members.

- Draw a picture in Kid Pix of how the area will look once it has been cleaned up and improved. Have students make proposals of what should be done with the area.

SOCIAL STUDIES

Helping Your Neighbors: Be alert to when families, teachers, or other school workers are ill, have babies, lose a family member, or are in need because of illness or a catastrophic event. In addition, follow the news to see whether the class can help in either a local or national catastrophic event. (As we write this book in 2002, it is a time when students and families are being invited to help schoolchildren in Afghanistan and the survivors and families of the September 11 attack.) Work with students to brainstorm ways they can help.

- Use Inspiration or Kidspiration to brainstorm ways to help.

- Look on the American Red Cross Web site (**www.redcross.org**) for areas that need assistance. Have students think about ways they can help, make a plan, and follow through.

Along the Way: Using the math activity How Far Away, determine what would be seen along the way as one traveled from one place to another. Examine the weather and climate. Ask students to pack a suitcase with the clothes they would need to live in the new place.

- Use the Weather Channel Web site (**www.weather.com**) to look up the current weather in the new location. Look at the weather history throughout the seasons. Look at the location's Web site to get a sense of what to expect.

- Select several points along the way to "stop" on a trip. Look at the Web sites for each location or the state's Web site. Decide what might be good to visit while passing through.

■ Use multiple Web sites to plan a trip to the new location. Create a budget (using Graph Club or Tabletop Jr.) for estimating the cost of buying gas, paying for food, staying overnight, and sightseeing.

Making New Friends: Read one of the books about new neighbors (*A Pig Is Moving In, Robobots, We Just Moved,* or *Who Will Be My Friend?*). Encourage students to make a list of fun and safe ways to be friendly with new people in the neighborhood or school. Try some of them out when new students and families arrive.

■ Use the Amazing Writing Machine to create a Welcome booklet for new students. Brainstorm all the information and ideas a new student would want to know when they arrive at the school. Have the students also brainstorm things they think parents of newly moved students should know that would make them feel better in their new location.

Assessment

FOR YOUNGER
LEARNERS

Select the area of neighborhood change most relevant to your community that was studied in this unit. Have students make a three-panel picture or story in which they identify something that needs to change, create a plan for making the change, and describe the anticipated outcome or results.

NOTE: For a description of the values "Not Interested," "Trying It," "Working on It," "Got it!," and "Helping Others," see chapter 4.

CRITERIA	NOT INTERESTED	TRYING IT	WORKING ON IT	GOT IT!	HELPING OTHERS
Area of needed change is identified.					
Change plan is explained.					
Outcome of change is described.					
Labels are provided throughout the picture or story.					

FOR MORE ABLE LEARNERS Ask students to write a news story about a change they think should happen in their neighborhood based on the topics studied in the unit. The news story should clearly identify the change that is needed and why, a plan to implement the change, and the anticipated results of the change. They may include pictures with their news story.

CRITERIA	APPROACHES TARGET	MEETS TARGET	EXCEEDS TARGET
Change needed	Is not related to an area discussed in class or does not make sense for the community	Is clearly identified and a rationale is provided	Is clearly identified with extensive rationale from a variety of perspectives
Plan to make the change	Is provided but is not clearly related to the problem or does not make sense	Is provided and makes sense	Is provided in great detail and/or has unique and creative solutions
Results	Are identified but may not be reasonable or make a positive contribution to the community	Are identified, reasonable, and make a positive contribution to the community	Are clearly identified, provide a unique and creative perspective on the problem, are reasonable, and make a positive contribution to the community
Pictures or labels	Are distracting or not related to the proposed results	Make a positive contribution to understanding the issue	Extend and further clarify the understanding of the issue

Assessment of technology use depends on the level of student use permitted, the technology available, and the age of the students. See chapter 4 for additional information on assessing technology use.

Additional criteria should be added focusing on writing. The criteria used for the rubric should reflect the objectives and expectations for the students.

theme culminating event

Neighborhood Block Party

Work with the children to plan a neighborhood block party. Set a date on the calendar. Create an invitation to send to the people who are to be invited, whether that includes the entire school, the young children, or the parents. Invite people in the neighborhood and community the children come in contact with (store clerk, recreation leader, bus driver, crossing guard, etc.). Invite school district personnel and city officials as well. Encourage each child to write and illustrate invitations to the people they choose to invite, sending the invitations by mail or e-mail. Ask guests to bring pictures of themselves working at their job and of landmarks of the neighborhood or community. Make the event a celebration of the character and features of the community.

PLAN THE EVENT

List the types of jobs the students have studied in this unit and let each student choose a job to represent (one they want to have when they grow up, their parent's job, or a job they've learned about). Have each student dress up as that type of community worker for the party.

Decorate the Gym or Classroom: Locate decorations for the room and tables, again using projects from the units (neighborhood maps or word quilts, traffic signs, recreation collages, etc.). Run the slideshows children created on the classroom computers in continuous loops.

STAGE THE EVENT

Host and Hostesses: Appoint several class hosts and hostesses to greet guests upon arrival. The hosts and hostesses should explain the type of community worker they represent; walk guests past the decorations, explaining each; and assign a student to sit with each guest or set of guests to fill out the guest book, look up their address in Yahoo! Maps, and add their pictures to the photo gallery bulletin board.

Guest Book: Create a guest book and have each guest sign in and list his or her name, address, and role in the community. Each guest may have several roles so leave several spaces for them to sign. The guest book could be an Excel spreadsheet that guests type into with a column for each piece of information.

Document: Take digital photos of the guests and students dressed up for the guest book or slideshows.

How Far?: Map out who traveled the farthest. Have students take turns at the computer typing the addresses of the guests into Yahoo! Maps to find out who traveled the farthest to the block party.

Community Sing: Sing songs from the community unit and invite the guests to sing along with the class.

When I Grow Up: Have groups of children take turns presenting what they want to be when they grow up and the changes they propose to make their community a better place to live.

Photo Gallery: Create a photo gallery bulletin board. In the invitations ask guests to bring pictures of themselves at their job and a landmark of the community to add to your community and neighborhood photo gallery. Put these pictures on a bulletin board as guests come in and save them to scan for next year's **Communities** units.

ARCHIVE THE EVENT

Videotape the Event: Videos can be transferred to VHS format to send home to parents to play on their VCRs. They may be burned on CDs. CDs can then be played back on CD drives in computers. These videos could also be burned on DVDs to be shown using a DVD player or a DVD drive in a computer. Other devices such as a Sony Play Station II also have the capability of showing DVDs.

theme 3

"One should eat to live, not live to eat."
—Cicero
(106 BC–43 BC)

Food

Children are very well acquainted with the notion of eating. It is an experience they all share. Why particular foods are served to them, how they come to the refrigerator or shelf, where they originated, and how they are made are generally ideas young children have not thought about. Since they have entered school, they have been able to make choices about what to eat and what to leave behind on the plate. The units in this theme will help students understand food and make better choices for themselves.

The initial study of nutrition orients children to the food pyramid and the notion of a balanced diet. Succeeding units focus on how food is grown or produced, where to find items in a grocery store, and the idea that not all people of the world eat the same food, but that diets are still balanced.

The following standards-based curriculum units enable students to explore the concepts of production, distribution, and consumption of food as they take part in the following activities. Students:

- Eat at a buffet, and record and analyze the foods they choose, with reference to the food pyramid.
- Examine the grocery store: how it is organized and how food gets there.
- Look at how foods go from the seed to the table and the complex set of steps they take to get there.
- Analyze the cultural or national origin of some of the most popular foods.

Unit Tools

SPOTLIGHT ON
TECHNOLOGY

Spreadsheet and Graphing: Spreadsheets and graphs are used to record and compare the weight of food before and after cooking, the costs of various foods, and the distances to countries that grow foods.

Word Processing: Writing is integrated throughout the unit by writing stories, listing steps in a process, and recounting family traditions.

Drawing Software: For emerging readers, drawing software is used to record their thinking, to reinforce patterning, and to create slideshows of student work.

Internet: Web sites are used extensively to provide additional information, to present places that cannot realistically be visited, to obtain grocery price information, to access maps, and to play games.

WRITING ACROSS
THE CURRICULUM

In the **Health and Nutrition** unit, students have the opportunity to write in a journal (using pictures or words) about the foods they eat, those they like and don't like, and their favorite recipes. The recipes can be published as gifts for holidays for their family members.

In the **Grocery Stores and Markets** unit, as in several other units, students create ABC books of items related to the topic. With the youngest students, pictures and the letter make the page. As students get older, pictures, letters, and words can be written. Eventually, simple definitions, related topics, and even recipes can be created.

In the **Growing and Producing Food** unit, students bring a piece of bread to school to demonstrate the type of bread most often eaten by their families. This provides an excellent opportunity for children to draw pictures, write captions, create slideshows, and share information about their home culture with the other students in the classroom.

In the **Foods Around the World** unit, students draw pictures and write about foods from various countries. Students can e-mail family members in distant places to ask the types of produce that is grown locally and how those foods are prepared. In preparation for a class celebration, the recipes can be prepared with student-created charts nearby telling about the foods.

TEACHER VOICES

About the Health and Nutrition unit

"My class was so excited to begin the unit by eating. The buffet activity caused them to stop and think about what they selected. The initial discussion focused on taking firsts and seconds of an item and why they chose to eat more of something. No one had ever had them record taking seconds of something. When we did it again at the end of the unit, I wish I had recorded the conversation. I had various children bring things according to the food groups. They looked at the choices on the table and were surprisingly deliberate about what they took. One of the children asked if we could rearrange the buffet by food groups!"

About the Foods Around the World unit

"My class is very multicultural. I have many students who speak other languages at home. This unit really celebrated their cultures and countries of origin. Being able to go on the Internet and see pictures, obtain maps, and get lots of information was an eye opener for the children.

"We even extended the unit by having an international feast. This was their idea. It was interesting that before we ate, the class wanted to examine each dish to classify the ingredients according to the food pyramid. And even those who usually are picky during snacks wanted to take a taste of many things. The day was a huge success in many ways."

CHILDREN'S LITERATURE   Each unit offers an extensive list of children's literature related to the growth, production, and consumption of food. The books have been purposefully selected to match young children's interest and the topic of the unit. Choose ones available in your school, personal, or public library and be sure to search for new ones on the market. Your search can be at the local bookstore or online.

WEB RESOURCES   An extensive Web Resources list accompanies every unit. All resources were current at the time of publishing. Because of the rapid growth of Internet use, sites can be expected to come and go. To keep the resources current, all software and online references are available online at **www.edtech4teachers.com** and will be updated frequently.

TEACHING TIPS   Teaching very young children requires a balance between holding discussions to clarify thinking and to practice oral language skills, and having students take part in active, hands-on activities to keep them exploring and engaged. The unit activities can be used as either center or whole-class lessons depending on the class and the amount of help available in the classroom.

Food is a universal. Because children seem to always be hungry, motivating them to participate in this theme is not difficult. The classroom management and safety issues concerning handling food and eating utensils, such as knives are, however, problematic at times. These things must be monitored. Set the standards firmly and fairly concerning who handles what and when. Be very insistent about washing hands, not touching the face when handling food, and general health concerns. Some school districts require students to wear plastic gloves when handling food. Check with the policies of your school or district before proceeding. Children comprehend the rationale for the cleanliness very easily. They have all had a stomachache at one time or another.

When doing the buffet or any of the cooking activities, be sure to have alternative, valuable activities students can engage in when their responsibility is complete. Organize the traffic pattern around the classroom so that all cooking or food handling occurs in one area where you can control what is happening, confine any mess, and not disturb alternative activities. Having baby wipes handy will keep students from parading in and out of the room to wash their hands and disturbing others.

LESSON EXTENDERS   For most of the lessons in this theme, children are investigating the foods that they eat, the origins of various foods, family traditions, and food preparation. Do lessons with teachers you know in other areas of the country or locate another class online that might do this activity with you. Share, compare, and contrast results.

Visit a nursing home and interview older members of the community about how they got their food and prepared it. Get permission from families to videotape the interviews that the children do with the residents. Archive them on a community, city, town, or county Web page to share with a wider audience. With the posting, provide your school e-mail address so that people can submit to you their food stories.

THEME CULMINATING EVENT

Have students work with the cafeteria manager to create a menu for a special school lunch. Although most school cafeterias have a set menu that is determined by the school district, many school cafeteria managers have some flexibility in rearranging items on the menu for special events such as this. Have the students help with the setting up of the tables and serving of the meal. Make posters of the menu, and correlate the menu with the food groups and the foods' country or culture of origin, if relevant. Have class slideshows of student work running automatically on an overhead screen as lunch is served to the rest of the school.

If this unit is being done with very young children, limit the lunch to serving other classes in their grade or age level, or to parents only. A complete plan for this activity is found at the end of the theme.

Health and Nutrition

UNIT OVERVIEW

One thing children do daily is eat food. They see it, they buy it, they eat it, they throw it away. However, many never think about organizing and maintaining a balanced diet, determining what foods are made of, or finding out where foods come from. The purpose of this unit is to investigate foods from a personal, cultural, and scientific perspective.

UNIT OBJECTIVES

At the end of this unit, students will be able to:

- Explain factors of food safety.
- Describe the food pyramid and the foods associated with the different groups.
- Examine their own food intake, analyze it using the food pyramid, and make recommendations for their own eating habits.
- Sort foods into food groups, natural foods, and processed foods.
- Reflect on their own food habits and make recommendations to themselves about the foods they need in their diet.
- Investigate ingredients and calories.
- Describe foods as sweet, sour, salty, or bitter.

STANDARDS ADDRESSED IN THIS UNIT

ISTE NETS for Students 1, 3, 4, 5, 6
IRA/NCTE English/Language Arts Standards 1, 5, 6, 7, 8, 12
NCTM Math Standards 1, 3, 4, 5, 8, 10
NAS/NSE Science Standards A1, A2, B1, F1, G1
NCSS Social Studies Standards 1, 4, 7

CHILDREN'S LITERATURE

Dim Sum for Everyone, Grace Lin
D.W. the Picky Eater, Marc Brown
Eat Your Peas, Kes Gray
Food Safety (Rookie Read-About Health), Sharon Gordon
The Grouchy Ladybug, Eric Carle
I Hate Lima Beans!, Rita Schweitz
I Love Food (My World), Tammy J. Schlepp & Alvin Granowski
It Looked Like Spilt Milk, Charles G. Shaw
My Breakfast: A Book About a Great Morning Meal, Heather L. Feldman
Nutrition, Lizzy Rockwell
The Peanut Butter Jam (allergies), Elizabeth Sussman Nassau

WEB RESOURCES

Health and Nutrition—General
Breakfast and Jump to It: www.dairycouncilofca.org/activities/breakfast.htm
Build a Food Guide Pyramid: www.kidfood.org/f_pyramid/pyramid.html
Dole 5-a-Day: www.dole5aday.com/Kids/K_Index.html

Fast Food Facts: www.olen.com/food/
Food Pyramid Game: www.dairycouncilofca.org/activities/pyra_main.htm
Food Pyramid Guide: www.nal.usda.gov:8001/py/pmap.htm
Foods: www.pdictionary.com/cgi-bin/browse.cgi?db=fruits
Kids and Families: Safe Foods:
   www.dairycouncilofca.org/kids/kids_safe_main.htm
Kids Cookbook: www.dole5aday.com/Kids/K_Index.htm
Kids Food Cyber Club: www.kidfood.org/kf_cyber.html
Nutrition Café: www.exhibits.pacsci.org/nutrition/
Sesame Street Parents: www.sesameworkshop.org/parents/
Songs: www.niehs.nih.gov/kids/music.htm
Vegetables: www.pdictionary.com/cgi-bin/browse.cgi?db=vegetables
Yahooligans: www.yahooligans.com

Picture Dictionaries

Internet Picture Dictionary: www.pdictionary.com
Little Explorers Picture Dictionary: www.enchantedlearning.com/Dictionary.html

SOFTWARE AND HARDWARE

Software

The Amazing Writing Machine, Broderbund

Dry Cereal, KidsClick Software

D.W. the Picky Eater, Broderbund (Living Books)

The Graph Club, Tom Snyder Productions, or Tabletop Jr., Broderbund

Kid Pix (English, Spanish), Broderbund

KidWorks

Kidspiration, Inspiration Software

TimeLiner (English, Spanish), Tom Snyder Productions

Hardware

Early learning microscope (such as DigiScope by Motic)

teaching
the unit

Getting Started

In preparation for the unit, send a letter home to explain the unit's purpose with an overview of the activities and expectations. Ask parents to (1) work with their children to complete an Intake Chart, (2) be prepared to send their child to school with no breakfast (or lunch if it is afternoon kindergarten) on a predetermined day, (3) save food boxes and food labels, and (4) make you aware of the child's food allergies.

Intake Chart: Ask parents to work with their child to record the foods eaten for one day (for more mature groups, ask for one week of data) including breakfast, lunch, dinner, and all snacks. Inform parents that children will be analyzing the data by classifying the foods they eat according to the food pyramid and discussing food choices that make a balanced diet. Send home a template for parent use and post the chart in PDF format on the class Web site for additional access. Parents can return the chart to school or return it as an attachment to an e-mail. (Be sensitive to cultural and economic differences that may make acquiring the data awkward.)

Motivating Activity

Checking first for food allergies in the class, set up a buffet for the children so that when they enter the classroom, they take care of their entry responsibilities (hanging coats, putting school supplies away, handing in notes, etc.) and go directly through the buffet line for breakfast (or lunch). Be sure to include all food types noted on the food pyramid. Allow students to select their own foods for their plates. On each child's desk, place a Breakfast Checklist (or Lunch Checklist) that contains the names or pictures of all the foods on the buffet followed by two columns (see next page). In the first column, students record all food items loaded on their plates during their initial visit to the buffet. The second column is for any second helpings. Their first responsibility is to place a circle in the "First Visit" column next to all those foods that they placed on their plate.

After eating, students must cross off the "0" in the "First Visit" column for any foods they selected but did not eat. Allow students to return for seconds if there is food left. In the "Second Visit" column, students must again first place a circle next to foods selected, and then cross off what they didn't eat. Collect the checklists.

As the food selected is being discussed, have students describe the foods as sweet, salty, sour, or bitter. Classify the foods on the buffet according to taste. Encourage students to use descriptive language throughout the unit.

Conclude the motivating activities with a story time focused on books about food safety such as *The Peanut Butter Jam* (allergies) or *Food Safety*, and about picky eating such as *I Hate Lima Beans!* or *Eat Your Peas*.

- Follow-up activities include accessing online sources where children build their own breakfast or salad:

  Breakfast and Jump to It: www.dairycouncilofca.org/activities/breakfast.htm
  Salad Toss, located at Dole 5-a-Day: www.dole5aday.com/Kids/K_Index.html

Breakfast Checklist

O = I put it on my plate

X = After I put it on my plate, I didn't eat it

FOOD	FIRST VISIT	SECOND VISIT
Hard-boiled egg		
Ham		
Tofu		
Carrots		
Celery		
Tomato		
Broccoli		
Apple		
Orange		
Banana		
Bread		
Cereal		
Bagel		
Tortilla		
Milk		
Yogurt		
Cheese		

Sesame Street Parents: www.sesameworkshop.org/parents/

■ The Breakfast Checklist can be loaded onto PDAs located at each child's desk. Students can use the stylus or touch screen to mark their foods. Be careful about having the PDAs too close to the food.

Multidisciplinary Activities

ART *Food Mobile:* Have students create a mobile of foods that mimics the food pyramid. The mobile can be created on a coat hangar or pipe cleaners to maintain the pyramid shape.

■ The pictures used in the mobile can be downloaded from a Web site or created using a drawing program. Students who are able to write can add descriptive language to each food added to the pyramid. The word-processed and drawn descriptions can be cut out in food shapes and hung on the pyramid with thread.

■ For more able children, extend the writing activity by having them describe the food as if they were a food writer for a newspaper. Make a word wall of descriptive language. Consult with the food section of various papers by looking online.

It Looked Like Spilt Milk: Read *It Looked Like Spilt Milk.* On a piece of construction paper, spill some colored water as if it were milk. The shape will soak into the construction paper. Ask students what it looks like. Turn the paper around in several directions to see if there are alternative ideas for what it looks like depending on the position of the paper.

■ Using Kid Pix, have children draw a puddle of spilt milk. Have them write a sentence about what their puddle looks like. This is a good opportunity to teach use of the pencil for creating a free-form drawing and the fill bucket for adding the consistent color of white.

■ Have students write a description in a text box of what they see, adding other features to the "spill" to help clarify their vision of what it is.

GROSS MOTOR *Twister:* Design a food or vegetable Twister game using an old sheet or shower curtain. Have children play Twister in groups of two to four.

HEALTH *Food Pyramid:* As an introductory health activity, examine the food pyramid. Discuss the rationale for the pyramid shape.

■ View the pyramid online (www.kidfood.org/f_pyramid/pyramid.html). Discuss foods from the opening activity food buffet or favorite foods in the context of the Dinner at My House activity.

■ As a follow up, students can take an online quiz (www.kidfood.org/ f_pyramid/q1.html) or play the Food Pyramid game (www.dairycouncilofca. org/activities/pyra_main.htm).

Dinner at My House: Use Kid Pix to draw a large circle or plate shape. Have students use the stamps and drawing tools to create their favorite family dinner. Have students consult the food pyramid to label the foods. Also have them record how they know the category in which the foods belong. For very young children, have an adult at the center to ask students questions about how they knew the category in which to place the food.

What Am I Eating?: Provide food boxes and food labels collected from parents in a center. Ask students to check and compare the nutrition information from several foods. Provide synonyms for the words on the back of the packages to help them understand the meaning of words such as fat, sugar, protein, carbohydrates, and vitamins. After some comparison and collaborative discussion, ask them to make a list or chart of foods, providing the names, calories, and other information. Have students write in their journals about what they learned about the foods they eat.

■ Using Kid Pix, have students draw a circle (plate) and a triangle (food pyramid). Have them draw or stamp what they had for dinner the night before on the plate. Copy and paste the foods into the food pyramid.

■ Use the Kidspiration activity Food Pyramid to plan a balanced diet.

Food Diary: Expand the students' knowledge of the food pyramid by looking at the number of servings of each food necessary to have a balanced diet for the day. Have students use their own Intake Chart completed at home to look at what is being eaten and how balanced the meals are. Have them tally the number of servings of each type of food and compare it with the recommended amount.

■ Using Graph Club, label the x-axis "Food Groups" and create a column for each group. Label the y-axis "Number of Servings." Show the number of servings required for each food group. Add another column next to the servings required and list the number of servings each student had from their food diary. Graph and compare the results.

LANGUAGE ARTS AND READING

Picky Eaters: Read a book about picky eaters (*D.W. the Picky Eater, Eat Your Peas,* or *I Hate Lima Beans*). Provide each child with a piece of paper on which to list or draw their three favorite foods and three foods they don't like (if they have any) using the language pattern _____ **likes** _____ or _____ **doesn't like** _____. Have students cut out the pictures or words and take them to circle time.

Discuss likes and dislikes in the context of changing opinions. As a homework assignment, have children ask their parents about food they didn't like when they were younger but do like now. Are there foods they used to like but no longer like?

Place a long strip of masking tape on the floor. Put up two signs: "I like" and "I don't like," one on each side of the tape. Ask children to place their pictures on one side or the other. Group the like and don't like pictures on separate sides of the line.

Continue to encourage students to use descriptive language such as sweet, sour, salty, and bitter. Encourage children to tell you the results.

- Using Kidspiration, create two boxes. Label one "Foods I like," the other, "Foods I dislike." Have students use the symbol library to fill the boxes. Have them think about when they've tried the food, why they didn't like it, and if they would try it again.

- Use the Amazing Writing Machine or other book-creating software to write a nutrition book. Have students write and illustrate pages showing their favorite foods, the foods they dislike, a balanced meal, the food pyramid, and other information they've learned during the unit. Add pages about what they have learned from their parents about changing likes and dislikes of food. Print the pages and fold them into a small book.

Class Cookbook: Ask each child to talk to his or her parents about how to make the child's favorite food. Use the information to construct a page for a class cookbook including the name of the food, directions on how to fix the food (in their own words), and a picture. Produce the book, one per family, as a special gift to families. For very young children, parent helpers can word process the children's descriptions with the children illustrating their own description.

- The descriptions and illustrations can be done using Kid Pix, KidWorks, or a similar tool.

- Introduce students to the Web sites designed for providing recipes to kids for cooking. Go to **www.yahooligans.com** to search for appropriate sites. This is a good opportunity to review with children how to search for something specific. Print out a few recipes for students to take home. If you print it off the Web site, the Yahooligans Web address will appear at the bottom of the printout to remind students of the site you used. Send a letter home to parents to have students make a healthy snack following a recipe. Instruct parents to have students either search for a new recipe on the Web or use a printout of one you found in class. Ask parents to write notes on the back of the recipe that tell how well their child followed the directions and what changes they may have made in the recipe.

The Little Red Hen: Read *The Little Red Hen.* Use the Amazing Writing Machine or other word processing software to write and illustrate the story. Encourage them to write a thank-you note to the school cooks or parents for preparing nutritious and healthy meals.

D.W. the Picky Eater: Discuss the book *D.W. the Picky Eater* and how a picky attitude can limit what you learn.

- Install the D.W. the Picky Eater software on the hard drive and place the icon strategically where students can quickly load the program. In Story Maker, students create stories by selecting pictures and phrases related to a specific theme. Food is one of the themes. Save the Garden allows students to chase a gopher from the garden. The Family Picnic presents the concept of food groups. Students help D.W. and Arthur set a balanced meal for a picnic. Sticker Fun requires students to match words and pictures from the stories.

MATH

Breakfast Checklist: Create one classroom chart that contains the names of students in column one and the names of breakfast foods across the top. Have students record what they ate for breakfast. Ask students to categorize the food according to the food pyramid. Have students examine the chart to make generalizations based on the data. Ask interpretive questions such as, "Which food group do we seem to eat the most of for breakfast?" Probe students to discuss issues of what they think they should be eating to have a balanced breakfast.

NOTE: Be particularly sensitive to students who come to school with no breakfast or are eating school-served meals.

NAME	SCRAMBLED EGGS	HASH BROWNS	ORANGE SLICES	MELON	TOAST	JELLY	MILK	ORANGE JUICE
Dylan	1	0	2	0	1	1	0	1
Sam	2	0	2	1	1	0	1	1

- Use Graph Club, TableTop Jr., or a different age-appropriate tool for developing the spreadsheet. With very young children, augment the breakfast foods listed with pictures. Add more columns to the chart if necessary. Evaluate the composite results by having the spreadsheet sum the number of responses in each type of food.

Fractions: Wholes, Halves, and Quarters: Provide foods that are easily cut with a plastic knife such as melon or prewrapped cheese. Have students place their food on a piece of waxed paper and cut the piece first into halves. Have students draw a picture of what it looks like and label the portions. Then have the students divide it into quarters, drawing pictures and sharing how the fruit looks after each cut. TIP: Be sure to slow down the process of cutting so that after the first cut they count the two pieces (two halves). After the second cut, there are three pieces, which are not all the same size (one half and two quarters). After the third cut, there are four pieces (four quarters). At the end, allow students to eat the pieces, one at a time, talking with their friends about the food or writing equations as they go.

- Create a Kidspiration activity using the Math symbol library that shows fractions and the Number symbol library that spells out the words for half, fourth, and so on. Have students drag the correct words beside the correct picture.

Whole and Parts: Peel an orange and see how many sections there are. Snap a pea to see how many peas there are. Cut an apple to see how many seeds there are. Peel several oranges and see how many sections each one has. Compare the results. Peel a big orange and a little orange. Does the big orange have more sections?

- Use the Graph Club to show the comparative findings of foods. Make a chart of how many sections, seeds, and so on various food have and whether the number in each is always the same.

- Using Kid Pix, create an animation of cutting a fruit. Have students draw a whole apple and save as apple1.gif. Then they draw an apple cut in half and label it apple2.gif. Have them continue this process until they have four drawings. Create a slideshow that shows the apple going from whole to fourths.

Calories and Serving Size: Discuss with students what a calorie is, what it measures, and why people pay attention to the number of calories in food. Post the calorie content of commonly eaten fresh foods. Teach the children how to read food labels from processed or premade foods. From the labels collected by parents, order the labels from foods with the highest calories to the lowest. Have children locate foods that are closest to 100 calories. Compare the size, shape, and weight of each 100-calorie food, paying close attention to the idea of serving sizes in packages. Compare and contrast.

- Have each student draw a picture of his or her favorite 100-calorie foods in Kid Pix. Create a class slideshow.
- Using the Graph Club, place the 100-calorie foods into the appropriate food groups. Ask the students to plan a balanced meal using 100-calorie foods. What is the total calorie count of the balanced meal?

MUSIC   *Food Tunes:* Do an Internet search for music related to food. Many manufacturers have Web sites with a subsection for children, such as Dole 5-a-Day (www. dole5aday.com/Kids/K_Index.html).

SCIENCE   *Foods Up Close and Personal:* Provide students with various foods and an array of scientific observation tools including magnifying glasses, measuring devices, and microscopes. Encourage students to thoroughly examine and describe at least one piece of food, documenting all observations as they examine it as a whole and as they take it apart and eat it. Encourage students to use descriptive language as they share their observations, such as sweet, sour, and salty, as well as texture words.

- Use an early learning electronic microscope attached to the computer to allow students to look at the food in great detail.
- Take a digital photo of each piece of food before, during, and after the observation and eating. Post with the written descriptions (using a corkboard or electronic bulletin board). Record information in a an electronic table with the name of the food on the left axis and the words "before," "during," and "after." Complete the cells of the table with the students' descriptions of the food.
- Use Kidspiration to create a web of the piece of food, placing the name or picture of food in the center and the descriptors at the arms of the web.

SOCIAL STUDIES   *Food Traditions:* Have students write a short story about any special food traditions they have to celebrate birthdays or an upcoming holiday. Ask parents to provide a photograph from a birthday or have students illustrate their most recent celebration including a description of the food served. Be sure to have them classify the food served according to the food pyramid.

- Enter the stories into word processing programs.
- Scan pictures and add them to the word processed stories.

- Draw and illustrate pictures using Kid Pix.
- Use Kidspiration to describe the foods that make that holiday special. Create a web or concept map with the name of the holiday in the center. Use the symbol library to find foods that make that holiday special. Write or record how that food smells and tastes.

The Grouchy Ladybug: This story is about a day in the life of a ladybug who does not want to share food. The ladybug spends the day moving along to larger animals as he feels the prior one is not up to the challenge of fighting to win the food. Discuss with students the attitudes and values displayed by the ladybug as well as the notion of sharing food when there is plenty available.

- Use TimeLiner to create a timeline based on whom the caterpillar meets.

Assessment

FOR YOUNGER
LEARNERS

Option 1: Ask children to write or draw a set of meals and snacks for a one-day intake that provides a balanced meal of healthy foods.

- Provide each child with a blank food pyramid template in Kidspiration and have them put their foods into the food pyramid, checking off each food as they go.

Option 2: Repeat the buffet that took place at the opening of the unit. Have children select foods that provide a balanced meal. Have them record their selections and classify them by the elements of the food pyramid.

NOTE: For a description of the values "Not Interested," "Trying It," "Working on It," "Got it!," and "Helping Others," see chapter 4.

CRITERIA	NOT INTERESTED	TRYING IT	WORKING ON IT	GOT IT!	HELPING OTHERS
Meals and snacks provide a balanced diet according to the food pyramid.					
Foods are labeled appropriately.					

FOR MORE ABLE LEARNERS Have students create one day of meals using some of their favorite foods. Meals should be balanced according to the food pyramid. Caution students that the meals for the day should not be high in calories. Have all foods labeled and classified. Allow students to organize their information either in a table form or in a narrative. Ask students to conclude by answering the question: Now that you know about healthy food, what is the most important change in your eating habits?

CRITERIA	APPROACHES TARGET	MEETS TARGET	EXCEEDS TARGET
Food selection is balanced.	The meals are not completely balanced, but some effort is shown.	Each meal is balanced and the total intake of the day is balanced.	Each meal is balanced, the total of the day is balanced, and there is good variety in the foods chosen.
Foods are categorized acccording to the food pyramid.	Categorization is incomplete and/or there are many errors.	Each food is categorized with only a few minor errors.	Each food is categorized with no errors.
Calories are taken into account.	Menu includes too many sweets or a high fat content.	Menu has only a few sweets.	There are very few high-calorie items, and these are spread throughout the day.
Changes in eating habits are discussed.	Discussion does not critically analyze eating habits. Surface level thinking. Student makes only one minor suggestion for change.	Reflection on eating habits is complete with recommendations for change.	Detailed, analytical reflection on eating habits is provided with valid suggestions for change.

Assessment of technology use depends on the level of student use permitted, the technology available, and the age of the students. See chapter 4 for additional information on assessing technology use.

Additional criteria should be added focusing on writing. The criteria used for the rubric should reflect the objectives and expectations for the students.

Grocery Stores and Markets

UNIT OVERVIEW   When asked about where foods come from, many young children will tell you that they come from the grocery store or market. For them that it true, unless, of course, they have grown foods in their gardens, on their patios, or on their farms. In this unit, students investigate grocery stores and markets to see the fresh and preserved or canned foods. They explore questions about how the foods are preserved or canned and how the foods get to the stores.

UNIT OBJECTIVES   At the end of this unit, students will be able to:

- Describe the functions of supermarkets and outdoor markets.
- Sort foods as they are arranged on store shelves.
- Understand the processing and canning of foods.
- Understand the interdependence between places that grow foods and those that sell foods.
- Determine the expense of various foods.
- Estimate grocery needs and expenses for a day or week.

STANDARDS ADDRESSED IN THIS UNIT
ISTE NETS for Students 1, 3, 4, 5
IRA/NCTE English/Language Arts Standards 1, 3, 5, 6, 7, 8, 12
NCTM Math Standards 1, 2, 3, 4, 5, 8, 10
NAS/NSE Science Standards A1, B3
NCSS Social Studies Standards 1, 3, 7, 8, 9

CHILDREN'S LITERATURE
Bakers Make Many Things, Carol Greene
Big Jimmy's Kum Kau: Chinese Take Out, Ted Lewin
Bruno the Baker, Lars Klinting
A Busy Day at Mr. Kang's Grocery Store, Alice K. Flanagan
Chef Ki Is Serving Dinner, Jill D. Duvall
Curious George and the Pizza, Margaret & H. A. Rey
Grandpa's Corner Store, Dyanne Disalvo-Ryan
Grociers Sell Us Food (Community Helpers Series), Carol Greene
Markets, P. Chamko
Produce Manager, Angela McHaney Brown
Sam's Pizza, David Pelham
Something Good, Robert Munsch
The Supermarket, Gail Saunders-Smith

WEB RESOURCES   Grocery Stores and Markets–General
Bring the Groceries: www.bringthegroceries.com
Earth Day Groceries Project: www.earthdaybags.org

Global Grocery List Project: http://landmark-project.com/ggl/
Home Canning: www.homecanning.com
Markets, Here and There: www.peacegallery.org
Songs: www.niehs.nih.gov/kids/music.htm
Tools: www.pdictionary.com/cgi-bin/browse.cgi?db=tools

Online Grocers
Albertsons: www.albertsons.com
KosherClub.com: www.kosherclub.com
Mexican Grocery Store: www.MexGrocer.com
NetGrocer: http://netgrocer.com
Oakville Grocery, Online Store: http://store.yahoo.com/oakvillegrocery/
Oriental Grocery: www.welcome-to-china.com/ogs/
Russian Foods.com: www.russianfoods.com
Yahoo Yellow Pages: Supermarket: http://yp.yahoo.com/py/
   yploc.py?Pyt=&clr=ypResults&stx=supermarket&stp=a&desc=supermarket

Picture Dictionaries and Reference
Ask Jeeves Kids: www.ajkids.com
Internet Picture Dictionary: www.pdictionary.com
Little Explorers Picture Dictionary: www.enchantedlearning.com/Dictionary.html

SOFTWARE   The Amazing Writing Machine, Broderbund
The Graph Club, Tom Snyder Productions, or Tabletop Jr., Broderbund
Kid Pix (English, Spanish), Broderbund

teaching
the unit

Getting Started

In preparation for the unit, send a letter home to explain the unit's purpose with an overview of the activities and expectations. Depending on the activities you select, ask parents to save and send (1) empty food containers, (2) grocery sacks, (3) grocery ads from a newspaper, and (4) coupon pages. If there is to be a trip to the grocery store, ask for volunteers to monitor a small group of children. Encourage parents to take their children to the store with them in the weeks before the unit, during the unit, and after the unit to explore what is there and eventually to hear from their children what they have learned.

Motivating Activity

Select one of the books from the Children's Literature list to start the unit. Ask children broad questions about grocery stores: What is a grocery store? Why do we have grocery stores? What is in a grocery store (money, people, departments, equipment, food)? How do foods get to the store so we can buy them?

Fill a grocery sack with a variety of things from the grocery store. Put enough items in for at least one object per child. Include fresh produce, bakery goods, cleaning supplies, canned goods, frozen food, dairy products, written material (cards, magazines, books), and paper products (napkins, paper towels, toilet paper). Make sure you have one item that when opened allows all children to have a "piece" (grapes, candy, cookies, etc.).

Sit children in a large circle on the floor. Peer into the grocery sack and pull things out one at a time and place them in the circle. As different items are identified, have children attempt to organize them in categories. Have children predict how the grocery store is organized based on the items in the circle. Ask them to look at how the store is organized the next time they go. Put questions on the board such as: What foods are along the walls? What is always by the checkout line? Why is the milk always along a wall? If you walk down the center of the store, what do you see? Why do you think those items are there?

A field trip to the local grocery store provides a great motivating or culminating experience for the children.

- An excellent alternative is a virtual field trip, developed by the teacher with a team of parents, taking just the right pictures for the other activities in the unit.
- Create a photo gallery of groceries, supermarkets, and outdoor markets from around the world for comparison. Show children that all people eat and that food can be purchased at many places.

Multidisciplinary Activities

ART   *Drawing to Demonstrate Knowledge:* To show what students know before the unit starts and have learned about groceries after the unit is over, ask children to draw pictures to show their grocery store. Instruct children to include as much about their grocery store in one picture as they can, labeling as many of the parts as possible. Be sure to have a word wall visible or encourage them to use invented spelling.

Miniature Store: Make a set of shelves from rulers and erasers. Ask children to make items for these shelves from clay or Play-Doh, sorting the items by type as they place them on the shelves. Create signs and prices for the items.

GROSS MOTOR

Stacking the Cans Relay: Divide students into four teams. Place 150–200 empty cans of various sizes and shapes in the center of the gym or playground. Strategically place the teams of students at what might be the four corners of a large square around this pile of cans. Create a circle adjacent to each team's corner where they must stack their cans. One student from each team runs to the center to get a can, returns to the team's home space, and stacks the cans in the circle, one on top of another. Set a three-minute time limit. See how many cans can be placed in the one stack in that three-minute period. Examine the stacks for size, number, and shape. Try it another couple of times.

- Try the activity again but increase the time and set the criterion for the winner as the one with the higher stack of cans or the stack that has the most cans in it.

LANGUAGE ARTS AND READING

Getting Groceries: Provide sentence strips for students on which to write or small squares of paper on which to draw the steps of the grocery shopping process, starting with making the list and concluding with putting the items on the shelves at home. Only one step is put on each sentence strip or square. Put the steps in sequence by moving the sentence strips around. Eventually each student should be able to use the strips or squares to illustrate her or his personal story of grocery shopping.

Groceries Getting to the Store: Complete another sequencing activity by having students figure out the steps necessary for an apple to get from a seed, to the store, to the grocery bag. Have students brainstorm the steps, create sentence strips, order the strips, the leave them out for an independent sequencing activity.

Change the final product to one that changes the raw ingredients into something processed, such as applesauce. Create another sequence of tasks to write on the sentence strips that describes the cooking, canning, and delivery processes.

- Create localized versions of the activity by changing the product to something that is grown locally. Take digital pictures of the process. Have the students order the pictures by dropping and dragging them into a Kid Pix activity.
- Have students create Kid Pix slides of the entire process of getting the product home, from seed to refrigerator.
- Use Kidspiration to create a sequencing chart with the symbols found in the symbol library.

Grocery Store Bags: Collect grocery bags from a variety of stores in the area. Ask students to search the newspapers and phone books for the names of groceries and cut them out. Have students sort the pictures, the names, and the other items that identify one specific store into the correct sacks.

Grocery ABCs: Create a grocery alphabet book or beginning dictionary of items found in a grocery store. Provide a consistent format for the language and layout of each page.

■ Use Kid Pix to create the pages in the ABC book. For a short activity, preassign each letter of the alphabet to a child. For an extended activity, have students create their own ABC books of grocery store items.

MATH   *Grocery List:* Have students work in five small groups to each create a grocery list for class snacks for one day. Use the newspaper to search for coupons for healthy snacks. Calculate the amount of each item that is needed. (How much milk for everyone to have a glass? How many boxes of crackers for everyone to have two?) Guess the cost or use the grocery ads to determine costs. Calculate the total amount of money needed to supply the healthy snack desired. Take a trip to the grocery store to purchase the items from the list, checking off the items when they are in the cart and noting the actual price on the grocery list next to the estimated cost. Ask the checker to provide the cost before coupons and tax, with coupons, and the tax amount. Compare the estimated and actual costs for each group.

■ Consult an online grocery store to find out the price of items. Children are fascinated by the "cart" function in the online grocery store and how it automatically adds tax on the relevant items.

The Shapes of Food: Using the empty boxes, cartons, and cans provided by families, have students sort food items by shape (cylinder, sphere, etc.). Within shape categories, order the boxes and cans by size. Have students communicate the process and results (verbally, with original pictures or photographs, or in writing).

Global Grocery List: Is the cost of food the same all over the world? Have students speculate about why or why not. What factors influence the cost of food in your area?

■ Participate in the Global Grocery List Project (**http://landmark-project.com/ ggl/**) to compare costs of food in your area with the average of those in the database.

Weighing Fruits and Vegetables: Use a scale to weigh different fruits and vegetables. List their price per pound. Add more of the items onto the scale to get to one pound. Have students calculate or estimate the cost of one piece of fruit or a vegetable. Discuss that a pound is divided into 16 ounces.

■ Use the Graph Club to create a graph of ounces. Graph the results of weighing the produce on the chart from the lightest to the heaviest.

The Grocery Store: Create a pretend grocery store in the classroom using the cans and boxes brought in by the students. Place prices on items. Give each child play money and have her or him purchase groceries. Have students take turns being the shopper and the storekeeper. Have students use a calculator or PDA to add up the prices.

MUSIC

Sounds in Cans and Bottles: Have students listen to the sounds made by tapping upside down cans with a drumstick. Compare the size of the can with the sound that is made. Organize cans by the pitch of the sound. Ask students to compare empty cans with partially filled cans. Arrange a set of cans to enable students to play a familiar song. Do the same activity with bottles of various sizes that are unfilled, partially filled, and filled.

- Videotape students as they create their songs. Group together several students to create an "orchestra." Capture digital video for insertion into a class video.
- If the school has an audiometer or probe ware that measures the frequency of sound waves, demonstrate to students the measurement of the sound wave to see if their ears are as good as the probe ware. This is a good time to introduce scientific measurement devices that attach to the computer.

SCIENCE

Bake a Cake: As a class project bake two different cakes, one using a boxed mix and the other from "scratch." (Ask students to find out where the phrase "from scratch" comes from. Encourage them to use Ask Jeeves Kids.) Compare the ingredients from the recipe with the ingredients required for the boxed cake. Look further into the actual ingredients of the mix.

- Experiment by dividing the cake ingredients in half. In one half of each leave out an ingredient (an egg or oil for the boxed mix and the active ingredient in the recipe such as soda or baking powder). Compare the results. Talk about following recipes exactly.
- Chronicle the baking of the two cakes using a video camera. Record students' reaction to tasting the cakes. For an alternative approach, assemble the two cakes in front of the video camera, baking both at the same time. Ask students whether they can tell why they look or taste different. Have students watch the videotape, looking for why they could be different.

Plant Seeds: In preparation for the **Growing and Producing Food** unit, plant some tomato, pumpkin, or other vegetable seeds early in the unit. Have a discussion with the class about what is necessary for the plants to be healthy: adequate sun, water, and nutrients. As the plants begin to mature, discuss how many plants are necessary to feed a family. Enter into a discussion on what happens when you have too much food, such as a farmer. This discussion provides an introduction to the canning section.

Canning Produce: Ask students why things come in cans. Bring some fresh carrots, canned carrots, and frozen carrots. Discuss why food comes in different forms. Using a hotplate, cook each type of carrot. Have students taste the difference. What tastes are evident in the canned version that are not in the fresh version? Once the students understand that canning and freezing are ways to preserve food beyond its natural freshness period, talk about how cans are sealed and what an unsealed can looks like. Remind students about the dates on foods, including some canned items, establishing the freshness period. If possible, demonstrate the canning of produce.

■ Go to the Home Canning Web site to look at how things are canned (www.homecanning.com).

Earth Day Groceries Project: Participate in the Earth Day Groceries Project (www.earthdaybags.org).

SOCIAL STUDIES

My Favorites: Divide a bulletin board into five columns, labeling each as a section of the grocery store (fresh produce, bakery goods, dairy products, frozen foods, canned goods). Provide five squares of paper for each child on which to record her or his favorite food in each category. Have students put their name or initials on the back of the sheet.

Jobs in the Supermarket: Write "help wanted" ads that describe the various jobs that are available in the supermarket. Have employees from the local grocery store come to class to explain their job, how they were hired, what they plan to do next, and whether they hold a temporary or part-time position.

Farmers' Market: Visit an outdoor or growers' market in the area. List the various parts of the market. Compare and contrast the farmers' market to the grocery store.

Comparing: Have students compare a farmers' market with a grocery store. Although most farmers' markets are open to the public, discuss why most parents do not buy the food at the farmers' market.

■ *Grocery Stores, Then and Now:* Go to Ask Jeeves Kids (www.ajkids.com). Ask: What is a grocery store? Examine the pictures of stores in various time periods. Compare and contrast those pictures with pictures of grocery stores today.

■ *Markets, Here and There:* View pictures of open-air markets from around the world (www.peacegallery.org).

Assessment

To see what students know and have learned about groceries, ask children to draw pictures at the beginning and end of this unit to show as much about their grocery store in one picture as they can, labeling as many of the parts as possible.

NOTE: For a description of the values "Not Interested," "Trying It," "Working on It," "Got it!," and "Helping Others," see chapter 4.

CRITERIA	NOT INTERESTED	TRYING IT	WORKING ON IT	GOT IT!	HELPING OTHERS
People are evident in their roles.					
Food is evident, sorted by type.					
Departments are noted.					
Various pieces of equipment are noted.					

Provide the same prompt for the more able learners. Ask students to write a narrative of their visit to the grocery store using their diagram as a reference. Remind them to be very observant as they share their visit orally or in writing.

CRITERIA	APPROACHES TARGET	MEETS TARGET	EXCEEDS TARGET
People are evident in their roles.	Very few people are evident. It is not clear if they are patrons or employees.	Employees are evident in their roles.	Employees are evident in every department and clearly described.
Departments are noted and food is organized.	Food is partially sorted, such as in the fresh produce department, but the entire store does not have a clear organization.	Food is sorted and store departments are clearly recognizable.	Food within departments is sorted, such as fresh fruit, canned vegetables, and meat.
Equipment is described.	Little equipment is evident or described.	Equipment is evident and described.	Equipment is evident and thoroughly described in the context of its function.

Assessment of technology use depends on the level of student use permitted, the technology available, and the age of the students. See chapter 4 for additional information on assessing technology use.

Additional criteria should be added focusing on writing. The criteria used for the rubric should reflect the objectives and expectations for the students.

Growing and Producing Food

UNIT OVERVIEW

Getting beyond the grocery store or market as a place where one gets food may be an abstract concept for many young children. Some, however, have helped with the family's vegetable garden or seen the neighbors growing vegetables or raising livestock. Some, too, may live on farms and be an active part of growing and producing foods. Exploring gardens and farms by taking field trips, going on virtual field trips, or planting seeds at school shows students how foods grow. Actually taking fresh ingredients to produce a common food (applesauce and bread) shows children the type of work that goes into the foods we buy in the store.

UNIT OBJECTIVES

At the end of this unit, students will be able to:

- Identify the origins of food (plants or animals).
- Explain the steps necessary for producing several foods.
- Take care of a plant as it grows.
- Understand what a plant needs to thrive.

STANDARDS
ADDRESSED
IN THIS UNIT

ISTE NETS for Students 1, 2, 3, 5, 6
IRA/NCTE English/Language Arts Standards 1, 3, 4, 7, 8
NCTM Math Standards 1, 4, 5, 8, 10
NAS/NSE Science Standards A1, A2, C2, F3
NCSS Social Studies Standards 1, 4, 5, 7, 10

CHILDREN'S
LITERATURE

Alejandro's Gift, Richard E. Albert
Alphabet Garden, Laura Jane Coates
The Children's Kitchen Garden: A Book of Gardening, Cooking, and Learning,
    Georgeanne Brennan
Cooking Tools, Inez Snyder
Food and Farming (Geography for Fun), Pam Robson
The Gardener, Sarah Stewart
Growing Vegetable Soup, Lois Ehlert
Jack and the Beanstalk, fairy tale
The Plants We Eat, Millicent E. Selsam
This Is the Sea That Feeds Us, Robert F. Baldwin
Tops and Bottoms, Janet Stevens
The Ugly Vegetables (a Chinese garden), Grace Lin
Uncle Willie and the Soup Kitchen, Dyanne Disalvo-Ryan & Myra Reisberg

WEB RESOURCES

Growing and Producing Food—General
    The ABCs of School Gardens (includes a slideshow): http://aggie-
        horticulture.tamu.edu/nutrition/schoolgardens/startagarden/abcintro.html
    Camp Silo: The Story of Corn: www.campsilos.org/mod3/index.shtml

Composting for Kids: http://aggie-horticulture.tamu.edu/sustainable/slidesets/
kidscompost/cover.html
CornCam: www.iowafarmer.com/corncam/corn.html
Corn Facts: www.ohiocorn.org/about_prod_facts.htm
DairyCam: www.dairycam.com
Dairy Facts (slideshow): www.mda.state.mi.us/kids/pictures/dairy/
Dole 5-a-Day: www.dole5aday.com
Emu Facts: http://home.golden.net/~walkabout/facts.html
Foods: www.pdictionary.com/cgi-bin/browse.cgi?db=fruits
Garden and Yard: www.pdictionary.com/cgi-
bin/browse.cgi?db=garden*and*yard
Getting Green Field Trip: A Virtual Field Trip: www.field-guides.com/sci/green/
index.htm
Great Plant Escape: www.urbanext.uiuc.edu/gpe/
Growing Plants Indoors: www.urbanext.uiuc.edu/gpe/case1/c1facts3a.html
Growing Wheat: www.waltonfeed.com/old/wheat.html
Honey Facts: www.honey.com/kids/
Kids Food Cyber Club: www.kidfood.org/kf_cyber.html
Kids Valley Garden: www.raw-connections.com/garden/
Learn About Plants: www.mhschool.com/student/science/mhscience/k/sims/
sim2.html
Lemonade Stand: www.littlejason.com/lemonade/index.html
Living Things: www.fi.edu/tfi/units/life/
Lizzy Visits the Sculpture Museum: www.nga.gov/kids/lizzy/lizzy.html
Songs: www.niehs.nih.gov/kids/music.htm
Vegetables: www.pdictionary.com/cgi-bin/
browse.cgi?db=vegetables

Picture Dictionaries and Reference
Ask Jeeves Kids: www.ajkids.com
Internet Picture Dictionary: www.pdictionary.com
Little Explorers Picture Dictionary: www.enchantedlearning.com/Dictionary.html

SOFTWARE   The Amazing Writing Machine, Broderbund
D.W. the Picky Eater, Broderbund (Living Books)
The Graph Club, Tom Snyder Productions, or TableTop Jr., Broderbund
Kid Pix (English, Spanish), Broderbund
Kidspiration, Inspiration Software
Sammy's Science House, Edmark
TimeLiner (English, Spanish), Tom Snyder Productions

teaching the unit

Getting Started

In preparation for the unit, send a letter to parents explaining the purpose of the unit. Ask parents to remind the children of times when they saw a garden, an orchard, or a farm where foods were being grown. This could be on a trip to a nursery or home improvement store to purchase the plants. Although this unit is specifically about food production, parents might also be encouraged to talk with their children about other types of gardens in their yards, the neighborhood, or area (rock, flower, sculpture, butterfly). Also, have parents talk to their child about the gardens their parents or grandparents had. Prepare parents to (1) send a vegetable to school on an appointed day and (2) transplant a vegetable plant that has been started at school.

Motivating Activity

On a field trip to the grocery store, make a point to purchase some fresh fruit or vegetable that is produced in the nearby area. Ask the students questions about how the food gets to the grocery store, who grows it or produces it, and so on. Use the information as a preassessment. Plan a field trip later in the unit to a garden, farm, or orchard at a time when the food is to be harvested to see where the food grows, how it is being grown, and how it is harvested. Caution children not to eat plants (leaves, berries, fruits, vegetables) without first consulting an adult about the safety of eating the produce and possible allergic reactions. Document the field trip using the digital camera.

- Upload the trip into a Web-based photo gallery or the school Web site, working with the children to title each picture and write a brief description of what is happening. If children are in the pictures, make sure you have parent permission to post the picture to the Web site, and use only their first names.

Multidisciplinary Activities

ART   *Nonproducing Gardens:* Create a rock or sculpture garden in an area of the classroom or schoolyard. Draw pictures to show its evolution. Contrast this garden with one that grows food or flowers.

- View Lizzy Visits the Sculpture Museum (**www.nga.gov/kids/lizzy/lizzy.html**) to see other types of gardens.

GROSS MOTOR   *This Is the Way We Plant Our Seeds:* Make up words and motions to "Here we Go Round the Mulberry Bush" that demonstrate the way various crops are planted, grown, harvested, cooked, and eaten.

Twister: Design a food or vegetable Twister game using an old sheet or shower curtain. Have children play Twister in groups of two to four.

LANGUAGE ARTS AND READING

Read to Learn: Place library books about how plants are grown and harvested on the reading table (see Children's Literature section).

- Have students read or model reading to learn by reading the information about several different farm and ranch products on the following Web sites:

  Corn Facts: www.ohiocorn.org/about_prod_facts.htm
  Emu Facts: http://home.golden.net/~walkabout/facts.html
  Dairy Facts (slideshow): www.mda.state.mi.us/kids/pictures/dairy/

- Use the Amazing Writing Machine to write and illustrate a Read to Learn book about a product grown in the area. Print it as a fold-up book. Alternative means of displaying the Read to Learn facts include creating:
  - a slideshow of the Read to Learn book using PowerPoint or Kid Pix,
  - a photo album documenting the facts, or
  - a photo gallery that combines the pictures and the written facts.

Family Bread: Have students bring a piece of bread to school that is an example of the type of bread their family most often eats. Ask them to draw a picture of it, explain how the family gets or makes it, and tell how often they have this bread for meals (routinely or for celebrations). Scan the pictures and use them in a slideshow.

MATH

Making Applesauce: Obtain 5–10 pounds of apples. Have students weigh the apples and record the weight in a table. Peel and cut apples, and place them in a cooking pot. With each cup of water added, weigh the cup of water and add it to the total weight of what has been added to the pot. Add enough water to about halfway cover the apples. Cook and stir. If sugar and cinnamon are added, be sure to weigh the amount before adding.

While the apples are cooking, discuss where the ingredients for the applesauce came from and the additional steps that it is taking to create applesauce.

- Have students create slides chronicling the process of making the applesauce. Considering breaking the class into groups to document the different steps in making the applesauce, from planting the seed to grow the apple tree, to buying the fruit at the grocery store, to cutting and cooking the apples.
- Use the Graph Club or Tabletop Jr. to record the weights and compare the results.

Before serving the applesauce, weigh the pot of applesauce. Compare the weight of the finished applesauce with the total weight of the ingredients. Don't forget to subtract the weight of the pot. (The applesauce should weigh less than the total of all the ingredients. Encourage students to think about the steam and the energy released in the cooking process.)

Making Bread: As a group activity, use a recipe for a traditional loaf of bread. Follow the teaching suggestions in making the applesauce. The bread has the added dimension of requiring several ingredients, each of which has its own manufacturing process before use. Be sure to have children measure the ingredients carefully.

- Have students use Kidspiration to describe the sequence of steps necessary to bring all the ingredients together to make bread. Small groups under the supervision of an adult can research on the Internet using Ask Jeeves Kids to find out how their assignment ingredient gets to the point of being ready for the bread recipe. (With very young children, an instant bread mix will suffice.)

- Use a spreadsheet to create a table that records each ingredient, the weight of the raw ingredient, and the total weight. (Like the applesauce, the weight of the bread will be less that the total weight of the ingredients.)

MUSIC

Old MacDonald Had a Farm: After singing this song, lead a discussion about how different animals have unique characteristics. For more advanced students, discuss how different animals have adapted to their environment.

SCIENCE

Keeping a Garden Alive: Explore the elements that are necessary for plants to survive. Purchase several plants. Separate them into four groups. Place one group in a closet that has no light. Place another on the windowsill but do not give it any water. Remove the dirt from another plant and place the roots in sand. Add any other variables students think will have an effect on the survival of plants. Place another group in the windowsill with adequate light, water, and plant material. Have students take digital pictures and record their findings in a journal each day as they observe the growth of the plants. Have students go home and assess the condition of plants around their home.

- Have groups create Kid Pix slideshows of each plant in the experiment. Have students record their conclusions in their science journals.

Our Own Bean Stalk: Soak lima beans in water over night. Read the story *Jack and the Beanstalk.* Taking a picture of each step of the process, plant bean seeds in a tall jar on a Friday. Fill the jar with 1–2 inches of water. Fold a set of paper towels in half and put the paper towels around the inside of the jar so that the bottom edge is in the water. Make sure there is enough water to saturate the paper towels and keep them moist thoroughout the weekend. Tuck beans between the towel and the jar, two to three inches above the water line. Place a yardstick into the jar or next to it. Check the seeds on Monday. Take pictures each day for several days. Pot the beans in soil (inside or outside or both), staking them so they can continue growing "up."

- Put a white carnation or a full celery stalk in water tinted with food coloring. Take digital pictures every hour to create a time-lapse photography movie. Discuss how the plant drank the colored water and why it changed the flower petals or leaf color.

- Insert the pictures into Kid Pix to create a slideshow.

- Have students draw several pictures showing the seed-to-plant cycle. Create a slideshow in Kid Pix.

- Use TimeLiner to create a timeline of the growth of the lima bean seeds. Add pictures, drawings, and student observations.

- Plant different types of seeds. Take pictures and measure the plants' heights at various stages of growth. Graph the various growth rates using the Graph Club. Create a timeline for each type of seed using TimeLiner. Merge the timelines together and compare the growth rates of each type of plant.

- Use PDAs and temperature sensors to take the temperature of the outside air and soil and note whether it is cloudy or sunny. Synchronize this information to a spreadsheet on the classroom computer and create a graph. Analyze the information. Have students determine the effect sunlight has on temperature.

- Put the pictures of the seed-to-plant cycle into a Kid Pix slideshow. Mix up the order. Have students drag the slideshow icons (trucks) into the correct order to make the cycle. When the pictures are in the right order, play the slideshow.

Planting: Use a sand table as a place to practice planting skills. Fill it first with some rocks for drainage and then mostly fill it with dirt, deep enough that students can actually plant seeds, seedlings, and small plants in it. Provide tools to till, dig, and water. Set up a helper chart with exact instructions for the "gardeners."

Food for the Animals: Read a book about gardens or try *Alejandro's Garden.* Research the types of birds, insects, and small animals indigenous to your area and the types of food they eat. Create a small garden that will attract butterflies, hummingbirds, or other creatures to your school where you can safely view them enjoying your produce.

- Put a bird feeder near a window or use one that sticks to the outside of the window with suction cups. Set up a Web cam connected to a motion sensor facing the bird feeder. Set the Web cam to take a picture every time it detects motion. Make a movie of all of the birds and other animals that eat at your bird feeder.

The Plants We Eat: Read one of the books that describes edible plants (*The Plants We Eat,* by Millicent E. Selsam, and *Tops and Bottoms,* by Janet Stevens). Show students the various parts of plants we eat, such as leaves (lettuce), fruit (apples), roots (potatoes). Provide several types of these foods for students to sort.

- Use Kidspiration to sort different types of food. Make a different box for the different ways we get foods: foods that grow under ground, foods that grow on trees, foods that come from animals, and so on. Have students use the symbols to fill the boxes.

SOCIAL STUDIES   *Making Vegetable Soup:* Have students work in task groups to (1) cut the vegetables for the soup, (2) clean and set the tables, (3) assemble the parts of the soup and stir it (under strict supervision, of course), (4) record the process both in photos and notes, and (5) read stories about soup with a reading buddy. As groups are assigned and the organization is explained, be sure to discuss with students the necessity of working together to complete a complicated task. Have children evaluate their cooperation at the end of the activity.

Read *Growing Vegetable Soup,* by Lois Ehlert; *Uncle Willie and the Soup Kitchen,* by Dyanne Disalvo-Ryan and Myra Reisberg; or any version of *Stone Soup.* Bring a soup bone, five precut onions, a bag of potatoes, a large can of tomato juice, and seasoning. Ask parents to each send a vegetable to school with their child, fresh or canned. Have a group clean and cut the fresh vegetables using plastic knives. Have children each use a potato peeler (under strict supervision) to peel a potato. Cut the potato in half for the children, and let them cube it.

Use a hot plate and a large canning pot to make the soup. Add a soup bone (for the stone in *Stone Soup*) and the five precut onions. Add all of the vegetables and tomato juice. Fill with water to cover the vegetables. Simmer until done.

- Chronicle the process using a digital or video camera. Have the recording group create a slideshow as the process unfolds.

Provide each child with a small taste. Arrange in advance to take the food to a local soup kitchen to share with those less fortunate. Discuss the importance of sharing food with those who are not able to provide for themselves. Make the parallel between the elements that are necessary for plants to thrive and elements, especially food, that are necessary for people to survive.

Assessment

FOR YOUNGER LEARNERS

Ask children to create a Food Chain picture, story, or timeline that shows food from the beginning (seeds) to the food we eat, labeling as many parts as they can.

NOTE: For a description of the values "Not Interested," "Trying It," "Working on It," "Got it!," and "Helping Others," see chapter 4.

CRITERIA	NOT INTERESTED	TRYING IT	WORKING ON IT	GOT IT!	HELPING OTHERS
Students start with seeds, and show the growth cycle, harvesting, and steps to the table.					
Roles of the humans in this cycle are noted.					
Labels clearly identify the process.					

FOR MORE ABLE LEARNERS

Ask children to write and illustrate a story that describes how food gets to the dining room table from seed to serving. Using knowledge they gained from the prior units, ask them to pick a vegetable or fruit.

CRITERIA	APPROACHES TARGET	MEETS TARGET	EXCEEDS TARGET
Steps in growth	Steps in growth are either incomplete or out of order	Begins with planting, showing growth to maturity	Includes detailed and logical steps or each set of steps for multiple ingredients
From farm to store	Neglects some of the steps and/or misplaces in store	Shows harvesting, packaging, transporting, and shelving correctly in a store	Includes detailed and logical steps or each set of steps for multiple ingredients
Food preparation	Neglects some of the steps in preparation	Includes refrigeration, cleaning, and cooking (if appropriate)	Includes preparation steps for a complex dish
Role of people	Shows food but does not include any people to describe the steps	Includes role of farmer, drivers, grocers, and adults in the home	Shows roles of many people and interdependence of people's tasks
Food selection	Selects appropriate food but neglects label or does not select appropriate food	Selects appropriate food—vegetable or fruit—and provides label	Selects an appropriate food that requires preparation with other ingredients. Accurately labels all ingredients by food group

Assessment of technology use depends on the level of student use permitted, the technology available, and the age of the students. See chapter 4 for additional information on assessing technology use.

Additional criteria should be added focusing on writing. The criteria used for the rubric should reflect the objectives and expectations for the students.

Foods Around the World

UNIT OVERVIEW

The **Foods Around the World** unit connects the study of foods to the study of the family, provides a glimpse into different cultures, discusses how things are transported, and expores basic world geography. Tracing the origin of foods builds a foundation for young children to study more abstract concepts of production, distribution, and geographic and economic factors in growing foods. Many families have food traditions that are connected to cultural traditions and national origins. Understanding this helps children understand and honor those traditions.

UNIT OBJECTIVES

At the end of this unit, students will be able to:

- Define and describe foods popularly attributed to various regions of the U.S. and other countries.
- Know the origins of vegetables and fruits of the U.S.
- Describe the connection between the growth and production of foods and the geography and climate of a region.
- Identify the original country of origin or culture of some common foods.

STANDARDS ADDRESSED IN THIS UNIT

ISTE NETS for Students 1, 2, 3, 4, 5
IRA/NCTE English/Language Arts Standards 1, 3, 7, 8, 12
NCTM Math Standards 4
NAS/NSE Science Standards F1, F3, F4
NCSS Social Studies Standards 1, 3

CHILDREN'S LITERATURE

Big Jimmy's Kum Kau: Chinese Take Out, Ted Lewin
Char Siu Bao Boy, Sandra S. Yamate
Dim Sum for Everyone, Grace Lin
Eating the Alphabet, Lois Ehlert
Food and Farming (Geography for Fun), Pam Robson
Food and Festivals Series (Brazil, Caribbean, China, France, Germany, India, Israel, Italy, Japan, Kenya, Mexico, West Africa), Linda Illsley
Food Found All Around, Janine Scott
The Story of Chopsticks, Ying Chang Compestine
Sun Bread, Elisa Kleven
This Is the Sea That Feeds Us, Robert F. Baldwin
The Ugly Vegetables, Grace Lin

WEB RESOURCES

Foods Around the World—General
Chinese New Year Recipes:
www.geocities.com/Wellesley/Garden/2790/cnyrec.htm
Enchanted Learning.com: www.EnchantedLearning.com/geography/

Food Network (New Year's, Oktoberfest, Passover, St. Patrick's Day, Sushi Party, Thanksgiving, Valentine's Day): www.foodtv.com/holidays/ho-g1/0,1948,,00.html

Foods: www.pdictionary.com/cgi-bin/browse.cgi?db=fruits

The Food Timeline: www.gti.net/mocolib1/kid/food.html

Globalwarming Kids Site: www.epa.gov/globalwarming/kids/gw.html

History of Eating Utensils: www.calacademy.org/research/anthropology/utensil/index.html

History: Where Food Crops Originated: www.mnh.si.edu/garden/history/

Holidays and Gatherings Kitchen (Chinese New Year, Christmas, Cinco de Mayo, Coffee Klatsch): www.pdictionary.com/cgi-bin/browse.cgi?db=kitchen

Kwanza Recipes: http://members.tripod.com/~Nancy_J/kwanzaa.htm

Lycos Travel: http://travel.lycos.com

Recipes Around the World: www.thinkquest.org/library/lib/site_sum_outside.html?tname=3195&url=3195/

Songs: www.niehs.nih.gov/kids/music.htm

Yahoo! Weather: http://weather.yahoo.com

Picture Dictionaries and Reference

Columbia Encyclopedia: www.bartleby.com/65/

Internet Picture Dictionary: www.pdictionary.com

Little Explorers Picture Dictionary: www.enchantedlearning.com/Dictionary.html

MapQuest: www.mapquest.com

SOFTWARE The Amazing Writing Machine, Broderbund

The Graph Club, Tom Snyder Productions

Kid Pix (English, Spanish), Broderbund

Kidspiration, Inspiration Software

teaching the unit

Getting Started

In preparation for the unit, send a letter to parents explaining the purpose of the unit. Ask parents to (1) talk with their children about some of their holiday food traditions and where they originated and (2) provide some favorite family recipes that have been handed down from grandparents or great grandparents. In addition, ask parents to send one fruit or vegetable to school for the opening motivating activity related to Lois Ehlert's book *Eating the Alphabet*. To ensure a variety, assign each child a different fruit or vegetable, perhaps even the ones in the story. Additionally, ask parents to work with their children at home to select four to eight photographs that depict the family celebrations that incorporate family food recipes. Be sure to have parents label the back of the pictures.

Motivating Activity

Select a variety of fruits and vegetables from the local market, some the children have probably seen and eaten before and some they have not. Place them all in a large fruit basket or, if there are enough, have each child hold one piece. Have close at hand a cutting board, paper plates, toothpicks, and napkins. Gather the children around. Read *Eating the Alphabet,* by Lois Ehlert. When you come to a fruit that is in the book, examine it closely with the students, asking them for descriptive words. (An aide or assistant can record the words for use in a later activity.) End each discussion of a piece of food with the statement, "I wonder where this came from," and listening to the answers that are given.

Whole-Group Activity

Food Tasting Party: Ask each child to bring one food (apple, orange, piece of bread, slice of cheese, cake, etc.). Provide a couple of potentially new foods yourself. In a center, have children cut the food into tiny pieces, put it on a paper plate, and cover it with plastic wrap. (Wash their hands. Use rubber gloves. Use a plastic knife.) Set all plates on a table. Give each child a paper plate and a toothpick. Have each child take one piece of each food to try. Take digital photos of the table and of each child tasting a food. Discuss the new foods that they tasted.

Multidisciplinary Activities

ART   *Where in the World?:* Place a world map on a bulletin board. Draw a picture of a food from the Motivating Activity and label it. Pin it to its country of origin. For example, the avocado comes from Mexico. Draw a picture of an avocado and label it. Place it on Mexico. If possible, purchase the foods and allow the students to taste each food.

   ■ Using the food assigned in the Motivating Activity or one chosen by each child, have students look up a food and its place of origin. Use an encyclopedi, or an online encyclopedia (Columbia Encyclopedia: www.bartleby.com/65/).

■ As an introduction to world geography, download and print maps of countries from Enchanted Learning.com (**www.EnchantedLearning.com/geography/**).

GROSS MOTOR

Upset the Fruit Basket: Make two sets of cards with the names of fruits you have discussed that come from other parts of the country and around the world.

■ Version 1: Give each child a card. Place the remaining cards randomly upside down on chairs, the floor, or in a circle on the playground. At the signal, have students find the matching name of their fruit and sit down where it is located.

■ Version 2: Pass out the pairs of cards to the students such that each student has one card but does not know who holds the matching card. Call out the name of one, two, or three fruits, and have students run to trade seats with their match.

LANGUAGE ARTS AND READING

Holiday Traditions: Create a class book by having each child select a family holiday tradition to draw or write about. The pictures sent by families noted in the Getting Started section can be used as a story starter. Select a near holiday or birthdays as the theme. Use information acquired from parents to tell about origins of the holiday or birthday traditions.

■ Scan the pictures sent by the parents into the word processing program and have children use the computers to write the stories.

■ Insert the pictures into Kid Pix. Ask the children to record the stories told to them by their parents. (All slides can be made into a class slideshow.)

ABC Book, Foods of the World: Create individual or class ABC books that tell of the places where foods originate. Use the language pattern "Avocados come from (or originated in) Mexico." Each child can make one page, or children can individually make a complete book using information from the Art activity described previously.

■ Use the Amazing Writing Machine or other book creation software to make books about foods of different countries. Write and illustrate the pages with a map of the country, the flag, and traditional foods. Have students tell whether they have tried these foods and whether they like them or not. If they haven't tried the food, would they like to?

MATH

Cooking: Each day for a week or more, select a holiday recipe to make as a classroom project (for recipes, access Holidays and Gatherings Kitchen: **www.foodtv.com/holidays/ho-g1/0,1948,,00.html**). Measure the amounts as a group, allowing every child to take part. Encourage students to have good manners as they taste the new and different recipes, taking a no-thank-you helping (a tiny bit) to try if they are not adventuresome.

■ Using the Kidspiration activity Patterns, substitute pictures of foods cooked in class from around the world for the pattern icons given in the activity. Have students finish a pattern and create their own.

- Keep track of the foods tried and how many liked or disliked them. Use the Graph Club to graph the results. Draw conclusions about the foods students like.

- Using MapQuest, obtain a map of some of the countries of origin of the foods selected. Use the World Atlas section of MapQuest. Have students guess how long it would take to get to that country. Look at the modes of transportation that might be necessary to get there. Pull up an airline schedule as a brief check on how long it might take to fly there.

MUSIC *Music of the Country:* To show different concepts about the country of origin, once the country is located for the foods in these activities, work with the music teacher to find and listen to the national anthems of each of the countries. Record the opening of the country's anthem or familiar folk music to insert as an audio file in a slideshow about food origins.

SCIENCE *What Is the Weather?:* In connection with the Art activity of drawing the fruit and printing a map of the food's country of origin, examine the climate and weather of that country. Current weather is available at Yahoo! Weather (http://weather.yahoo.com). (Use adults or older children to read these pages.) The climate of the country can be found through Lycos Travel (http://travel.lycos.com). Type in a country in Search for a Destination. Click on Environment in the Overview section of the country page. Definitions of climate and weather are available at the Environmental Protection Agency's Web site for kids (www.epa.gov/globalwarming/kids/gw.html).

- Use Kid Pix to create a picture that shows the country and the food.

- Insert a sound file of the national anthem of the country into a Kid Pix slide of the food and the country.

SOCIAL STUDIES *History of Foods:* Making the connection between what foods used to be like and what they have evolved to today helps young children see that change happens over time and in everyone's lifetime. Looking at food is a tangible way to examine differences. Assign each child in the classroom one food from the list of Old World and New World foods located at History: Where Food Crops Originated: www.mnh.si.edu/garden/history/.

- Have children make a Food History book using the Amazing Writing Machine by writing or quoting a brief story about the origin of each food discussed. (Use this opportunity to teach students how to write about a topic by reading and saying it in their own words or quoting the original source.)

Does Everyone Use a Fork?: Read *The Story of Chopsticks.* Many young children assume that all children of the world eat foods with the same utensils they do. Many cultures use other utensils in addition to and instead of forks to eat their food. Have students discuss chopsticks, bowls, hands, and so on. (With the discussion of hands, insert the importance of washing hands both before and after eating.) Have children try eating different foods with different utensils.

- Share the Web site History of Eating Utensils (www.calacademy.org/research/anthropology/utensil/index.html).
- In Kid Pix have children draw themselves eating with something other than a fork. Write a sentence about the experience. Create a classroom slideshow with all of the pictures.

The Food Pyramid: Different cultures also have different favorite foods. Study different cultures' foods and discuss how they still fit into the food pyramid. Select meals of cultures different from the predominant one of the class. Have students classify the foods according to the pyramid.

- Create a new symbol library in Kidspiration with different cultures' typical food pictures. Using the Kidspiration activity The Food Pyramid, have students drag food from the cultural foods symbol library to the appropriate food group in the food pyramid.

Recipes Around the World: Bring various cookbooks to school. Discuss how cookbooks are organized and usually written according to a theme, such as vegetarian, Italian, dessert, and so forth. Have students create a list of the foods they would put in a class recipe book that would represent the class.

- Show students the ThinkQuest Web site created by kids, Recipes Around the World (www.thinkquest.org/library/lib/site_sum_outside.html?tname=3195&url=3195/). Have students create a Venn diagram noting the similarities and difference between their food list and those from the Web site. (Be sure to select only recipes that are comprehensible by the class. Narrow the selection of the recipes depending on the maturity of the students and their familiarity with creating Venn diagrams for comparing and contrasting ideas.)

Create a Healthy Day: Use the food pyramid as a guide and have students complete a healthy set of meals for one day.

- Examine and record the origins of the foods they have selected. For information, access History: Where Food Crops Originated: www.mnh.si.edu/garden/history/.

Assessment

FOR YOUNGER
LEARNERS

Ask children to create a story or picture telling of a family tradition that involves a meal. Encourage them to write about the tradition and tell the country of origin for the foods involved.

NOTE: For a description of the values "Not Interested," "Trying It," "Working on It," "Got it!," and "Helping Others," see chapter 4.

CRITERIA	NOT INTERESTED	TRYING IT	WORKING ON IT	GOT IT!	HELPING OTHERS
Tells the tradition surrounding a family meal					
Names the foods					
Names the origins of the foods					
Provides labels throughout the picture					

FOR MORE ABLE LEARNERS

Ask students to create a daily menu using food from other regions of the country and other countries for the time of year in which you are teaching the unit. They can include three meals and snacks. Instruct students that the meal must be balanced according to the food pyramid. The items in the meals should be labeled with the region or country of origin. The foods should also be classified according to which element of the food pyramid they are attributed to. Decide whether writing skills are going to be assessed. If so, set the expectations for conveying their one-day menu (list, narrative, illustrated pictures, etc.).

If assessment is to be done electronically, use Kid Pix or the Amazing Writing Machine. Assess students' technology skills in entering information and printing it out. Permit students to access Web sites covered in activities to research information to compose their menu.

CRITERIA	APPROACHES TARGET	MEETS TARGET	EXCEEDS TARGET
Food selection	Does not clearly demonstrate understanding that foods are different for countries and cultures	Selects foods representing other regions and other countries or cultures	Selects foods from around the world, purposefully showing an array of cultures
Food availability	Selects some foods that are out of season or not currently available	Selects foods that are all currently available and not out of season	(Not applicable)
Completeness of menu	The menu is incomplete.	The menu covers the entire day with time or meal (e.g., breakfast) specified.	The menu covers three meals and snacks including drinks.
Food groups	Some foods are not labeled or labeled incorrectly.	Each dish in the meal is labeled with the food group.	(Not applicable)
Menu balance	The total intake is not balanced.	The total intake for the day is balanced according to the food pyramid.	(Not applicable)

Assessment of technology use depends on the level of student use permitted, the technology available, and the age of the students. See chapter 4 for additional information on assessing technology use.

Additional criteria should be added focusing on writing. The criteria used for the rubric should reflect the objectives and expectations for the students.

Fun Facts About Foods Feast

theme culminating event

Work with the children and the cafeteria managers to plan a special meal. Set a date on the calendar. Create an invitation to send to the groups that are to be invited whether they include the entire school, the young children, or the parents. Encourage each child to write and illustrate invitations to the people they choose to invite, sending the printed invitations by mail or e-mail.

PLAN THE EVENT

Consultant: Invite the cafeteria manager or the person who will be responsible for making the foods for the meal into the classroom to help create the menu. Although most school cafeterias have a set menu that is determined by the school district, many school cafeteria managers have some flexibility is rearranging items on the menu for special events such as this.

Shopping List: Make a shopping list of the items that will be needed. Allow a few of the students to go to the grocery store with the manager. Keep the grocery store receipts, sacks, and labels. Make those into a collage to serve as part of the decorations for the Fun Facts About Foods Feast.

Decorate the Cafeteria: Locate decorations for the room and tables, again using projects from the units (Food Mobile, It Looked Like Spilt Milk, etc.). Find background music about foods (visit the Dole 5-a-Day site for selections). Post on the walls items such as:

- *The Menu:* List the calories for the foods and portions and other information of interest to the children. Provide recipes for each child or guest of the foods that are served (with fat content, sugar content, and energy).

- *A Fun Facts List:* Find fun facts about the foods that will be served during the "feast." Use activities from the units (Intake Charts, Food Pyramid, etc.).

- *How Things Grow Pictures:* Post sequence pictures of the foods from growth, through production, to how they look when prepared, using information learned in the units (see the **Growing and Producing Food** unit).

- *An ABC Chart:* Create an ABC chart that has the ABCs of this meal posted with the letter, the word, and a brief definition of each.

STAGE THE EVENT

Hosts and Hostesses: Appoint several class hosts and hostesses to greet guests upon arrival and walk them past the decorations, explaining each. Assign a student to sit with each guest or group of guests to answer fun facts about the foods at the feast.

ARCHIVE THE EVENT

Videotape the Event: Videos can be transferred to VHS format to send home to parents to play on their VCRs. They may be burned on CDs. CDs can then be played back on CD drives in computers. These videos could also be burned on DVDs to be shown using a DVD player or a DVD drive in a computer. Other devices such as the Sony Play Station II also have the capability of showing DVDs.

On the Go

Young children have been carried or ferried around extensively in their short lives. As their world expands to looking beyond the neighborhood, different modes of transportation become intriguing. This theme explores how people get from one place to another, from short distances to space.

This series of units builds from vehicles with wheels that are familiar to students to other modes of transportation that may be less familiar and certainly not within their current experience, vehicles used for space travel. Noting the similarities and differences between the modes of transportation, the purposes for the type of transportation, and the force or energy that propels the vehicles draws upon students' critical thinking as they develop their content-area skills.

The following standards-based curriculum units enable students to explore the concept of transportation as they take part in the following activities. Students:

- Investigate why hills make cars go fast.
- Investigate gauges in cars.
- Practice safety rules.
- Learn why some things sink while others float.
- Explore flight and developments in space.

Unit Tools

Spreadsheet and Graphing: Spreadsheets and graphs are integrated into the study of transportation with the exploration of airline costs, travel times, and so forth.

Word Processing: Writing is highlighted in the Language Arts and Reading activities by having students create descriptions of things, procedures, and imaginary events. Take-home books are created for reinforcement.

Drawing Software: For the emerging readers, drawing software is used to record their thinking, reinforce patterning, and create slideshows of student work.

Digital Still and Video Cameras: Visual images are used to record events that take place inside and outside the classroom. Additionally, video is used to record a train traveling by for later study.

Internet: Web sites are used to reinforce classroom discussion and offer further exploration. Virtual tours of places, such as the International Space Station, provide students with access to information and experiences they cannot obtain locally.

In the **Things That Go on Land** unit, students can create travel brochures that describe the various sites along a chosen path. Sites of interest can be discovered using various map searches. The brochures offer the opportunity to develop pictures, definitions, and brief descriptions. Students can use productivity software to create the brochures. Creating a bike or car manual offers students the opportunity to explain how things are fixed according to them.

In the **Things That Go on Water** unit, students use Web cams to view scenes in faraway places. They also experiment with objects that sink (anchors) and float (buoys). Documenting what they saw allows them to record scientific information in a slightly different language than that used for creative writing. Letter writing to various places where boats travel or where boats are sold allows them to make personal connections with those who live differently than they do.

In the **Things That Go on Rails** unit, students create a circus train as an art project. The writing connection allows the creation of flyers announcing the circus, newspaper reports of the circus events, and letters to their favorite clowns. Students' investigation of steam offers many opportunities to write predictions and outcomes. The explorations of various states can be extended into travel guides, brief history books, and descriptions of fun places to see.

In the **Things That Go in Air and Space** unit, the I Want to Be... books and A Day in the Life series provide a format to write about their parents' and other family members' occupations or to write letters to NASA requesting information about the various jobs available on the International Space Station. The investigation of inventions over the years allows a creative writing experience that explores what might be possible in years to come with smart cars, smart appliances, and smart robots.

About the Things That Go on Rails unit

"I had never used a video camera to photograph a train passing by. My students and I enjoyed watching the video over and over again becoming aware of patterns in the cars and the sounds on the track, as well as the visual shapes as the cars passed. For weeks after doing the unit, my students would tell about trains they had seen going by and what the trains were carrying. The parents really appreciated the discussion on railroad track safety as we have unmarked railroad track intersections around town."

About the Things That Go in Air and Space unit

"I was initially skeptical about having my students study any more about space than the fact that a space ship is different from an airplane. I was amazed at how fast my students were able to navigate the NASA Web site and what great resources were there for teachers. My students had their parents come into the classroom to look at the pictures of the International Space Station. The parents requested a list of the Web sites I was using in class, as they were interested in the information, too. The most popular activity was being able to take a virtual tour of the International Space Station. I still have not removed the button to that site on the computers as the students still go there to check out what is going on. Their interest has continued long after the unit is over."

CHILDREN'S LITERATURE   Each unit includes an extensive list of children's literature related to land, water, rail, air, and space transportation. The books have been purposefully selected to match young children's interest and the topic of the unit. Choose ones available in your school, personal, or public library and be sure to search for new ones on the market. Your search can be at the local bookstore or online.

WEB RESOURCES   An extensive Web Resources list accompanies every unit. All resources were current at the time of publishing. Because of the rapid growth of Internet use, sites can be expected to come and go. To keep the resources current, all software and online references are available online at www.edtech4teachers.com and will be updated frequently.

TEACHING TIPS   Teaching very young children requires a balance between holding discussions to clarify thinking and to practice oral language skills and having students take part in active, hands-on activities to keep them exploring and engaged. The activities can be used as either center or whole-class lessons depending on the class and the amount of help available in the classroom.

Students love to use the computer. Be sure to make clear that each computer station is reserved for a particular task. Because many Web sites on transportation can be handled independently by students, create a shortcut to access these sites off the computer desktop. Before the sites can be accessed by a shortcut button, however, be sure to introduce the site as a whole-class activity, setting the expectations and limitations of using the site.

LESSON EXTENDERS   Create a transportation bulletin board. Use different pieces of the students' artwork and digital photos to separate the board into rails, land, water, and air.

Find out how mail travels. Create your own postcards in Kid Pix or Word, or bring in ready-made postcards. Have students locate a place on the map that they would like to send their postcard. Discuss how the mail might get that postcard to its destination. By mail truck, plane, boat? Have them write a story of the travels their postcard will make. Send e-mail postcards online and discuss how those travel to their destination. How many modes of transportation are involved in getting the letter from one place to another? Make a visit to the post office to help children understand how the mail is handled and all the ways that mail travels.

THEME CULMINATING EVENT

By the end of the theme, students will have made ABC books for various activities. In the culminating activity, Travel Guide Show: Transportation Stations, students display ABC slide books and slideshows that illustrate all they have learned about transportation. Set the slideshow on automatic play accompanied by a recording of the students singing some of the transportation songs they have learned. A complete plan for this activity is found at the end of the theme.

Things That Go on Land

UNIT OVERVIEW
Many young children ride someplace each day of the week, whether by car, bus, or subway. The vehicles they ride in and see as they travel provide a convenient source of meaningful exploration. In their examination of things that go on land they start with their own means of transportation (wagons, tricycles, bikes, rollerblades) and move on to those that are driven by adults (cars, trucks, buses, and perhaps even snowmobiles and sleighs). (Subways, cable cars, monorails, and trains will be covered in a separate unit.) Most vehicles they know about are pleasure vehicles. However, daily they also see working vehicles (mail trucks, delivery trucks, tow trucks, moving vans) and rescue vehicles (fire trucks, ambulances, police cars, state troopers). This unit focuses on vehicle parts, their purposes, some careers associated with land vehicles, and safety when riding in wheeled vehicles.

UNIT OBJECTIVES
At the end of this unit, students will be able to:

- Categorize vehicles as those that travel on land, on rails, in the air, or on the water.
- Sort vehicles and name them by the number of wheels they have.
- Describe the various parts of bikes, cars, and trucks.
- Name the different pleasure, working, and rescue vehicles.
- Describe the different jobs associated with land vehicles and their maintenance.

STANDARDS ADDRESSED IN THIS UNIT
ISTE NETS for Students 1, 3, 5
IRA/NCTE English/Language Arts Standards 1, 2, 3, 4, 5, 7, 8, 12
NCTM Math Standards 1, 4, 8, 10
NAS/NSE Science Standards B2, E2, G2
NCSS Social Studies Standards 1a, 1d, 2b, 2d, 7e, 8a, 8b, 10b, 10c

CHILDREN'S LITERATURE
Moving on Land—General
Big Book of Things That Go, Caroline Gingham, Ed.
The Greedy Triangle, Marilyn Burns

Bikes
Bikes, Anne F. Rockwell
Curious George Rides a Bike, Margaret & H. A. Rey
The Mystery of the Stolen Bike, Marc Brown

Bus
Fluffy's School Bus Adventure, Kate McMullar
School Buses, Dee Ready
Wheels on the Bus, Raffi

Cars

Are We There Yet? (CTW Sesame Street), Sarah Albee
The A-To-Z Book of Cars, Angela Royston
At the Auto Repair Center, Justine Korman
Big Book of Cars, Caroline Bingham, Ed.
Big Book of Cars, Trevor Lord
Cars, Anne F. Rockwell
Cars, Gail Saunders-Smith
Cars (Inside and Out), Angela Royston & Roger Stewart
Cars (Transportation Around the World), Chris Oxlade
Fill It Up: All About Service Stations, Gail Gibbons
Gas Station Charlie, G. Kraushaar
Henry Ford, Lola M. Schaefer & Gail Saunders-Smith, Ed.
Let's Build a Car, Margaret A. Schaefer
The Little Auto, Lois Lenski & Heidi Kilgras
The Little Red Car, K. K. Ross
Little Red Car Gets Into Trouble, Mathew Price
Little Red Car Has an Accident, Mathew Price
Little Red Car in the Snow, Mathew Price
Police Cars, Steven James Petruccio
What Makes a Car Go?, Sophy Tahta

Trucks

Big Book of Trucks, Caroline Bingham, Ed.
Big Joe's Trailer Truck, Joe Mathieu
Big Truck and Little Truck, Jan Carr
Big Wheels, Anne F. Rockwell
Construction Trucks, Jennifer Dussling
Construction Trucks, Betsy Imershein
Dumpy the Dump Truck, Julie Andrews Edward & Emma Hamilton
Pickup Trucks, James Koons
Trucks, Byron Barton
Trucks, Betsy Imershein (Illustrator)
Trucks: Giants of the Highway, Ken Robbins
Truck Stop, Bonnie Dobkin
Trucks (Transportation Around the World), Chris Oxlade
Trucks Trucks Trucks, Peter Sis
The Usborne Book of Trucks, Harriet Castor
What's Inside Trucks, D.K. Publishing

WEB RESOURCES
Transportation
Songs: www.niehs.nih.gov/kids/music.htm
Transportation Inventors: www.inventorsmuseum.com/transportation.htm
Transportation Wonderland: http://education.dot.gov/k5/gamk5.htm
Virtual Tours of Transportation Sites: http://education.dot.gov/k5/tours.htm
What Is Transportation?: http://education.dot.gov/k5/whatis.htm

Bikes
Bike Helmet Safety: www.cpsc.gov/kids/kidsafety/correct.html
Cycling: www.transcycle.org/cycling/cycling.html
Four-Wheel Bikes: www.rhoadescar.com/jumpshow.htm
Indonesian Becak: http://minyos.its.rmit.edu.au/~dwa/Becak1.html
Know Your Bike, Bike Parts: www.state.il.us/kids/isp/bikes/knowbike/default.htm
Malaysian Trishaw: http://minyos.its.rmit.edu.au/~dwa/Trishaw.html
Recumbent Bicycles: www.bikeroute.com/Recumbents/
Safety: http://education.wichita.edu/m3/tips/health/first/safety/webqstfrm.htm
Samlor of Thailand: http://minyos.its.rmit.edu.au/~dwa/Samlor1.html
Unicycle Page: www.unicycling.org

Bridges
Super Bridges: www.pbs.org/wgbh/nova/bridge/

Buses
Museum of Bus Transportation (slideshow): www.busmuseum.org
Rosa Parks and the Montgomery Bus Boycott: www.holidays.net/mlk/rosa.htm
Wheels on the Bus: www.niehs.nih.gov/kids/lyrics/wheels.htm

Cars
Beetle Cars and Kombi Vans: www4.tpgi.com.au/users/kstrong/
Build an Online Race Car: www.pbs.org/tal/racecars/build.html
Built for Speed: Automobile History: www.pbs.org/wgbh/amex/kids/tech1900/car.html
A Celebration of Motoring (79 vehicle types represented): http://cars.motorcities.com/main_vehicletypes.html
Everything About Construction Equipment: www.kenkenkikki.jp/special/e_index.html
Hot Wheels: www.hotwheels.com/kids/2001/index.asp
How Does It Work?: www4.tpgi.com.au/users/kstrong/howwork.htm
Land Vehicles: www.transport-pf.or.jp/english/land/index.html
Lego Car: www.lego.com/advanced/level1.asp
Muppet Car Games: www.sesameworkshop.org/parents/activity/article/0,4117,14975,00.html
Tire Treads: www.pbs.org/tal/racecars/ttreads.html
Way Back in U.S. History: www.pbs.org/wgbh/amex/kids/tech1900/

Motorcycles
Honda Motorcycle Models: www.hondamotorcycle.com/models/index.html

Rollerblades
Rollerblade History: www.discovery.com/stories/history/toys/SKATEBOARD/shoulda.html
Rollerblade Safety: www.somersetborough.com/Police/rollerblading_safety.htm

Safety
Bike Safety: www.state.il.us/kids/isp/bikes/
Bike Safety: Gun Safety, Call 911: http://members.bellatlantic.net/~louis2/tips.html
Buckle Up Baby (songs): www.state.oh.us/odps/kids/html/songs.html

Elmer's Seven Traffic Safety Rules: www.safety-council.org/info/child/
elmer/7rules.html
Florida Children's Safety Center: http://legal.firn.edu/kids/kids.html
Journey With Care (several countries): www.careusa.org/vft/bolivia/
Otto Club: www.ottoclub.org/kids/ottosplayland/index.html
Road Safety (bike, walk, bus, car): www.roadsafety.net/KIDS/HTML/
licence.html
School and Neighborhood Safety: www.dot.state.tx.us/kidsonly/SafetyPg/
Safety.html
Scooter Safety: www.cpsc.gov/kids/kidsafety/scoot.html
Steering Your Way to Bike Safety: http://kidshealth.org/kid/watch/out/
bike_safety.html
Traffic Signals and Signs: www.dot.state.tx.us/kidsonly/SafetyPg/
Safety.html

Simple Machines
Inclined Plane: http://library.thinkquest.org/J002079F/plane.htm
Inclined Plane: http://weirdrichard.com:80/inclined.htm
Simple Machines (inclined plane, wheel, and axle): www.smartown.com/
sp2000/machines2000/main.htm
Wheel and Axle: http://library.thinkquest.org/J002079F/wheel.htm

Trucks
Everything About Construction Equipment: www.kenkenkikki.jp/special/
e_index.htm

Wagons
Across the Plains in '64: http://flag.blackened.net/daver/1sthand/atp/atp.html
Classic Wagons (wagons, wheelbarrows, bikes, scooters, tricycles):
www.classicwagons.com
Prairie Schooners: www.endoftheoregontrail.org/wagons.html

Dictionaries
Internet Picture Dictionary: www.pdictionary.com
Little Explorers Picture Dictionary: www.enchantedlearning.com/Dictionary.html
Merriam-Webster's Word Central: www.wordcentral.com

SOFTWARE
AND CDS

The Amazing Writing Machine, Broderbund
Falling in a Black Hole, The Space Place
The Graph Club, Tom Snyder Productions, or Tabletop Jr., Broderbund
Kid Pix (English, Spanish), Broderbund
Kidspiration, Inspiration Software
Roamer Robot, TerrapinLogo
Tonka Garage, Hasbro
Tonka Search and Rescue, Hasbro
Travel the World With Timmy, Edmark

Music CD
"Go," Daniel Kirk

teaching the unit

Getting Started

In preparation for the unit, send a letter to parents explaining the objectives and outcomes of the unit. Their child is likely to have questions about cars, in particular. Encourage parents to talk with their child about the type of car they have, how and why they bought this car instead of another, as well as car care and safety. If parents bring children to school, ask them to come prepared to stop, park, and have their child's picture taken beside the family car on a specified day. Ask parents to search through family albums looking for pictures of other cars, cars of parents, cars of grandparents, and cars of other family members, as well as any pictures of friends or family members getting out of a car for a special occasion such as the first day of school, a vacation, or a prom.

Motivating Activity

Bike Parade: Read several of Anne Rockwell's books (*Bikes, Cars, Big Wheels*). Use the computer with a projector or SMART Board to examine Asian bikes (see Web Resources) to see how they decorate their bikes. Decorate tricycles, bikes, and wagons for a parade in the schoolyard. Invite a police officer to participate and have a bike safety inspection. Give students a reward if they bring their bike helmet to school. Note the number of wheels on the bikes, who rides them, and the idea that bikes can be ridden by everyone.

Multidisciplinary Activities

ART   *Bikes:* Have students draw a picture of a bike and label its parts before any instruction or experiences have occurred about bikes. Save the pictures. After having them explore various types of bikes (read *Bikes*, by Anne F. Rockwell), and bike parts (view Know Your Bike, Bike Parts: www.state.il.us/kids/isp/bikes/knowbike/default.htm), ask students to again draw a picture of a bike, label its parts, and tell of its use. Show students how much they have learned by the difference in the two drawings. Place the two pictures in an assessment folder.

Paint a Truck: After discussing 18-wheel trucks, provide paint on the easel to paint large trucks. Allow two or three sheets of paper, as students might want to make up a double- or triple-trailer truck. Be sure to have students label the side of the truck with what is being carried inside or the name of a trucking company. Some students enjoy being creative with the naming and logo of the company. Post on a "highway" in the hall.

GROSS MOTOR   *Tire Rolling:* To explore the physics of things that roll, obtain various sizes of tires from a tire store and bike store. Provide students with tires of various sizes to roll on the playground, catch in relays, or roll against a fence or wall.

Load 'em Up? Head 'em Out?: Load up wagons and wheelbarrows to move materials from one place to another. This loading and unloading can be done to help someone or as a relay race that involves blocks.

LANGUAGE ARTS AND READING

ABCs on the Go: Read one or more of the ABC books about things that go on land. Create ABC books with cars and other wheeled vehicles.

- Create picture dictionaries using Kid Pix. Have students save pictures and definitions to be printed out for a book and displayed as a slideshow.

All Kinds of Bikes: Using pictures from *Bikes* (by Anne F. Rockwell) and the Web Resources at the beginning of this unit, ask students to describe various bikes and how they think they are used.

- Create an All Kinds of Bikes book, slideshow, or online photo gallery.

Car Manual: Have children design a car manual. Pages in the book would include a child's experience with cars, but could also include a diagram with parts labeled and information on getting it started, driving, parking, changing the oil, and getting gas. It might make a good gift for parents. One related book is *What Makes a Car Go?*

- Children can create the pages in the book using the Amazing Writing Machine or Kid Pix as a center activity. Each page in the book can be a different rotation through the center.

Computer Station: Set up a word processing document that directs children to visit these sites and record what they learn:

Build an Online Race Car: **www.pbs.org/tal/racecars/build.html**
Transportation Wonderland: **http://education.dot.gov/k5/gamk5.htm**
Virtual Tours of Transportation Sites: **http://education.dot.gov/k5/tours.htm**
What Is Transportation?: **http://education.dot.gov/k5/whatis.htm**

MATH

All Kinds of Bikes: Use the pictures students created in the All Kinds of Bikes Language Arts and Reading language activity to classify and sort bikes by the number of wheels or by the function.

Number Line: Move a wheeled vehicle on the playground along a giant number line. Give directions in terms of the number of steps forward and backward. Debrief the activity in the classroom by making number sentences.

- Using TerrapinLogo's Roamer Robot, program the Roamer to take a trip. Make a number line on the floor. Program the Roamer to go forward 3 steps and then go forward 2 steps. What number does the Roamer end on? Now have the Roamer go backward 1 step. What number does it end on? Continue using the Roamer to predict addition and subtraction facts. Older children can program the Roamer for longer and more complicated trips, maybe even providing music along the way.

The Shapes of Signs: Take a walk in the neighborhood. Take pictures of all the traffic signs the children see. Ask children to tell you what the signs mean, the color, and the shape. Show the pictures in class, having the students affix the correct geometrical label to the shape of each sign.

- Import the sign pictures into the Kidspiration symbol library. Sort the pictures into circles by shape. Look in the symbol library and find other pictures that are similar in shape to sort.

Bus Problem: Give students unifix cubes or a different manipulative to solve the following problems:

A mini-bus is taking children on a field trip. Nineteen children are going on the field trip. The van has seven seats. How many children will have to sit two on a seat and how many will have to sit three on a seat? (Use the problem several times, changing the number of seats and the total number of students. Watch how students count and verify their solutions.)

The entire first grade is going on a field trip. The teachers have to request buses to take the class. There are 64 children in first grade. If a bus holds 42, how many buses will they need? (Extend the question by asking the number of children that should go on each bus and whether chaperones can be accommodated. Add a discussion about bus safety rules.)

A Day in the Life of a Car: Create a sequence of what the children think their parents' cars do all day long, from the time they head out until they are parked again for the night. Have students offer all the activities as you record them on cards. Have students help you put the pictures in order from the beginning of the day to the end. Older children can record approximate times on the pictures. Related books include *At the Auto Repair Center, Fill It Up: All About Service Stations, Little Red Car Gets into Trouble, Little Red Car Has an Accident,* and *Little Red Car in the Snow.*

- Recreate the day's events using Kid Pix. Place each event in a truck that can be rearranged so that students can print out the sequence as they try the activity at the computer center.

Why Are Wheels Circular?: Ask why the wheels on vehicles are not triangles, squares, or hexagons. Have the students roll pattern blocks along the table surface and discuss what the difference is between rolling a shape with sides and corners and one that has no corners. What would the ride be like? (A related book is *The Greedy Triangle,* by Marilyn Burns.)

MUSIC *Music About Moving:* After singing these songs, students can compare the different types of transportation mentioned in each tune.

"Are We There Yet?," Discovery Toys
"Bicycle Built for Two": www.niehs.nih.gov/kids/lyrics/daisy.htm
"London Bridge Is Falling Down": www.niehs.nih.gov/kids/lyrics/london.htm
"She'll Be Comin' 'Round the Mountain": www.niehs.nih.gov/kids/lyrics/mountain.htm
"The Wheels on the Bus": www.niehs.nih.gov/kids/lyrics/wheels.htm

SAFETY

Safety Posters: The Web Resources section includes several online resources on safety. Review the sites. Have students design a set of safety posters to post in the room and online. Include sidewalk, car, bike, skateboarding, and fire safety, as well as safety signs.

- Create safety posters in Kid Pix. Make a safety slideshow out of all the pictures or import the pictures into a writing program and print a Safety book for each child.

SCIENCE

Gauges and Equipment: Take digital pictures of the gauges and technological equipment in several different cars. Examine each and determine its use. Sort the pictures so that the speedometers are in one pile, the radios in another, and so on. As the gauges are being sorted, discuss the purpose of each and what it measures. Be sure to focus on the vocabulary difference between speedometer and odometer.

How Far?: Build various sizes and types of cars from Legos. Provide materials for an inclined plane. Allow the cars to go down the inclined plane three times, marking or measuring the distance each time. Adjust the slope of the inclined plane (both up and down) and measure the distance of the cars. Discuss why the cars go faster when the slope is steep rather than flat. Have students draw pictures or write about the process, recording each step and the conclusions.

- View a full-sized Lego car (**www.lego.com/advanced/level1.asp**).
- Examine online information about simple machines (see Web Resources).
- Have the students graph the results from their three trials. Take a digital picture of each child's Lego car. Print the picture and the graph and hang on a bulletin board.

SOCIAL STUDIES

On a Trip: Plan a field trip that is related to one of the other units, such as a trip to the grocery store, farm, or some other location. Before you go, have the children brainstorm a list of things they think they will see while traveling. Create small pictures of each item. Produce a copy for each child. Have them mark off things as they see them and add things they see that are not on the list.

- Create the small pictures in Kid Pix as icons. Save the icons for use later in other activities.
- Program the Roamer Robot to take a trip. Use masking tape on the floor or draw a map outside with sidewalk chalk. Create different places along the map for the Roamer to visit. Program the steps it will take the Roamer to get to each destination.

Buses: Depending on the part of the country in which the children live, they may or may not have ever ridden a city bus. Take a field trip to ride the city bus somewhere. Discuss safety concerns for riding a city bus versus a school bus. Have students observe the kinds of seats on the bus, how the money is taken, and what the driver does besides drive. From memory, draw a bus picture (any kind of a bus).

- View the Museum of Bus Transportation slideshow (**www.busmuseum.org**). Compare the buses of yesterday with the buses of today. How are they the same? How are they different?
- Read the story of Rosa Parks and the Montgomery Bus Boycott (**www.holidays.net/mlk/rosa.htm**). Discuss the issues of bus etiquette and the rights of people to sit where they choose.

Rescue Vehicles Save the Day: Ask each child to create a story or picture that tells how a rescue vehicle saves the day.

- Scan their pictures into Kid Pix and record their voices telling the story. Create a classroom slideshow.

Building a Community: In a blocks area, provide community map rugs with roads, blocks, cars, paper, and crayons so children can build cities, roads, bridges, and street signs.

- Use Tom Snyder's Community Construction Kit software to create and print buildings that children can cut out and paste together to create a city. Pay close attention putting roadways in that have two-way traffic. This is a good time to discuss the difference between solid dividing lines on streets and dashed lines.

Assessment

FOR YOUNGER
LEARNERS

Ask children to create an On the Bike, In the Car, or On the Bus word or picture story on the computer that includes the vehicle, a labeled drawing, safety rules, and places to go.

NOTE: For a description
of the values "Not
Interested," "Trying It,"
"Working on It," "Got it!,"
and "Helping Others," see
chapter 4.

CRITERIA	NOT INTERESTED	TRYING IT	WORKING ON IT	GOT IT!	HELPING OTHERS
Vehicle is present and parts are labeled.					
Safety rules are clear and appropriate.					
Story includes places to go.					
Computer skills are evident.					
Writing is clear.					

FOR MORE ABLE
LEARNERS

Have students describe an adventure or ride in a vehicle. Ask them to include a description of the vehicle, where they are going, and safety rules they will follow.

CRITERIA	APPROACHES TARGET	MEETS TARGET	EXCEEDS TARGET
Vehicle	Describes the vehicle with few parts labeled and/or some incorrectly labeled	Describes the vehicle correctly, labeling the major parts	Describes the vehicle accurately including all parts covered in the unit as well as a detailed gauges
Safety	In the context of the story, mentions only a few safety rules. The rules are not complete.	In the context of the story, describes how safety rules are followed	In the context of the story, follows the safety rules with both procedures and rationale. May even describe safety measures taken for others
Story	The adventure uses the vehicle in a way that is unrealistic. It is unclear what the student knows about the use of the vehicle.	The adventure uses the appropriate vehicle in the appropriate way.	The adventure uses the appropriate vehicle in the appropriate way. The child may introduce additional vehicles, which are all used appropriately.

Assessment of technology use depends on the level of student use permitted, the technology available, and the age of the students. See chapter 4 for additional information on assessing technology use.

Additional criteria should be added focusing on writing. The criteria used for the rubric should reflect the objectives and expectations for the students.

Things That Go on Water

UNIT OVERVIEW   The vehicles children ride in and see provide a convenient source of meaningful exploration. For some, bodies of water (streams, rivers, ponds, lakes, oceans) are close and provide an excellent way to introduce transportation by water. For others, those bodies of water are far away, making the study of transportation by water more abstract for very young children. Just like other vehicles, some water transportation vehicles are for pleasure, some for work, and some for rescue. This unit focuses on the various ways to travel on or under the water, the purposes of those crafts, some careers associated with them, and safety.

UNIT OBJECTIVES   At the end of this unit, students will be able to:

- Categorize vehicles as those that travel on land, on rails, in the air, or on the water.
- Name several different types of water vehicles.
- Describe the purposes of various vessels.
- Explain the jobs of the people who pilot or in other ways work on water vehicles.
- Explain their experiences with objects that sink and float.
- Describe life on board a ship.
- Explain how to be safe on a boat.

STANDARDS
ADDRESSED
IN THIS UNIT

ISTE NETS for Students 3, 4, 5
IRA/NCTE English/Language Arts Standards 1, 2, 3, 4, 7, 8, 12
NCTM Math Standards 1, 3, 4, 8, 10
NAS/NSE Science Standards A1, A2, B1, B2, F5
NCSS Social Studies Standards 1a, 1d, 2c, 3e, 3h, 3j, 7e, 8a, 9b,

CHILDREN'S
LITERATURE

Beacons of Light: Lighthouses, Gail Gibbons
The Boat Alphabet Book, Jerry Pallotta
Boat Book, Gail Gibbons
Boats, Byron Barton
Boats, Anne F. Rockwell
Boats, Gail Saunders-Smith
Boats on the River, Marjorie Flack
Boat Rides (Let's Go), Pamela Walker
Busy Boats, Tony Mitton
Eyewitness Books: Shipwreck, Richard Platt, Ed.
Ferries, Lola M. Schaefer
Ferryboat Ride!, Anne F. Rockwell
Ferry Rides (Let's Go), Pamela Walker
The Great St. Lawrence Seaway, Gail Gibbons

Harbor, Donald Crews

Homes on Water, Alan James

How Do Big Ships Float?, Isaac Asimov

I Love Boats, Flora McDonnell

Mail by the Pail, Colin Bergel

My Grandpa Is a Tugboat Captain, Ken Krisler

Nicola's Floating Home, Bobbie Kalman

Riding the Ferry With Captain Cruz, Alice K. Flanagan

Row Row Row Your Boat, Iza Trapani (Illustrator)

Sail Away, Donald Crews

The Sailor's Alphabet, Michael McCurdy

Sea House, Deborah Turney Zagwyn

Ships, Robert B. Noyed & Cynthia Fitterer Klingel

Some Boats Have Wings (I Didn't Know That), Clare Oliver

Steamboat! The Story of Captain Blanche Leathers, Judith Heide Gilliland

Tugboats, Lola M. Schaefer

Warships, Iain MacKenzie

WEB RESOURCES **Water Transportation—General**

Boatsafe Kids: www.boatsafe.com/kids/

Canadian Coast Guard Photo Gallery: www.pacific.ccg-gcc.gc.ca/EPAGES/ PHOTGALL/PHOTGALL.HTM

Dragon Boat Festival: www.sandiego-online.com/forums/chinese/htmls/ dragboat.htm

Exploratorium Roof Cam (Golden Gate Bridge): http://cams.exploratorium.edu/ CAM2/index.html

The First Thanksgiving: http://teacher.scholastic.com/thanksgiving/index.htm

Grand Princess Deck Plans: www.honeymooncruiseshopper.com/ grand_deck_plans/grand_princess_deck_plans.htm

Kids in Boats (Boats Now and Then): www.anzsbeg.org.au/kids.html

Kids in Boats (Safety Saves Lives): www.anzsbeg.org.au/kids.html

Lifeboats: www.rnli.org.uk/young.asp

Lusitania: Diagram of a Colossus: www.pbs.org/lostliners/diagram.html

The Mayflower: http://teacher.scholastic.com/thanksgiving/Mayflower/tour/ navig.htm

Mayflower II: www.plimoth.org/Museum/Mayflower/mayflowe.htm

Momma's Sink or Float: www.ipfw.edu/educ/e328jn/wplesson/start.html

Monterey Bay Aquarium Webcam: www.mbayaq.org/efc/cam_menu.asp

Nautical Know How: Boating Basic Glossary of Terms: www.tcmall.com/ nauticalknowhow/GLOSSARY.htm#A

NOVA, Experiment with Sonar: www.pbs.org/wgbh/nova/lochness/sonar.html

Practice Safe Boating: www.uscg.mil/hq/g-cp/kids/safeboat.html

Rescue Gear (QuickTime movie): www.uscg.mil/news/PerfectStorm/swimmer.avi

Rub a Dub Dub: www.arts-letters.com/rubadub/rubadub.html

Rub a Dub Dub Rebus Story: www.enchantedlearning.com/Rubadub.shtml

Sea Vehicles: www.transport-pf.or.jp/english/sea/index.html

Ships Across the Ocean: http://www.dot.state.mn.us/aero/aved/publications/ TEA_elementary.htm

The Ships of Christopher Columbus: www.ci.corpus-christi.tx.us/services/ museum/a_ships.htm

Ship Speak: www.unc.edu/courses/rometech/public/content/transport/
ships/merch_02.html
Ship Vocabulary: www.mariner.org/age/histvocab.html
Songs: www.niehs.nih.gov/kids/music.child.htm
Steamboat Calliopes: www.steamboats.org/ecaliope.htm
Steamboats and Paddlewheelers: www.steamboats.org/eexhibit_pure1.htm
Steamboat Whistles: www.steamboats.org/eblow.htm
Tall Ship Model Gallery: www.tallshipmodels.com/nina.htm
Theodore Tugboat's Official Web Site: www.cbc4kids.cbc.ca/getset/tugboat/
default.html
Transportation Inventors: www.inventorsmuseum.com/transportation.htm
USPS Flag Etiquette: www.usps.org/f_stuff/etiquett.html
World Time Zone Map: http://aa.usno.navy.mil/faq/docs/world_tzones.html

Dictionaries

Internet Picture Dictionary: www.pdictionary.com
Little Explorers Picture Dictionary: www.enchantedlearning.com/Dictionary.html
Merriam-Webster's Word Central: www.wordcentral.com

WebQuests

Shipwreck Adventure: www.richmond.edu/academics/a&ts/education/projects/
webquests/shipwreck/
Weather Watchers: www.sbcss.k12.ca.us/sbcss/services/educational/
cctechnology/webquest/weather.html

SOFTWARE   The Amazing Writing Machine, Broderbund
Elmo's Deep Sea Adventure, Mattel Interactive
The Graph Club, Tom Snyder Productions, or Tabletop Jr., Broderbund
Kid Pix (English, Spanish), Broderbund
Kidspiration, Inspiration Software
Pirate Ship (JC), Fisher Price

teaching
the unit

Getting Started

In a letter sent to the home, prepare parents for the unit by explaining the objectives and outcomes. The student is likely to have questions about boats. Encourage parents to point out boats whenever they see them on television, in magazines, in the newspaper, and in other media. Instruct parents to experiment at home with items that sink and float. Toys, kitchen items, and even food provide lots of opportunities for children to think about the attributes of materials that sink and float. Ask the parents to let you know whether they have a relative or friend in the Navy on a ship or out of the country who is able to receive e-mail and would like to communicate with the class. If boating does not take place in the vicinity, ask parents to focus their reading aloud selections on water-related books. Some parents may enjoy a list of the Web sites being used for the unit. Consider posting the unit-related Web sites on a class or school Web site.

Motivating Activity

Following the unit on homes, read children's books about living on the water: *Homes on Water, Nicola's Floating Home,* or *Sea House.* Near Thanksgiving, you might want to use some of the sites mentioned in Web Resources to investigate the trip of the pilgrims on the Mayflower. Compare and contrast life on the water and in the children's own homes, making comparisons of living quarters, play areas, school, and walking and traveling places. Questions may emerge about the size of the boats or ships, recreation, food, and safety.

Multidisciplinary Activities

ART   *At the Easel:* After students have had exposure to the various kinds of boats, provide large painting paper on which students can paint a picture of a boat or ship and name it (writing the name on when the painting is dry). Cut them out and put them on a hallway "ocean" (made of blue paper, either from rolls of blue bulletin board paper or painted by the children).

GROSS MOTOR   *Safety First:* Provide life jackets for the children to practice putting on while they play.

- View information about boat safety at the computer station (Boatsafe Kids: www.boatsafe.com/kids/).

Ships Across the Ocean: Play a tag game in which some students are captains and others are "ships." Play the game as described at this Web site: www.dot.state. mn.us/aero/aved/publications/TEA_elementary.htm

Ring Toss: Cut several pieces of paper or cloth into one-foot squares and place them around the playground. From a spot designated as the shore or the ship, have children attempt to toss a life-saving ring (or any ring attached to a rope) and land it on the spot.

LANGUAGE ARTS AND READING

Nursery Rhymes: Learn the nursery rhymes associated with boats and ships.

- To practice skills with the mouse, use Rub a Dub Dub: **www.arts-letters.com/ rubadub/rubadub.html**
- A rebus story can be downloaded for children to print and follow: **www.enchantedlearning.com/Rubadub.shtml**

Ocean Web Cams: View marine life using the Web cams underneath a boat at the Monterey Bay Aquarium (**www.mbayaq.org/efc/cam_menu.asp**). Discuss pleasure boats that go whale watching. Connect this discussion of sea animals with previous discussions of endangered species and the environment. Create a class slideshow.

- Using Kid Pix, have students draw a picture of themselves in a boat and write a sentence about what they might see underneath their boat. Demonstrate by drawing a waterline high on the paper as a place to begin.

Mail by the Pail: The story *Mail by the Pail* (by Colin Bergel) tells about getting mail in buckets while out on a lake. Write letters to imaginary friends away at work on a ship. Place them in a bucket with a couple of paperclips on them. Have each child "fish" a letter out, respond to it, and send it out by bucket at the time of the next mail delivery.

- Many children have a connection to someone in the military. Rather than sending traditional letters, many branches of the service have instituted e-mail as a way for family and friends to keep in touch. Ask students if they have any friends in the Navy. Get permission for the class to send e-mail to a service person who is out at sea.

Ship Language: Read an ABC book of ships, boats, or other water vehicles (such as *The Sailor's Alphabet,* by Michael McCurdy). Have a toy engine-driven and a sail-driven ship. Have students help you label the parts of the ships.

- View Ship Speak (**www.unc.edu/courses/rometech/public/content/transport/ ships/merch_02.html#forestay**) or Nautical Know How: Boating Basic Glossary of Terms (**www.tcmall.com/nauticalknowhow/GLOSSARY.htm#A**) to determine the names of the various parts of a ship. Draw a diagram and label its parts. How many of the terms can be applied to other boats or ships?

Boat Parade: Many Chinese coastal communities have a dragon boat festival. Provide children a boat to decorate like an animal, choosing animals whose names start with letters from A to Z. Place the boats on an alphabet line (made to look like blue water), arranging the decorated boats to match the letters. This would make a good interactive bulletin board if placed low where the children could reach the letters.

- View online information about a dragon boat festival (**www.sandiego-online.com/forums/chinese/htmls/dragboat.htm**).

MATH

Time Zones: As ships travel through the waters of the various oceans, they cross many time zones. For children, the notion of time not being the same in every part of the world is a difficult concept until it is tied to how the sun moves across the sky. Many maps have the time zones marked with the lines of latitude. Select several voyages (Great Britain to the U.S.; Australia to Chile). Note the time in one port. Determine the number of time zones the ship will pass through. Determine the time in the second port. Count as you move across the time zones.

- View the Web site World Time Zone Map (aa.usno.navy.mil/faq/docs/world_tzones.html) for a detailed time zone map.

What Is Weight?: Have children weigh different items in the classroom using a handheld spring scale. Discuss the importance of knowing the weight of the amount of cargo and people in a ship. (This leads to the discussion of what sinks and what floats.) Have students guess the order of items from lightest to heaviest. Compare the items by using a pan balance.

- Record the weights of each item in a spreadsheet.
- Obtain a small boat that fits into a water table or a tub. Have some small classroom items of which there are many available, such as counters, paper clips, pencils, and so on. Guess how many of an item already weighed could be put in a boat in the water table before the boat sank. Make a table to record the maximum number of the item before the boat sank.
- Extend the lesson by asking how many boats it would take to transport a given number of items. After the students have estimated and used manipulatives to verify their answers, use the spreadsheet to show the exact amount.

MUSIC *Boat Songs:* Have students sing songs such as "Michael, Row Your Boat Ashore"; "My Bonnie Lies Over the Ocean"; "Row Row Row Your Boat"; "Sailing Sailing"; and "On the Good Ship Lollipop" (www.niehs.nih.gov/kids/musicchild.htm). Afterward, have students discuss their experiences on boats.

SAFETY *Safety Vests:* Pass out some Lifesavers candy. Have students examine the shape of the candy and discuss why the circle is the best shape for a floatable cushion to save someone's life. Look at life vests that are used by water skiers and boaters. Talk about the floatable substance that is contained inside the vest. Introduce the word "buoyancy." Ask the manager of a sports store or a boating club to bring several life vests to class for students to try on and discuss.

- Visit the Australian Boating Association Web site, which has explanations of boating safety rules for children (www.anzsbeg.org.au/kids.html).

Lifeboats: Discuss what lifeboats are and why they are on large ships. Emphasize that a safety vest is also required when on a large boat in addition to a lifeboat. Have students create a sequence of the events that should take place if an emergency happens on a large ship.

- Lifeboat is also a term used for boats that rescue people at sea. Have students explore the British site www.rnli.org.uk/young.asp. The site focuses on lifeboats used along the coast of England and shows student work related to activities posted on the site.

SCIENCE

Sink and Float (Anchors and Buoys): Fill tubs or a water table with water. Ask children to collect items from the playground to see whether they sink or float. Guess first and record those responses. Test the items and record the actual results for each. Look for similarities (wood, stone, leaf, etc.). Find other like items and test them.

- View Momma's Sink or Float activity, which provides a virtual water table and items to try to float (**www.ipfw.edu/educ/e328jn/wplesson/start.html**). After doing the virtual sink and float, try the items in the classroom to see whether Momma is right.

Bridge Building: Using Legos or other building blocks, have students build bridges. Discuss how different types of vehicles use bridges. Vehicles go under, they go over, they go across, and so on. What do boats do? What do airplanes do?

- Take digital pictures of bridges in your area. Have students label the kinds of vehicles that go over and under the bridges.
- Have students look at the bridges on the Web sites and the bridges around their area. For example, look at the Golden Gate Bridge at **http://cams. exploratorium.edu/CAM2/index.html**. What geometric shape do they see in the construction of the bridge? What is the shape that keeps the bridge up? What makes a bridge strong? Have students examine the bridges they make out of Legos to see whether there is a way to make those bridges stronger. Have students put weights on the bridges to see which design can hold the most weight.

Sonar Technology: Sonar is one of the technologies ship captains use to be sure that they are traveling in water that is deep enough for their vessel. Explore the use of sonar technology, which measures the depth of water and the fish swimming in it.

- Sonar technology is being used by a NOVA project to study the legend of the Loch Ness Monster. Use the Web site graphic at **www.pbs.org/wgbh/nova/ lochness/sonar.html** to show students the capabilities of sonar technology.

Magic Boats: Boats are powered by either a fuel-driven engine or the wind. Discuss the difference between the two in terms of structure and navigation. Tell students that there are other forces that can make an object move. Make a boat out of a cork, toothpick, and two thumbtacks. Use magnets to sail the boats across the water (**www.dot.state.mn.us/aero/aved/publications/TEA_elementary.htm**).

SOCIAL STUDIES

Flags of the Ships: There are many ways to communicate when out on a boat. The radio is the most common way to communicate. However, before radios were invented, ships communicated by flying flags. Ships fly flags to tell others of their place of origin and purpose. Make the comparison of country flags, as a symbol of citizenship or ownership, and signal flags, which send a specific message. Have students tell you about the flag shapes and symbols they are familiar with.

■ View USPS Flag Etiquette (**www.usps.org/f_stuff/etiquett.html**). Put children in teams to investigate, draw, and make reports about different flags.

Bodies of Water: Draw students' attention to the names of common lakes, rivers, ponds, streams, and oceans. Have the students identify the attributes of each. Show some of the pictures of the boats you have discussed. Where would they belong? Make a Venn diagram of boats that travel in rivers and boats that travel on the ocean. Note that some boats can travel in both.

■ Use Kidspiration to brainstorm the attributes of various bodies of water. Include the names of familiar bodies of water.

■ Use Kidspiration or Kid Pix to create the Venn diagram.

Where Are We Going?: Ask students how a ship finds its way once it is out on the ocean and land is no longer in sight. Have children use compasses to find a certain place. Have the students hold the compass in front of them and follow directions such as the following: Walk 10 steps to the north. Turn to the west. Walk 10 steps west. Have students find "treasure" or practice geometry with the turns.

■ Use the TerrapinLogo Roamer Robot as a ship in the sea. Have students program the robot to get to a destination in the same way a ship would be given directions when at sea.

Nina, Pinta, and Santa Maria: Learn about the ships of Christopher Columbus online. Compare these ships with the ships students have already studied. Compare the size of the ships by marking out the length on the playground. Have students compare the ship with a cruise liner. Discuss the differences in jobs and accommodations on ships of varying sizes.

■ Look at these Web sites: The Ships of Christopher Columbus (**www.ci.corpus-christi.tx.us/services/museum/a_ships.htm**) and Tall Ship Model Gallery (**www.tallshipmodels.com/nina.htm**). Compare the ships with those students have studied so far.

The Jobs People Do: Toward the end of this unit, examine the jobs of people aboard ships, their attire, and their tools. Several of the children's books provide descriptions: *My Grandpa Is a Tugboat Captain; Riding the Ferry With Captain Cruz; Steamboat! The Story of Captain Blanche Leathers; Tugboats;* and *Warships.* Discuss the kinds of jobs found on cruise liners and those needed in the Navy. Look at the differences in functions of cruise ships, naval vessels, racing sailboats, and cargo ships.

Assessment

FOR YOUNGER LEARNERS

Ask children to write or draw a story about traveling from their home to an island or continent they are familiar with, such as Bermuda, Australia, Hawaii, or islands out in the harbor. Assess their work by marking the following rubric.

NOTE: For a description of the values "Not Interested," "Trying It," "Working on It," "Got it!," and "Helping Others," see chapter 4.

CRITERIA	NOT INTERESTED	TRYING IT	WORKING ON IT	GOT IT!	HELPING OTHERS
Methods of transportation to get from home to the continent or island are noted.					
Description of life on board ship is supplied.					
Parts of the ship are labeled.					
Safety issues are evident.					

FOR MORE ABLE LEARNERS Have students write about a trip from their home across the ocean to Australia, Hawaii, Africa, or an island in the Caribbean. Tell them that they must take a boat across the ocean for part of their journey. Ask them to describe the trip, the safety measures they take, and life on the ship. Have them draw a picture of the ship with the parts labeled.

CRITERIA	APPROACHES TARGET	MEETS TARGET	EXCEEDS TARGET
Going from home to the destination	Includes only driving when other modes of transportation would be more appropriate	Includes efficient forms of transportation to get to the ship	Includes taxis, airlines, etc. Is very detailed in thinking through the modes of transportation necessary to get to the ship
Life on the ship	Limited to description of one aspect of being on a ship such as eating or sleeping. Does not include any of the people working on the ship	Describes eating, sleeping, and appropriate daytime activities on the ship. Mentions some of the people who work on the ship	Describes every aspect of life on the ship including eating, sleeping, and daytime activities. Includes the idea of multiple days on the ship and changes daytime activities. Mentions the employees of the ship in their jobs
Parts of the ship	Provides minimal labels for the ship including hull and cabin	Labels hull, cabin, propeller or sail/mast, portholes, and several other items	Provides a detailed picture with many labels including the hull, cabin, propeller or sail/mast, portholes, and others with a high level of detail
Safety	Includes only a life vest or a lifeboat	Includes both a life vest and a lifeboat	Details the procedure, including the order of putting the life vest on first and going to the lifeboat, waiting in line, etc.

Assessment of technology use depends on the level of student use permitted, the technology available, and the age of the students. See chapter 4 for additional information on assessing technology use.

Additional criteria should be added focusing on writing. The criteria used for the rubric should reflect the objectives and expectations for the students.

Things That Go on Rails

UNIT OVERVIEW

Haven't most of us stopped at a railroad crossing as the long trains slowly pass by, frustrated by being delayed, only to hear the children counting the cars, commenting about their colors and words, and waving to the engineer and brakeman? Trains fascinate young children. The waving person at the beginning and end of the train only perpetuates that fascination. For many schools, trains, subways, monorails, or cable cars are close by. Teaching the children about the safety issues around these vehicles is as important as teaching them about the good things that trains do.

UNIT OBJECTIVES

At the end of this unit, students will be able to:

- Categorize vehicles as those that travel on land, on rails, in the air, or on the water.
- Describe the various parts of a train.
- Name the different types of trains.
- Describe the different jobs associated with rail vehicles and their maintenance.

STANDARDS ADDRESSED IN THIS UNIT

ISTE NETS for Students 1, 3, 5
IRA/NCTE English/Language Arts Standards 1, 2, 3, 4, 5, 7, 8, 12
NCTM Math Standards 1, 4, 8, 10
NAS/NSE Science Standards B2, E2, G2
NCSS Social Studies Standards 1a, 1d, 2b, 2d, 7e, 8a, 8b, 10b, 10c

CHILDREN'S LITERATURE

Moving on Rails—General
The ABCs of Trains
All Aboard ABC, Doug Magee
All Aboard!: Trains, Trains, Trains, Phil Wilson
Big Book of Trains, Caroline Bingham, Ed.
Big Book of Trains, Christine Heap
The Caboose Who Got Loose, Bill Peet
Circus Train, Joseph A. Smith
Country Crossing, Jim Aylesworth
Crossing, Philip E. Booth
Freight Trains, Adele D. Richardson
Freight Trains, Darlene S. Stille
Gus and Grandpa Ride the Train, Claudia Mills
Henry the Green Engine, C. Reginald Dalby
I'm Taking a Trip on My Train, Shirley Neitzel
The Little Engine That Could, Watty Piper
The Little Red Caboose, Steve Metzger
The Little Train, Lois Lenski

Long Train: 101 Cars on the Track, Sam Williams
Mr. Putter and Tabby Take the Train, Cynthia Rylant
My First Train Trip, Emily Neye
Passenger Trains, Allison Lassieur
Percy the Small Engine, C. Reginald Dalby
Railways (History Series), Colin Hynson
Really Useful Engines, Christopher Awdry
Superpower: The Making of a Steam Locomotive, David Weitzman
Thomas the Tank Engine (several books), Watty Piper
Toby the Tram Engine, Wilbert Vere Awdry
Tommy's Train Ride on the Alaska Railroad, Bonnie Pennington
Train Rides (Let's Go), Pamela Walker
Trains, Byron Barton
Trains, Gail Gibbons
Trains, Phyllis Jean Perry
Trains, Anne F. Rockwell
Trains (First Discovery Book), Gallimard Jeunesse
Trains (Transportation Around the World), Chris Oxlade
Trains (Transportation Machines at Work), Hal Rogers
Train Song, Harriet Ziefert
Train to Somewhere, Eve Bunting
Trouble on the Tracks, Kathy Mallat
Two Little Trains, Margaret Wise Brown
Where the Sidewalk Ends, Shel Silverstein ("The Little Blue Engine")

Cable Cars
The Cable Car and the Dragon, Herb Caen
Cable Cars, Lola M. Schaefer
Kerby the Cable Car, Arturo Lara Garcia
Maybelle the Cable Car, Virginia Lee Burton

Subways
Down in the Subway, Miriam Cohen
Subway Rides (Let's Go), Pamela Walker
Subways, Allison Lassieur
Subway Sparrow, Leyla Torres

WEB RESOURCES   Rail Transportation—General
Age of Steam Railway Museum Online Photos: **http://dallasrailwaymuseum. com/collection.html**
America's Lost Trains: Streamliners: **www.pbs.org/wgbh/amex/streamliners/ Land**
Central Pacific Railroad Photographic History Museum: **http://cprr.org**
Color Tracks Game: **www.webeans.net/hutt/educ/colortracks.htm**
Down by the Station: **www.niehs.nih.gov/kids/lyrics/station.htm**
George Stephenson, Father of Railway Transportation: **www.jaam.ee/eng/ history.rw.2.php**

Global Story Train: http://storytrain.kids-space.org/
Golden Gate Railroad Museum: www.ggrm.org/
How Steam Engines Work: www.howstuffworks.com/steam.htm
It's Just Railroad Talk: www.uprr.com/aboutup/rrtalk/
I've Been Workin' on the Railroad: www.niehs.nih.gov/kids/lyrics/railroad.htm
Jump the Tracks Game: www.webeans.net/hutt/educ/jumptracks.htm
New York Transit Scenes, Past and Present: www-tech.mit.edu/Subway/
North American Light Rail Association: www.lightrail.com
Railroad Crossing Signs: http://members.aol.com/rcmoeur/r15.html
Railroads and States: www.aar.org/AboutTheIndustry/StateInformation.asp
Railroad Web Cams: www.railcams.com
Seattle Monorail History: www.seattlemonorail.com/history.htm
The Train Era: www.transitpeople.org/lesson/train.htm
Trains In, Around, and Through Maryland: www.intandem.com/NewPrideSite/
  MD/Lesson2/Lesson2_1.html
Transportation Inventors: www.inventorsmuseum.com/transportation.htm
Union Pacific Railroad Photo Gallery: www.uprr.com/aboutup/photos/
Vehicles: www.transport-pf.or.jp/english/land/index.html

Dictionaries

Internet Picture Dictionary: www.pdictionary.com
Little Explorers Picture Dictionary: www.enchantedlearning.com/
  Dictionary.html
Merriam-Webster's Word Central: www.wordcentral.com

SOFTWARE, TOYS, AND VIDEOS

Software

The Amazing Writing Machine, Broderbund
The Graph Club, Tom Snyder Productions, or Tabletop Jr., Broderbund
Kid Pix (Enligh, Spanish), Broderbund
Kidspiration, Inspiration Software
Thomas and Friends, Trouble on the Tracks, Infogrames

Toys

ABC Animal Train, Pockets of Learning
Alphabet Train Floor Puzzle, Lights, Camera, Interaction
Alphabet Train Peg Puzzle, Lights, Camera, Interaction

Videos

Let Me Tell You All About Trains, Traditional Images
Lots and Lots of Trains (Volumes 1 and 2), Superior Home Video
Toy Trains and Big Trains, Tom McComas

teaching
the unit

Getting Started

In a letter, let parents know the objectives and desired outcomes for the unit on trains. Have the parents and grandparents share stories about their own experiences with trains. Ask parents and grandparents to write, e-mail, or tape their story for a classroom learning experience. Additionally, ask parents to volunteer to take a digital video of a passing train for use in the lessons. Share with the parents how you are going to use the video in class, as some may want to replicate the activity at home. In preparation for the art and math activities that utilize shoe boxes, ask parents to send at least one shoe box to school as well as any extras they might have.

Motivating Activities

Set up the classroom as a movie theater and provide an afternoon at the movies. Start this unit with a video about trains, showing the various types of trains: passenger and freight trains, real and model trains, and on-, under-, or above-the-ground trains. This experience, combined with their conversations about trains with their parents, should bring forth plenty of excitement for a study of trains. Plan either an introductory or culminating visit to a train museum, a train in a zoo, or an engine in a park. Take a trip to see the train. Visiting a real train is especially informative if students are allowed to investigate, touch, climb in, and see what it really looks like.

Multidisciplinary Activities

ART   *Shoe Box Train:* Provide each child with a shoe box to decorate as a train car. The engine and the caboose can be class projects, with groups of students taking care of each. In a large class, different types of trains can be constructed (passenger, freight, mail). Different sizes of boxes can be used to show the various sizes of trains (real and model) and also to show the different rail gauges of model trains. Encourage students to decorate their cars with the details that real train cars have. Look at the various kinds of cars.

   ■ The Union Pacific Museum Photo Gallery, www.uprr.com/aboutup/photos/, has an excellent collection of train photos that can be printed and displayed for ideas.

   Circus Train: Read *Circus Train* (by Joseph A. Smith) to discover just what a circus train is. At the art center, have students make paintings of all the animals they think are in the circus. Make a bulletin board of all the animals in the circus, lined up from one end of the room to the other. Use brown craft paper or butcher paper to make individual cars for each type of animal. Fit the size and shape of the paper to the size and shape of the animal. Cover the animals with the cars. Windows could be made to see the animal (and allow it to breathe).

GROSS MOTOR

Building a Human Train: Play Follow the Leader (have children put their hands on the waist of the person in front of them) with the leader wearing a train engineer's hat. Discover how hard it is to turn corners and stay together. Make "chug chug" and "choo choo" sounds while playing. Have children move their free hand in a circle to mimic the wheels on a train moving together. Couple and uncouple the cars of the "train" as students go around the circle. For example, have student "train cars" uncouple in groups of two, three, or more.

LANGUAGE ARTS AND READING

Word Train: Read and learn train terms from It's Just Railroad Talk, **www.uprr.com/ aboutup/rrtalk/,** which describe trains from many perspectives. Use the language throughout the unit to name the ideas children are describing. Create a Word Train— an engine that has Word Train on its side and several cars. Each car describes a different category of train words (train terms, yard terms, types of trains, engineering terms, terms for places, transportation terms, and mechanical terms).

- Use the electronic dictionaries for further information.
- Use Kidspiration to initially organize the known words and establish the categories for sorting words.

ABC Train: Give each student a large train car cut out of construction paper with a unique letter of the alphabet on it. Just as different train cars carry different merchandise, the cars of this ABC train carry very specific items. Have students cut out magazine pictures of things that start with the letter they were given and paste them onto the car. String all the cars together with yarn and hang the string on the wall. Discuss why trains have a caboose.

Train Encyclopedia: Read with students *The ABCs of Trains, The Big Book of Trains,* or one of the other information books listed to discover as many things as you can about trains. For each fact discovered and verified, have students draw a picture, label it, and write a telling description of the fact. Alphabetize all of the findings into a Train Encyclopedia.

- Use Kidspiration to brainstorm words that could become part of the encyclopedia. Categorizing the words as they are recorded helps students clarify the meaning of the words.
- Make a Kid Pix slideshow of all the facts about trains. Record the students chanting train chugs in the background.

MATH

Load the Car: Make a shoe-box train with the open end of the box facing up. Place the numbers being studied on the outside of the cars. Have students sort counters or written equations into the boxes to indicate the correct number of items.

How Much Cargo?: Each train car that carries cargo is marked with the maximum weight (LD LMT means load limit) and minimum weight (LT WT means lightest weight) of loads that they can carry. Have children learn to state a range by indicating that the weight of the cargo ranges from the LT WT to the LD LMT.

- Take digital pictures of the passing train video or use still pictures of box cars, tank cars, flat cars, or other cars that show the weights.

Color Tracks: Use computational facts or number recognition as a way to move along the tracks on the game board Color Tracks. Access the Web site to print out the game board and playing cards to create the Color Tracks game (**www.webeans. net/hutt/educ/colortracks.htm**). Practice addition, telling time, and counting money using this game.

Jump the Tracks: Like Color Tracks, Jump the Tracks is a game that provides students a way to practice their basic facts in a fun format. Print out the game board and playing cards to create the Jump the Tracks game (**www.webeans.net/ hutt/educ/jumptracks.htm**). Practice addition, telling time, and counting money using this game.

Counting Cars: Give each student a large train car cut out of construction paper with a unique number on it. Have the students cut out magazine pictures that equal the number on their car and paste them onto the car. String the cars together with yarn and hang them on the wall.

- Create a box train in Kidspiration by placing several number boxes together in a row. Have students use the symbol library to put items in the boxes to match the number. Add the numbers on all of the train cars together and type that number on the engine.

- If the school is located near a train route, take a video of the train. Have the children watch the video with you and count the number of cars. Have each child record the number of cars they counted. Rewind, review, and recount. Record the second number. See if the counts are the same. Have students count by twos as they watch the train cars pass.

- Many of the train cars will have some sort of identification on them, such as Union Pacific, Lincoln Grain, or Cargill Foods. Some have only letter identifications: NAHX, DGHX, FLIX, CTRN. Use the train video from above. Identify the companies noted on the cars. See how many of each type there are. Place the types and numbers in a spreadsheet and create different kinds of graphs.

Train Schedules: Log on to a train Web cam (such as **www.railcams.com**). Keep the computer camera on during the day. Record the time a new train enters the view. If you are in an area where trains, subways, and cable cars run on schedules, get copies of the schedule for the classroom. Teach the students how to read the schedule from the table. Determine how long there is between trains throughout the day. Speculate why the time between trains varies.

MUSIC   *Trains at Work:* Post various train-related pictures before students sing these songs.

- "Little Red Caboose": visit **http://community.webshots.com** and search for "Little Red Caboose."

- "I've Been Working on the Railroad": **www.niehs.nih.gov/kids/lyrics/ railroad.htm**

■ "Down by the Station": www.niehs.nih.gov/kids/lyrics/station.htm

SAFETY   *Train Safety:* Examine the Web Site on train safety signs (**http://members.aol.com/ rcmoeur/r15.html**). Clearly identify what each means. Include in this study the arms that come down to keep cars from passing. Provide paper and markers in a student construction center so children can create appropriate crossing and stop signs.

SCIENCE   *What Is Steam?:* Steam was one of the first forms of energy for trains. How do we get steam? Show students the different properties of water. Freeze water and make ice. Boil water and make steam. Show how water becomes steam using an iron or a teapot. See how the steam escapes and moves. Discuss how this might power a train.

■ Show how steam is used to create power with this How Steam Engines Work Web site: **www.howstuffworks.com/steam.htm**

■ Discuss the electric light rail trains that are often found in big cities. Have students think about how the train gets the electricity. Go to the North American Light Rail Association Web site (**www.lightrail.com**). Look at the pictures of rail systems. They are sorted by city. Find a city close to the school. Compare the light rail with the diesel locomotive. Look at issues of purpose, distance traveled, speed, noise level, employees needed, and cost to ride.

SOCIAL STUDIES   *Where's It from?:* Train cars travel all over the country. Take a digital video of a passing train. Play the video for the children. Freeze the frames. Examine the company names on the cars. Locate the companies on maps. Place a map pin on the city or state to mark the spot. Determine whether you can figure out where the train came from and where it might be going. How many different places are identified by the cars on one train?

In My State?: Draw an outline of your state to post in the classroom. Examine maps of various railroads to see which pass through the state. Place the names of those train lines on the outline of the state.

■ The Web site Railroads and States (**www.aar.org/AboutTheIndustry/ StateInformation.asp**) will show the tracks through each state. Use the search engine on the site to seach the term "passenger trains" and locate several trains and maps throughout the world. Give students an opportunity to look states up on the Web site and find the location of railroad lines that are close to the residences of family and friends.

All Aboard: The history of railroad development is extensive. Students who are developing a sense of history may have a hard time understanding that the railroad has been in existence a long time but did not always look the way it does today.

- Take the students through the Web site Trains In, Around, and Through Maryland to learn more about trains and railways (www.intandem.com/ NewPrideSite/MD/Lesson2/Lesson2_1.html).

- Share this photographic history museum with the students: http://cprr.org.

I Think I Can: Read the story of *The Little Engine That Could*. Discuss difficult things that students really have to work on, and then chant, "I think I can. I think I can." To show that you can't always do something just because you think you can, read Shel Silverstein's poem "The Little Blue Engine," from *Where the Sidewalk Ends*. The poem ends with "Just thinking you can isn't always enough."

- Have each student draw a Kid Pix slide of her- or himself doing something "they think they can" do. Record their voices saying "I think I can..." Create a classroom slideshow.

Jobs on the Train: Have students think about all the people who are necessary to make a train run well and on time. If you are taking a long trip on a train, what are the expectations of services available on the train?

- Use Kidspiration to brainstorm the type of people who would be working on a train on a long trip. Make an additional diagram of those who would be on a freight train. How does the number of workers differ? Why?

Assessment

FOR YOUNGER
LEARNERS

Ask children to draw a folding train book with each page a new car. Encourage them to label the parts of the train and to write simple sentences or a short story about the kind of train it is and where it is going.

NOTE: For a description of the values "Not Interested," "Trying It," "Working on It," "Got it!," and "Helping Others," see chapter 4.

CRITERIA	NOT INTERESTED	TRYING IT	WORKING ON IT	GOT IT!	HELPING OTHERS
Train engine and caboose are evident.					
Train cars are evident and labeled appropriately.					
A story line is provided.					
Labels are provided throughout the story.					

FOR MORE ABLE LEARNERS Ask students to draw a folding train book with each page a new car. Specify that each car in the train must be different. Ask students to label the parts of the train. Have students write a story to accompany the picture that tells where the train started, where it will end its trip, and what will happen along the way.

CRITERIA	APPROACHES TARGET	MEETS TARGET	EXCEEDS TARGET
Train cars	Drawing shows multiple cars that are mostly the same. Limited or no labels are provided.	Drawing shows the engine and the caboose with at least three additional cars on the train. Accurate labels are provided.	Drawing shows more than seven types of cars, each of which is unique. Labeling goes beyond type of car to include weight range, place of origin, engine type, and other items of interest.
Train type	The kind of train is not clearly identifiable.	The train is clearly labeled and labels are consistent with the drawing. The engineer and brakeman are included in the picture or description.	The train is clearly labeled. Story line more fully explains the function of the type of train and includes information about those who work on the train.
Train story	The story refers to a function of the train that is not consistent with the type of train. The starting point and destination are specified but no additional details are provided.	The story tells where the train started and where it is headed. The story is compatible with the type of train identified.	The story includes a purpose that is consistent with the type of train. The story contains details that include many functions and stops for the train.

Assessment of technology use depends on the level of student use permitted, the technology available, and the age of the students. See chapter 4 for additional information on assessing technology use.

Additional criteria should be added focusing on writing. The criteria used for the rubric should reflect the objectives and expectations for the students.

Things That Go in Air and Space

UNIT OVERVIEW

Events involving planes and aircraft appear almost daily on the news. Although most young children don't sit down to watch the evening news, they can't help but see much of it as their parents watch. Air and space travel will be an increasingly large part of young children's lives, more so than for any of their parents and teachers. Whether seeing and hearing about them, traveling on them, or imagining life as an astronaut, children are intrigued by planes and spacecraft. Air- and spacecraft can be categorized into pleasure, working, and rescue vehicles, much like those that travel on land. This unit focuses on air and space vehicle parts, purposes, careers, and safety.

UNIT OBJECTIVES

At the end of this unit, students will be able to:

- Categorize vehicles as those that travel on land, on rails, in the air, or on the water.
- Sort air and space vehicles.
- Describe the various parts of the air and space vehicles.
- Name the different purposes of air and space vehicles, such as for pleasure, work, or rescue.
- Describe the different jobs associated with air and space vehicles and their maintenance.

STANDARDS ADDRESSED IN THIS UNIT

ISTE NETS for Students 1, 3, 5
IRA/NCTE English/Language Arts Standards 1, 2, 3, 4, 5, 7, 8, 12
NCTM Math Standards 1, 4, 8, 10
NAS/NSE Science Standards B2, E2, G2
NCSS Social Studies Standards 1a, 1d, 2b, 2d, 7e, 8a, 8b, 10b, 10c

CHILDREN'S LITERATURE

Air Flight
Air and Flight, Sally Hewitt
Aircraft (Draw It), Patricia Walsh
The Airplane Alphabet Book, Jerry Pallotta
Airplanes, Robert B. Noyed & Cynthia Fitterer Klingel
Airplanes, Gail Saunders-Smith
Airplanes (True Book), Darlene R. Stille
Airplanes and Flying Machines, Pascale De Bourgoing
Airplanes: Transportation Machines at Work, Hal Rogers
All Aboard Airplanes, Frank Evans
The Berenstain Bears Fly-It!: Up, Up, and Away, Stan Berenstain & Jan Berenstain (Contributor)
Big Book of Airplanes, Caroline Bingham, Ed.
Flight: Fliers and Flying Machines, David Jefferis

Get Around in Air and Space, Lee Sullivan Hill
How Do Airplanes Fly?: A Book About Airplanes, Melvin Berger
How to Draw Wings and Wheels, Georgene Griffen and Karen McKee
How to Fly for Kids!, Natalie Windsor
I Fly, Anne F. Rockwell
Kids' Paper Airplane Book, Ken Blackburn & Jeff Lammers
Lisa's Airplane Trip, Anne Gutman & Georg Hallensleben
Look Inside Cross-Sections: Jets, Hans Jenssen & Moira Butterfield
The Magic School Bus Taking Flight: A Book About Flight, Joanna Cole & Gail
   Herman
Plane Rides, Pamela Walker
Planes, Byron Barton
Planes, Anne F. Rockwell
Richard Scarry's A Day at the Airport, Richard Scarry
Some Planes Hover (I Didn't Know That), Kate Petty
Tell Me Why Planes Have Wings (Whiz Kids), Shirley Willis

Space Flight
Floating in Space, True Kelley (Illustrator) & Franklyn Mansfield Branley
Get Around in Air and Space, Lee Sullivan Hill
If You Were an Astronaut, Virginia Schomp
The International Space Station, True Kelley (Illustrator) & Franklyn Mansfield
   Branley
Liftoff!: A Space Adventure, Rosanna Hansen
Man on the Moon, Anastasia Suen
Moonwalk: The First Trip to the Moon, Judy Donnelly
My First Book of Space, Ian Graham
Space, Will Osborne & Mary Pope Osborne
Spacebusters, Philip Wilkinson
Space Station, Accident on MIR, Angela Royston
Touchdown Mars!: An ABC Adventure, Peggy Wethered & Ken Edgett

Careers
Astronauts Today, Rosanna Hansen
Astronauts Work in Space, Carol Greene
Buzz the Little Seaplane, Wendy Cheyette Lewison
Christa McAuliffe, Patricia Stone Martin & Karen Park
A Day With Air Traffic Controllers, Joanne Winne
Flying an Agricultural Plane With Mr. Miller, Alice K. Flanagan
I Want to Be an Astronaut, Byron Barton
The Picture World of Astronauts, Norman Barrett
Pilots, Elizabeth Dana Jaffe
Pilots Fly Planes, Fay Robinson

WEB RESOURCES   **Teacher Resources**
Aerodynamics General Information: www.lerc.nasa.gov/WWW/K-12/airplane/
    bga.html
Chasing the Sun: www.pbs.org/kcet/chasingthesun/
Encyclopedia Astronautica: www.astronautix.com
Science Fun With Airplanes: www.ag.ohio-state.edu/~flight/
Songs: www.niehs.nih.gov/kids/music.htm
Testing a New Spacecraft Material: http://spaceplace.jpl.nasa.gov/
    nmp_action.htm
Transportation Inventors: www.inventorsmuseum.com/transportation.htm

Air Flight
Air Force One: www.boeing.com/defense-space/military/af1/
Air Force One: Fact Sheet: www.af.mil/news/factsheets/
    VC_25A___Air_Force_One.html
Air Force Planes of Different Countries: www.geocities.com/CapeCanaveral/
    Hall/5536/johns_pages/planes.htm
Careers in Aeronautics: www.allstar.fiu.edu/aero/career1.htm
Charles Lindbergh: www.dot.state.mn.us/aero/aved/publications/
    skyslimit/lindbergh.html
Flying Free: Flying Firsts: www.pbs.org/saf/1109/
Greatest Achievements: Timeline: www.greatachievements.org/
    greatachievements/ga_3_3.html
History of Aeronautics: www.allstar.fiu.edu/aero/history1.htm
How Things Fly: www.nasm.edu/galleries/gal109/NEWHTF/HTF050.HTM
Jay, Jay, the Jet Plane: http://pbskids.org/jayjay/
Knowble: www.knowble.com/K_browser.html
Plane Math: www.planemath.com/activities/pmactivitiesall.html
Sky Vehicles: www.transport-pf.or.jp/english/sky/index.html

Space Flight
Building the International Space Station: http://school.discovery.com/
    schooladventures/spacestation/
A Day in the Life of the ISS: http://ali.apple.com/events/iss/
How Space Stations Work: www.howstuffworks.com/space-
    station.htm/printable
I Don't Want to Live on the Moon: www.niehs.nih.gov/kids/lyrics/nomoon.htm
International Space Station (photos, drawings, and video clips):
    http://spaceflight.nasa.gov/gallery/images/station/index.html
International Space Station Location: http://liftoff.msfc.nasa.gov/temp/
    StationLoc.html
International Space Station Slideshow: www.hq.nasa.gov/osf/funstuff/
    stationoverview/npage1.html
International Space Station Suit: www.cnn.com/interactive/space/9907/
    spacesuit/frameset.exclude.html
International Space Station Virtual Tour: http:// spaceflight.nasa.gov/gallery/
    vtour/index.html
Launch a Rocket: http://spaceplace.jpl.nasa.gov/ds1_mgr.htm
Living in Space: http://spaceflight.nasa.gov/living/index.html
Living in Space, Design a Space Station: www.childrensmuseum.org/
    cosmicquest/spacestation/a1.html

NASA Astro-Venture Career Fact Sheets: http://quest.arc.nasa.gov/projects/
astrobiology/astroventure/teachers/fact_sheets.html
Skylab (first U.S. space station): www.astronautix.com/craft/skylab.htm
Skylab Cutaway: www.astronautix.com/graphics/s/skylcuta.jpg
The Space Place: http://spaceplace.jpl.nasa.gov/
The Space Shuttle Clickable Map: http://seds.lpl.arizona.edu/ssa/docs/
Space.Shuttle/index.shtml
Space Station: www.pbs.org/spacestation/
Space Station Assembly: http://spaceflight.nasa.gov/station/assembly/
index.html
Stationed in the Stars: www.pbs.org/wgbh/nova/station/
Wheels in the Sky: http://science.nasa.gov/headlines/y2000/
ast26may_1m.htm

Dictionaries

Internet Picture Dictionary: www.pdictionary.com
Little Explorers Picture Dictionary: www.enchantedlearning.com/Dictionary.html
Merriam-Webster's Word Central: www.wordcentral.com

WebQuests

Come Fly With Me: www.murarriess.qld.edu.au/webquests/planequest/
index.htm
Weather Watchers: www.sbcss.k12.ca.us/sbcss/services/educational/
cctechnology/webquest/weather.html

SOFTWARE AND VIDEOS

Software

The Amazing Writing Machine, Broderbund
Bill Nye the Science Guy: Stop the Rock, Pacific Interactive
The Graph Club, Tom Snyder Productions, or Tabletop Jr., Broderbund
Kid Pix (English, Spanish), Broderbund
Kidspiration, Inspiration Software
Magic School Bus Discovers Flight Activity Center, Microsoft/Scholastic
Magic School Bus Lands on Mars, Microsoft/Scholastic
PowerPoint
Space Academy GX, Edmark
Space: A Visual History of Manned Spaceflight, Sumeria

Video

Airplanes A to Z (for children 3–8), East Texas Distributing

teaching the unit

Getting Started

In a letter, prepare parents for the unit by providing the objective and desired outcomes. Because many children may have parents in the military or connections to tragic events that involve air travel, ask parents to prepare their children for the unit and make you, as teacher, aware of any personal issues. Encourage parents, as planes fly overhead or are seen on the news, to bring their child's attention to them as appropriate.

Motivating Activity

View the video *Airplanes A to Z*, visit the Air Force One Web sites (see Web Resources), or read *The Airplane Alphabet Book* (by Jerry Pallotta) as a way to introduce this unit. The children may want multiple viewings of this video and site, and readings of the book throughout this unit. There is much to learn in each. Initiate conversations with students to determine what they know about air and space travel. Use that information as a springboard into further learning, tying it to books, videos, Web resources, and appropriate software.

Multidisciplinary Activities

ART   *Airplane Hangings:* After children have had some exposure to the types of planes and space vehicles, ask each to paint and label a picture of their favorite airplane or space vehicle. When they are dry, cut out two copies—the picture and a blank piece of paper. Staple the edges except for about 8" on one edge. Paint the back. When it is dry, stuff it with wadded newspaper. Staple shut. Hang the airplanes and space vehicles from the ceiling.

Clay Models: Provide Play-Doh and airplane and rocket cookie cutters to cut air travel shapes. Older children may actually mold or sculpt airplanes and rockets. With some adult help, children can shoot digital stills and create a clay animation of the airplanes taking off and landing and the rockets lifting off.

Winged Vehicles: After reading *How to Draw Wings and Wheels,* provide students with the materials to make pencil drawings of winged vehicles.

- Have students create an animated space vehicle or airplane that flies in Kid Pix. Draw the first picture of the vehicle and name the slide airplane01. Open that picture and use the moving van tool to begin moving the airplane into flight. Add some jet smoke and save as airplane02. Continue drawing and moving the plane until the student has drawn several slides and made the airplane fly across the screen. Put these slides into the slideshow, setting the timing for one second each. The slideshow will show the airplane flying through the air. For older children, have them draw the background, including people waving goodbye, and add the sound of the airplane taking off.

GROSS MOTOR   *Why People Can't Fly:* Place a wooden box in the sand on the playground. Tell the students the story of the Wright brothers. Have student test "their wing" to show why humans cannot fly by jumping off the box. Encourage students to flap their wings (arms) as much as possible.

HEALTH   *Space Food:* Bring in everyday food and space (freeze dried) food for the children to examine and taste. Discuss why food in space must be freeze dried and how it is reconstituted. Discuss why backpackers carry freeze-dried food as astronauts do.

- Learn more about clothing and food in space at Living in Space: http://spaceflight.nasa.gov/living/index.html

LANGUAGE ARTS AND READING   *I Want to Be:* Read some of the children's books about jobs related to air and space travel. Set up some software in the computer station, such as Magic School Bus Lands on Mars or Magic School Bus Discovers Flight Activity Center. Have children identify a job they might like to have when they grow up and create an eight-page book. The first page will state, "I want to be a/an _____ when I grow up." It should include a picture of the child as an adult, dressed for the job. Each page after should start with "I will..." On those pages, students describe the different things they will have to do as part of their job. Print out the NASA Astro-Venture Career Fact Sheets and read them to students. Discuss how their parents' jobs are similar to or different from the children's selected careers (**http://quest.arc.nasa.gov/projects/ astrobiology/astroventure/teachers/fact_sheets.html**).

- Create the book in the Amazing Writing Machine or create a slideshow in PowerPoint.

A Trip in the Air: Have each child create a drawing of a different type of airplane or space vehicle, then type a sentence telling where they will go on their flying machine.

- Have students use Kid Pix to create their drawing. Create a classroom slideshow of all of the slides, with a recording of the children's voices telling a story of where they are going to go on their vehicle.

Concentration: Make a set of Concentration cards by downloading pictures of air- and spacecraft. Make two copies of each picture. Glue onto cards. Play Concentration with the cards. More advanced readers can match pictures with words or words with definitions.

MATH   *Paper Airplanes:* Make paper airplanes. Test the flight length and time for several different models in different places (inside in the gym or hallway, outside on the playground on a windy or calm day).

- Measure the flight length and time and record them in a spreadsheet. Graph the results. Speculate on each plane's design and the length and time it flew. Make one change to the design and fly again. Did that make the flight longer or shorter? Why?

Where in the World?: Have students select a country they would like to visit, one that would require an air flight to get there. Check the airfares from the local airport to the country and compare airfares and the length of time that it would take to get there, allowing two hours for check in at the airport and one hour for baggage claim and customs.

- Look up the airfares on the Internet using several airlines that are familiar to the class or ones that fly out of the local airport. Compare the length of time the trip would take for each airline's itinerary by making a graph and plotting the time for each trip.

The Space Shuttle: The vehicle we use to travel to space from the earth is currently aboard one of the space shuttles. Children often have an inflated sense of how big the space shuttle is. Have children estimate how long the space shuttle is by making marks on the playground as if the shuttle nose touched the fence. Have students measure out the shuttle's actual length and width with a yardstick, meter stick, or trundle wheel.

- To provide more information on the shuttle and to have students search for the actual length and width of the shuttle, go to **http://seds.lpl.arizona.edu/ ssa/docs/Space.Shuttle/index.shtml.**

MUSIC   *I'd Like to Visit the Moon:* Have students sing "I'd Like to Visit the Moon" (available at **www.niehs.nih.gov/kids/lyrics/nomoon.htm**). The teacher can lead a discussion by asking the students what they would bring to the moon if they were able to visit.

SCIENCE   *Rocket Power:* Students wonder how huge rockets carrying the space shuttle can go straight up in the air. Make rockets out of cylindrical 35mm camera film containers. Decorate the lid with a small construction paper rocket. Outside, put vinegar and baking soda in the container, put the lid on, shake it, and set the container down. Watch as the lid explodes off and the paper rocket flies. Discuss power and what caused the explosion. How are rockets powered?

- Have students write about what happened using Kid Pix or Kidspiration. Take a short digital movie or digital pictures of the experiment. Put the movie at the writing center or post the pictures to help students remember what they saw as they write.

Science Experiments: Discuss with students the differences in purpose between airline travel and space travel. Because we know so little about what can grow and survive in space, have students think of some of the questions concerning space that they would like answers to. How would they conduct the experiment? Focus on the scientific method as you record their thinking.

- Use Kidspiration to record students' thinking. Organize their ideas around topics with further clarification by procedure.

- Use the Web sites Science Fun with Airplanes, Testing a New Spacecraft Material, and Launch a Rocket as the jumping off points for science experiments.

- Use the Amazing Writing Machine or Kid Pix to have students record and illustrate the process and the results of experiments.

- The International Space Station is the hub of collaborative experiments. Spend some time taking a virtual tour of the International Space Station (http:// spaceflight.nasa.gov/gallery/vtour/index.html).

Wheels in the Sky: Space travel has evolved immensely in the last 30 years. Look at the history of the inventions of space travel on the Internet (http:// science.nasa.gov/headlines/y2000/ast26may_1m.htm). Have students design their own spacecraft.

- Have students draw a slide in Kid Pix of their design. Record their voices pointing out special features. Create a classroom slideshow.

- Students can also animate their design to fly (see the Winged Vehicles Art activity). Add that to the slideshow.

Things That Fly: Brainstorm a list of things that float in the air or fly. Sort them into natural and manmade. Describe the similarities and differences.

- Use Kidspiration to brainstorm and then sort the items.

SOCIAL STUDIES

Life in Space: Learn about the history of space travel. The software Space: A Visual History of Manned Spaceflight provides a good introduction. Examine the International Space Station (see Web Resources) to see what life on the space station might be like. Ask children to draw a picture of their home and a space station home to show what life on earth is like and what life in a space station might be like.

- Check the location of the space station daily (International Space Station Location: http://liftoff.msfc.nasa.gov/temp/StationLoc.html). Take a screenshot of the information at the same time each day and make a timeline in the hallway.

Traveling Abroad: Have students select a country they would like to visit, one that would require an air flight to get there (see the Where in the World Math activity). Determine what they would need to make the trip (tickets, identification, currency from the other country, passport, visa, shots, etc.). Construct a travel brochure that tells the highlights of the country or a scrapbook of pictures of the key points of interest. Complete the Traveling Suitcase activity as follows:

- Determine what you would need to wear if you were going to the selected country. Pack an imaginary suitcase.

Assessment

FOR YOUNGER
LEARNERS

Ask children to write and illustrate an imaginary air or space story that contains as many facts as possible.

NOTE: For a description of the values "Not Interested," "Trying It," "Working on It," "Got it!," and "Helping Others," see chapter 4.

CRITERIA	NOT INTERESTED	TRYING IT	WORKING ON IT	GOT IT!	HELPING OTHERS
Vehicle or station is present and parts are labeled.					
Safety rules are clear and appropriate.					
Actual abilities of the vehicle are used.					

FOR MORE ABLE LEARNERS Have students describe an adventure from their home to the International Space Station and back. Be sure to give them directions to include as many facts as possible, including what they intend to accomplish while on the trip.

CRITERIA	APPROACHES TARGET	MEETS TARGET	EXCEEDS TARGET
Vehicle	Describes the airplane, space shuttle, and space station with few parts labeled and/or some incorrectly labeled	Describes the airplane, space shuttle, and space station with many parts labeled correctly	Describes the airplane, space shuttle, and space station with detailed labeling of parts. Labeling and narrative indicate understanding of what the parts do.
Air travel	Includes only space shuttle or airplane	Includes both conventional air travel to get to the shuttle launch site as well as the rocket and space shuttle	Includes both conventional air travel to get to the shuttle launch site as well as the rocket and space shuttle, and describes the difference between the two
Purpose	Describes purpose of trip but does not describe doing experiments while in space	Describes purpose of trip including conducting experiments while in space	Describes purpose of trip. Includes details in conducting experiments both inside and outside the space station
Safety	Mentions only few safety rules. The rules are not complete.	Describes completely how safety rules are followed within the context of the story	In the context of the story, follows the safety rules with both procedures and rationale. Describes safety measures taken . for others
Story	The adventure uses the vehicle in a way that is questionable, making assessment of what the student knows about the use of the vehicle unclear.	The adventure uses the appropriate vehicles in the appropriate way.	The adventure uses the appropriate vehicles in an appropriate way. The child may introduce additional vehicles, which are all used appropriately.

Assessment of technology use depends on the level of student use permitted, the technology available, and the age of the students. See chapter 4 for additional information on assessing technology use.

Additional criteria should be added focusing on writing. The criteria used for the rubric should reflect the objectives and expectations for the students.

Travel Guide Show: Transportation Stations

Work with the children to plan a Travel Guide Show highlighting different transportation stations. Set a date on the calendar. Create an invitation that looks like a travel brochure to send to the groups that are to be invited, whether they are the entire school, the young children, or the parents. Encourage each child to write and illustrate different ways to travel and different destinations on their travel brochure invitations. Send the printed invitations by mail or e-mail.

PLAN THE EVENT

Long-Distance Travel: Invite long-distance guests by e-mailing friends, family, and other classrooms invitations to the Travel Guide Show. Attach in an e-mail copies of the students' ABC books. Have students share with their long-distance guests how their ABC books could have traveled if they hadn't arrived through e-mail. Ask the long-distance guests to e-mail the class back a review of their books including information on how their books could have traveled back to the classroom if they weren't traveling through e-mail.

Four Stations: Set up four different areas in the classroom or gym, one for each type of travel: wheels, rails, air, and water. Use the children's ABC books and other items to decorate each transportation station. Play a slideshow of the children's ABC pictures or other slideshows they've created in the unit in a continuous loop at each center. Have students create maps of the classroom or gym showing each transportation station and where it is located to hand out to the guests as they arrive.

STAGE THE EVENT

Travel Guides: Have children greet guests at the door, giving them a map and taking them on a tour of the Travel Guide Show. Have students explain each type of transportation and where one might travel using it. Have students read and share their ABC books at each transportation station. Have guests circle their favorite type of transportation on their map and hand them back to the students.

Graphing: Graph the results of the guests' choices of favorite type of transportation. Also, graph the types of transportation their ABC books would have taken to and from their long-distance destinations if they hadn't traveled through e-mail.

ARCHIVE THE EVENT

Take videos of children participating in the activities. Videos can be transferred to VHS format to send home to parents to play on their VCRs. They may be burned on CDs. CDs can then be played back on CD drives in computers. These videos could also be burned on DVDs to be shown using a DVD player or a DVD drive in a computer. Other devices such as the Sony Play Station II also have the capability of showing DVDs.

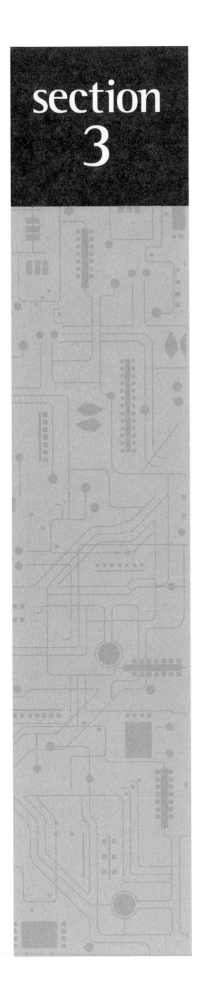

section 3

Strategies for Managing Technology

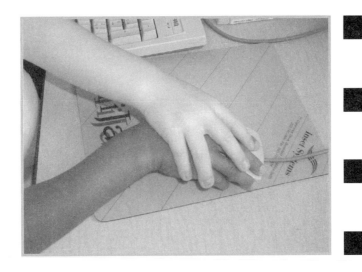

chapter 5

TONYA WITHERSPOON

Computers and Young Children

In the age of technology, many of us are like young students, curious about technology yet not nearly as fearless. As adults, we are experiencing things that no one before us has experienced. We are exploring in ways no others have explored before us. As adults, we are student explorers ourselves as well as guides and experts for our students. How do we translate all this information into workable learning for young children? How do we teach about what we know little about or did not experience as young students? We can!! And this book will show you how.

Introducing computers in the early childhood classroom is similar to introducing any new tool, game, or activity. Consider using a Montessori approach when introducing computers and software to young children. Montessori suggests that a small replica of adult work tools, not toys, be used in classrooms of young children (Carinato, Cluxton, McCarrick, Motz, & O'Connor, 1999, p. 7). Even though the computer is not a small replica of an adult tool, but the actual tool itself, a Montessori approach can still be applied. A Montessori demonstration, which is a clear set of methodical steps to introduce children to new activities, provides a good process for introducing young children to these sophisticated and expensive tools.

Teachers, like students, must be clear on how to handle and respect the equipment, how it will be used for the proposed activity, and how and when students should ask for help. Check with building or district technology support personnel for appropriate Internet filters and any policies that need to be followed when using computers, including acceptable use policies (AUPs) signed by students, staff, and parents.

Introducing Computers to Young Children

Based on the Montessori process for demonstrations, the following activity was developed to introduce the computer to children by taking it out of the box and setting it up.

1. Carry the computer box to the demonstration area and set it on the floor with the children.

2. Examine all sides of the box, reading the words and describing any pictures.

3. Carefully open the box.

4. Lift each item out of the box and place it on the table on which the computer will be housed.

5. Unwrap each item, placing the wrapping under the item. Band the cords (see the following section, Handling and Respect).

6. Find the instruction booklet. Pick it up, read the instructions out loud, and follow the instructions one by one to set up the computer.

7. Read and follow the instructions on how to start the computer.

8. Demonstrate the use of the mouse to locate, select, and open various items on the computer screen.

9. Give children a chance to use the mouse (see the instructions in the Using the Equipment section, later in this chapter).

10. Shut down the computer.

11. Place all extra items, books, cords, and cables in one large ziplock plastic bag for safekeeping.

12. Place all packing materials back into the box.

13. Return the box to the appropriate person.

Handling and Respect

ORGANIZING COMPUTER CORDS

Keep computer cords banded together and out of the way. Use colored tape to color-code the cords so that you can follow their path from device to device and to electrical sources. If using laptops, lay power strips in front of or in the middle of the group of children. Plug laptops into the power strips so that all power cords are in plain sight and not running behind students on the floor. Require that students always ask before plugging or unplugging any cords.

TEACHING COMPUTER OPERATION AND CARE

Show students how to respect the computer and other equipment. Demonstrate how to turn computers on and off properly. Teach students to identify whether the computer is turned *off* or simply *asleep*. Demonstrate the sleep mode by first putting the computer to sleep and then shaking the mouse to wake up the computer. Explain that students must be careful with the mouse and keyboard. They must not bang on them or use them roughly. They should not touch the monitor and leave fingerprints. Require that students carry laptops, cameras, and other equipment with both hands. Teach students to handle disks and CDs with proper care and not to print without permission.

KEEPING THE EQUIPMENT CLEAN

Use alcohol wipes to clean the screen, the body of the computer, the mouse, and the keyboard. Clean them frequently, just as you would the toys and manipulatives in your rooms. Use carpet cleaner to clean the mouse pad and a small vacuum attachment to clean keyboards. Have students wash their hands before using the computer, either by taking a bathroom break or by using baby wipes or hand sanitizing gel kept beside the computer. (More details on keeping the equipment clean are provided in the following section.)

Using the Equipment

Most computer hardware is designed for adults. When introducing young children to technology, extra steps have to be taken to ensure that small children can use the technology effectively. Below are some tips that teachers can use to make sure technology hardware is accessible to young children, but also protected from young users.

MONITORS

MAKING THE MONITOR READABLE

Setting up the monitor so that young children can easily view the screen is very important. When using tabletop computers, placing the computer on a small table so that children can sit on chairs with their feet touching the ground is ideal. Make sure that the monitor is set up and tilted at the appropriate height for young children. Place the computer where there is no glare on the monitor from the windows. Check the brightness and contrast settings. Adjust the resolution of the monitor in the system controls. Use a lower resolution, 800x600, for young children. This will make things appear much bigger. Adjust the font or text zoom in the preferences of the individual software programs so that students can see and read easier. For example, in Internet Explorer the font size can be adjusted by clicking on the View menu and choosing Text Zoom on a Mac and choosing Text Size in Windows. If young children share a lab with others, teach them to make many of these adjustments themselves and to put the computers and settings back the way they found them when they're done.

USING LAPTOPS

Laptops are a good option to consider in the early childhood classroom because they can be set up easily using the classroom's regular tables and centers and then put away or shared with other classes when not in use. The screens are easy to tilt and adjust for optimal viewing. When giving the children instructions, ask them to lower the lid of the laptop and put their hands in their laps so that you may have their full attention.

CLEANING THE MONITOR

Teach children not to touch the monitor and leave fingerprints. Keep a screen buddy (a stuffed Beanie Baby with a tummy made of chamois to clean the screen) on top of the monitor to use for frequent cleaning. Make slipcovers for your monitors to keep them clean between uses. Put a happy face on one side and a sad face on the other. Use these faces to signal when the computers may be used.

THE MOUSE AND OTHER POINTING DEVICES

KEEPING THE MOUSE CLEAN

Keeping the inside of the mouse clean and lint free is very important so that the mouse moves smoothly. While the computer is off, turn the mouse over and twist open the cover on the bottom. The ball inside the mouse is *not* a superball toy. The mouse won't work without this ball. Clean the inside of the mouse and contact points with alcohol wipes and replace the ball and cover. An optical mouse does not have a ball inside and doesn't need the interior to be cleaned. Consequently, it is much easier to use and requires less care. An optical mouse doesn't require a mouse pad but it is good to use one anyway. Reflective tables can cause the optical mouse to work incorrectly, and the mouse pad defines for young children the area in which to move the mouse.

CHOOSING A MOUSE

The ease with which young children learn how to navigate menus and items on the screen is related to how comfortable they are using the pointing device or mouse attached to the computer. Some mice have many different buttons, balls, wheels, and shapes. These extras tend to confuse young children. For young students, a small, simple mouse is easier to use. Many alternative mice can be purchased to make students more comfortable. If the mouse plugs into the keyboard, look to see whether the mouse may be plugged in on either side to accommodate left- and right-handed students.

DEMONSTRATING USE OF THE MOUSE

Adjust the mouse or pointer settings in the system control panel to select different sensitivity tracking and to vary the size and shape of the pointer. The settings can be changed to allow for a slower time between clicks for a double-click. The mouse cursor on the screen can also be changed to different pictures and sizes. Very young students often have trouble moving the mouse at first, especially when they have moved the mouse to the end of the mouse pad. Have the child place his or her hand on top of yours on the mouse as you lift the mouse, set it down in the middle of the mouse pad, and continue rolling. Sometimes putting the mouse inside a small box lid with one end cut out for the child's wrist and hand helps if they are moving the mouse around too much. This allows the child to move the mouse around inside the confines of the box, which provides a boundary or guide.

DEMONSTRATING SINGLE-CLICK, DOUBLE-CLICK, AND CLICK-AND-DRAG

Macs have only one button or one place to press down and click the mouse. Windows mice have a left- and a right-click button. Point this out to children and teach them to left-click with their pointer finger first. Teach them to right-click only after they have fully mastered left-clicking. Double-clicking and single-clicking can confuse young students. First teach them to single-click and watch the screen for something to happen or for the hourglass that tells them that the computer is thinking and working. Then demonstrate the rhythm of double-clicking by having the child place his or her hand on your hand while you hold the mouse and move your finger in a double-click rhythm.

Clicking-and-dragging is another mouse skill students must learn. To click-and-hold while moving the mouse can be tricky. Have the child place his or her hand on top of your hand on the mouse. Click-and-hold while rolling the mouse, and then release the button. Practice this several times with the child's hand on top of yours so that she or he can get the feel of click-and-drag. Afterward, let the child practice alone.

"MOUSING" WITH A LAPTOP

Most laptops have track pads. Young students usually can maneuver these more easily than adults. The track pad gives the student a defined area of movement, unlike the mouse, which can be moved as far as the cord will allow. Young children have small fingers and hands. Teach them to use their thumb to hold their other fingers back while they use their pointer finger on the track pad. Show children the relationship between the location of their fingertip on the track pad and the cursor on the monitor. If students have trouble clicking and pointing, teach them to use one hand to click on the button and the other to point. This is also helpful when selecting and dragging. Have them use one hand to click-and-hold the button down and a finger on the other hand to drag across the track pad. Track pads are easier to use while sitting at a desk, on the floor, or at other locations where there is no room for a mouse.

Keep the track pad dry. If it becomes moist, *do not* use heat on it. Instead, use air or a fan to dry it. If using laptops, have extra mice available to plug in as an option for those who need them.

USING ALTERNATIVE POINTING DEVICES

Alternatives to the traditional mouse are available to use with all computers. Graphic tablets are an option for pointing and mouse movement. These tablet and pen sets allow students to grip a pointer similar to a pencil and press and draw to maneuver the cursor as if writing on a tablet. The tablets allow children to trace a drawing into the computer, sign their name, or write instead of type. The Graphire2 tablet from Wacom is inexpensive and suitable for use with young children through adults. Touch screens, switches, and voice control software are also available for use with young children or children with special needs. If a student is having trouble adjusting or navigating with the traditional mouse, some investigation is warranted to determine whether a different pointing device would be more appropriate.

PRACTICING WITH SIMPLE SOFTWARE

After demonstrating different techniques for using a mouse, allow children to practice skills to become more comfortable with the mouse. Use software such as the Living Book or Reader Rabbit series to allow children to explore how to navigate and click and control the mouse. Or try the Peter Rabbit site (www. peterrabbit.com). The Living Book series reads a book aloud while allowing students to click-and-drag to see movement, make choices, and hear more sounds. Reader Rabbit software allows children to click-and-drag or respond to simple alphabet letters, colors, numbers, and shapes. Peter Rabbit activities use mouse movement and click-and-drag actions to help Peter Rabbit escape Mr. MacGregor. Other software that allows students to click and select or drag and drop while practicing simple tasks are helpful in reinforcing skills.

Don't try to teach a new computer skill and a content skill at the same time. That is too stressful. Always practice a technology skill while reinforcing a topic or idea that students are familiar and comfortable with.

KEYBOARDS

USING KEYBOARDS WITH YOUNG CHILDREN

Place stickers on important keys to give students a visual clue of what the key is used for. Put a green sticker on the location for turning on the computer and a red sticker on the location for turning off the computer. If a software program uses certain keys for commands, use stickers to indicate these as well.

The ergonomic or split keyboards that are made to help relieve typing fatigue are not appropriate for young children. The split keyboard is hard for children to read and their hands are small and cannot span the full-size keyboard. Most children are not ready to type with correct hand and key positions until their hands have grown and their dexterity develops. Children who have been exposed to piano lessons or other fingering exercises might be ready earlier. As with teaching other skills to young children, watch for and be prepared for the teachable moment. If a student shows a real interest in correct keyboarding, then demonstrate correct fingering and hand positions. Young children can be taught to use two hands, keeping the right hand on the right side of the keyboard and the left hand on the left side of the keyboard; to use all fingers, not just their index fingers; and to become familiar with the location of the keys. Have students find the number keys, the letter keys, the arrow keys, and the Command key on Macintosh computers.

CONSIDERING KEYBOARD ALTERNATIVES

Large print stickers may be placed on the keys to increase the size of the characters for easier reading. Skins may be purchased that cover the keys and replace the uppercase characters with upper- and lowercase characters so that young students can recognize the letter keys easier. Alternative keyboards made for small hands, sometimes with built-in track pads or track balls, may be purchased if using the keyboard is difficult for younger children. Many early childhood programs use the mouse for navigation and the keyboard is unnecessary. Move keyboards out of the way when not in use.

CLEANING KEYBOARDS

Clean keyboards with a vacuum attachment made specifically for keyboards or a mini keyboard vacuum, a can of compressed air, and a damp cloth.

SPEAKERS AND HEADPHONES

EQUIPPING THE CLASSROOM FOR SOUND

Many early childhood software programs require sound. Have at least one set of external speakers so that when demonstrating a skill or sharing a computer program with a group everyone can hear the sound well. When the computers are not being used as a group, use earphones to keep the noise down in the classroom. A dual earphone adapter allows two earphones to be plugged in to one computer at the same time. This is very handy when students are sharing a computer and working together. Use stick-on hooks for earphones to keep the cords from becoming tangled. Place the hooks on the edges of the computer.

CLEANING
EARPHONES

Clean the earphones regularly. In case of lice, put all earphones in ziplock plastic bags and keep them closed tightly for 48 hours. This will delouse them.

DESKTOP, FILES, AND FOLDERS

MANAGING FILES

It is very important that you have a system for saving and finding files on your computer. Your computer's hard drive is like a filing cabinet. Folders are a way to keep everything organized. Create folders on your hard drive in which to put individual files. This is similar to putting pieces of paper in labeled folders in your filing cabinet. Create file names that are short and make sense.

The properties of a file tell you the kind of file it is—whether it is a Word document or an Excel file—and the last date the file was accessed. To find the file properties on a Windows machine, right-click on the file and choose Properties. On a Mac, select the file and then pull down from the File menu to get general information. Use the Search or Find command to search your hard drive for files, using file names, file types, or the date the file was created. Files can be moved from folder to folder or rearranged at any time—just drag and drop. Leave the things on your desktop that you are currently working with. Create shortcuts or aliases for programs and files on the desktop to allow students to access them more easily. Keep all of your teacher files in folders on your hard drive.

OPERATING SYSTEMS

LEARNING ABOUT
OPERATING
SYSTEMS

It is a good idea to learn more about your computer's operating system so that you can use it more efficiently and comfortably. Ask your building or district tech support for a list of workshops or suggestions on how you may learn more. *The Little Mac Book,* written by Robin Williams, is an excellent beginning book on the Mac operating system. The author has written several editions, one for every version of the Mac operating system. Microsoft's educational Web site, **http://microsoft.com/education**, has a database of software tutorials for teachers, staff, and students. The site also offers templates and technology integration lesson plans for the Windows operating system along with Word, Excel, PowerPoint, and FrontPage.

WORKING TOGETHER AND SHARING

SCHEDULING
COMPUTER ACCESS

Young children shouldn't become deeply absorbed and addicted to the computer any more than they should isolate themselves in a corner reading a book for long periods or sit at the art table all day long. Computer use does not have to be an individual activity. Encourage children to work in pairs to explore, collaborate, and help each other. Two young children can easily sit closely together and "share the chair," two bottoms per chair, when working with computers. A computer center with two computers can easily accommodate four or more children.

TIMING
COMPUTER USE

Use an egg timer to measure the amount of time each child controls the mouse or track pad. When the egg timer runs out, the student in control passes the mouse to the next student and turns over the egg timer. Place egg timer near the computer to help control the time on task.

TASK CARDS

Use a task card to introduce the students to the process you would like them to follow at the computer. Screenshots of menus and icons can help students follow step-by-step instructions or provide reminders after verbal instructions have been given. Clock pictures remind students they only have three minutes at the computer. Hang task cards or papers from paper arm holders that are attached to the monitor or put a stick with a clothespin in a can of plaster on top of the monitor and clip the papers onto the clothespin.

ILLUSTRATING
EXPECTATIONS

The following is an example task card for helping a student create a square in a draw program.

STEPS FOR DRAWING A SQUARE

Wash your hands.

Open the draw program.

Draw a square.

Complete the picture in the given time.

Asking for Help

Montessori saw that "children worked better when left to themselves with a minimum of adult interference, for children are not small adults but essentially creatures of a different order, and too much adult interaction upsets their own rhythms of work" (Carinato, et al., 1999, p. 7). Once they are introduced to the computer and are closely supervised in their initial explorations, young students can be left to work alone, after being instructed on how to attempt initial problem solving and how to ask for help when it is needed.

Learning to troubleshoot technical problems is a skill that children need to see modeled and be allowed to explore. It can be very exciting to solve a problem on your own. A lesson using the computer can quickly turn into a series of raised hands and questions that a teacher can't keep up with if the teacher hasn't set the stage for the students to try to figure out problems before asking for help. Teachers can model troubleshooting by asking the questions aloud, talking themselves through, and trying a variety of possible solutions while asking for student input. Contact the building tech support for help when necessary.

SIGNALING FOR HELP

Stack one small green plastic cup on top of one small red plastic cup and set the stack on top of or beside each computer. Have students place the red plastic cup on top to signal to the teacher that they need help. When using laptops, if cups are cumbersome, have students place a red Post-it note on the lid of the computer to signal for help. Students use a cup or Post-it note rather than raising their hands, which allows them to signal quietly and continue working to solve the problem while they wait. This management method can be used throughout the classroom, not just at the computer center.

FOLLOWING A REGULAR PATH

Teachers should not try to help the students in the order that they put up their red cups. They should make a regular path through the room and help students as they come upon them. This allows the teacher to continue to give positive encouragement to all students as well as help those who have asked for help. Create a diagram of the room, draw the regular path you will take on it, and post it on the wall. This allows students to know when their turn will come. If they are confident about the order in which they will be helped, then they will be more comfortable continuing to work to solve their own problems. If a student solves his or her problem without help and is able to flip the green cup back on top before you get there, give the student special praise and a sticker or other reward. When using this system, soon you will have many students flipping their cups from red to green without any teacher help.

STUDENTS HELPING STUDENTS

In the second semester, start a student tech group and add a third cup to the stack. The yellow cup signals "I need help from a student." Students who have been assigned to be tech helpers watch for yellow cups and may leave their computers to try to help another student who has signaled with a yellow cup. If the student can't solve the problem, then the red cup is placed on top to signal for the teacher. This student tech group is another rotating job just like watering plants, turning off the lights, closing the doors, and so forth. Students learn from helping.

TROUBLE JOURNAL

When a technical problem can't be solved by the students or the teacher, put a Post-it note on the computer with a short explanation of the problem for the building technical support. Keep a trouble journal noting the student and computer having the trouble, the software being used when the problem occurred, and the action or error message that was displayed. Also list any troubleshooting that was tried and failed. When tech support solves the problem, add this to your trouble journal. Soon you will have a rich history to look back on that will give teachers and students new strategies for troubleshooting. This trouble journal can also help tech support to see a pattern of problems with a certain computer or software that might lead to a better solution. The trouble journal will also give the teacher a history of student use so that if a particular student shows a pattern of trouble, that student can be given additional help. Reading through the trouble journal with the tech support solutions occasionally with the class will help everyone gain new troubleshooting strategies. In addition, the journals can help staff decide on professional development and inservice topics.

Reference   Carinato, M. E., Cluxton, A. J., McCarrick, A., Motz, M., & O'Connor, M. (1967; reprint 1999). *Montessori matters*. Cincinnati, OH: Sisters of Notre Dame de Namur.

chapter 6

JERI CARROLL AND TONYA WITHERSPOON

Managing Computers in Different Settings

Based on vision, needs, and budget, stakeholders and administrators for each state, district, school, and classroom will have different expectations for students and teachers that require different configurations of computers in the classrooms. The number of computers available for students—only 1 or sets of 5, 15, or 25—is not important; it's what is done at the computer that makes the difference. In this chapter we investigate several scenarios of computer use and provide additional ways the computer can be used with and without peripherals.

One-Computer Classroom

SCENARIO

All the teachers in the building were given a new computer two years ago. Each was connected to a school server, but had no Internet connection. Mr. Mellow, the first-grade teacher, got a new computer along with all the other teachers. He placed it on his desk and used it to write his lesson plans; to keep track of standards taught, assessed, and met for each student; and to design weekly newsletters for parents. Until recently, Mr. M. saw few other ways to use his one computer. That was until a student teacher arrived who had other ideas.

Ms. Wow was assigned to Mr. M. for a semester of student teaching. She spent her first week mostly observing and talking with the children during center time, recess, and lunch. At the end of her first week, she asked Mr. M. if she could use the computer with the children. Being quite skeptical, yet not wanting to thwart her enthusiasm, he consented. After taking inventory of the computer and software available in the school and having chats with her university supervisor over the weekend, Ms. Wow arrived on Monday with a cable, an extra TV her folks had in their basement, and several CDs.

DEMONSTRATIONS AND PRESENTATIONS

One computer is an excellent tool for classroom demonstrations and presentations. It can be hooked to a TV with an inexpensive scan converter box and cable, or a digital projector can be used to project the computer screen onto a large white screen, but the latter can be very expensive. Typically before establishing centers, teachers introduce each center and what is to be done. The centers could by introduced using a single computer screen hooked to a TV or projector. Using a TV screen, teachers can demonstrate software or an Internet site and how it is to be used to the group.

Teachers can create a Kid Pix slideshow or PowerPoint presentation to introduce a unit or activity to students. Teachers can create an All About Me slideshow in Kid Pix, inserting pictures of their home, pets, things they like to eat, things they like to do, and so forth. The slideshow can be shared with the children to introduce themselves. It can be run as a continuous loop on the computer during open house for parents. The slideshow then becomes a model for the students to follow when they create their own All About Me slideshows.

CLASSROOM COMPUTING

Projecting to a TV or other large screen can also allow teachers to use one software CD with the entire class instead of purchasing a lab or site license. Many content software packages are very applicable to a unit or a lesson, but a classroom budget may not allow the purchase of software for an entire lab. However, this software can be used with a group on a single computer with a TV as a monitor. Students can take turns coming up and controlling the mouse as the class gives feedback and interacts. Choose software that encourages critical thinking skills and encourages group interaction and discussion. Internet sites may also be used on one computer to stimulate collaborative group thinking.

INTERACTIVE GROUP COMPUTING

Using an interactive whiteboard with the computer allows the teacher to demonstrate to the group while permitting the students to become more interactive with the software. A computer projector can project the computer screen onto an interactive whiteboard or SMART Board. Instead of using the mouse to click, students can use their hands to touch icons and menus on the whiteboard and click-and-drag to navigate.

DIGITAL RESEARCH OR COMMUNICATION STATION

One computer can be used as the hub of a learning station. A WebQuest (http://webquest.sdsu.edu) can direct a group of students to preselected Web sites that give information and pictures on a topic. Several students can sit around a computer sharing turns controlling the mouse while others take notes and draw pictures of what they see. Students can also communicate their learning by working together to create a Kid Pix slideshow. Working from their prewritten notes, students can take turns choosing the background colors; typing or recording themselves reading their notes; and adding pictures, graphics, and transitions. Students can also get involved in Internet projects by e-mailing another classroom or participating in a group discussion board set up ahead of time and approved by the teacher.

TEACHER PRODUCTIVITY AND COMMUNICATION

Mr. M could enhance and expand his ability to communicate with other teachers, building and district administrators, and parents if the one computer in his classroom was connected to the Internet. Unlike the telephone and postal service, e-mail allows for communication to take place when it is convenient for each person at a split second speed. Parents enjoy connecting with teachers through e-mail. This allows for quick notes and communication to take place without disrupting the classroom or invading personal evening time at home. Teachers are often isolated in their classrooms, having little time to communicate with other teachers and associates. E-mail allows collaboration and communication to happen during a teacher's planning period—whether the recipients have that same time free or not!

Three to Five Computer Classroom

SCENARIO

Ms. Hasnot is an inventive preschool teacher. Her students enjoy an extended free play time each day with multiple centers set up where they have choices of activities and a variety of levels of skills. Colorful pictures and posters adorn the walls. Materials and supplies are labeled with picture word cards. While the other teachers in the elementary building have been allotted money for new computers, she has not. Until last year, two 20-year-old computers on a small table were all she had. But those two computers were in use all day long. During free choice time, the students sat four at the table, two to use the computer and two who watched and talked with their partner as they solved problems. The preschoolers handled the 5' floppies (which were really floppy) with care, and played seemingly archaic games with adroit agility.

This year, Ms. H. received one of the hand-me-down computers from the kindergarten teacher. The children were quite excited when she brought the box into the room. They explored the outside of the box and its contents as Ms. H. took the computer out of the box and set it up in the classroom inside a cupboard. When the cupboard door was closed, no one would know there was a computer in the classroom. When the double doors were opened, the computer miraculously appeared. The keyboard tray pulled out with a small ledge for the mouse. On the inside of one of the doors were vocabulary picture cards with pictures and names of various parts of their computer. On the inside of the other door was a chart of children's names for monitoring the use of the new computer. Ms. H. had been prepared for the students to "fight" over this new computer. But no such problem. Not only was the new computer with its color monitor and CDs in use all day long, so were the two 20-year-old computers.

With the new technology initiatives in the district, Ms. H. will have one connection to the Internet. She has her eye on an electronic whiteboard, a wireless connection, and more hand-me-down computers. Ms. H. definitely does not see herself as a "has not."

LEARNING STATIONS

Three to five computers in the classroom can be used in many of the same ways as a single computer. Teachers can use the computers for productivity, presentation, and demonstration. Teachers and students who have a learning station with multiple computers will be able to produce more in less time than those with only one computer because of the greater access additional computers allow.

Computer stations for young children should be developed to fit their needs—physical, cognitive, and social. According to Angie Dorrell (2002), "The American Academy of Pediatrics recently highlighted a study that supports the importance of adjustable workstations for young children. Studies found that poor posture, primarily due to the monitor and keyboard or mouse being too high, is associated with neck, shoulder, back, arm, and hand discomfort." Dorrell (2002) further states, "All chairs in the computer learning center should have appropriate back support and fit under the computer table properly. In addition, the children's feet should be flat on the ground when sitting in the chair and their eyes should be level with the monitor."

True integration occurs when the three to five computers in the classroom become an extension of the curriculum and the tools already available in the classroom. Davis and Shade (1994) point out that "without proper integration of computers into the curriculum, the benefits of technology to foster children's learning cannot be fully achieved, regardless of the creative potential of any software used." Three to five computers can be used as learning stations throughout the day. The computers can be used as a single station for one center, separated into a couple of different stations with multiple activities happening, or used as an open station for students to work on or produce at as time allows.

Correct positioning of the computers is a factor in successful integration. According to Dorrell (2002), "The computer table should be placed against a wall with direct access to a power source. The computer center should also be safely away from any water source (such as the sand and water table), magnets (even small ones typically found in the science center), and windows that might cause a glare on the computer screen."

Just as they would rotate through any learning centers, students can rotate to the computers, working on projects, researching and gathering information on the Internet, and communicating with others. Using a rotation chart and an egg timer is a good way to monitor the time spent in the learning station so that all students can have a turn.

Computer Lab

SCENARIO

Having no computers in the classroom, but a nicely equipped and wired computer lab, Ms. NoNonsense was somewhat dismayed when all teachers were assigned two periods in the lab each week. It wasn't enough that she felt compelled and was required to test the students frequently to monitor progress toward content standards, but now there were technology standards and the computer lab, too. And the teachers were required to go to the lab with the students. Just what she needed—another interruption in her already hectic day.

During the first couple of sessions in the lab, Ms. NoNonsense took along paperwork to do while the computer teacher taught her children how to use the computers—turn them on, turn them off, use the mouse, insert the CD, share the chair. She perked up her ears when she heard lots of chatting, chuckling, and numerous boings, bongs, sirens, and whistles. She shook her head and went back to grading.

The computer teacher asked Ms. NoNonsense what they were studying in class. She told her they were studying about community helpers, wondering what that had to do with anything. When she arrived with her students at the end of the week, she knew. The monitors in the room were brightly lit up with firetrucks, fireboats, police uniforms, stop lights, safety signs, a picture of the city post office, and a rescue helicopter. Where had all this come from in so short a time? Her eyes were as big as the children's. Put those papers aside. Grab a seat. Have some fun. This was no nonsense.

FOCUS OF COMPUTER LABS

Usually computer labs in elementary schools are geared for grades K–5, which means the chairs are too big, the monitors are set to traditional settings, and the walls are decorated with materials designed for older children. Scheduling the classrooms of young children into the lab in clumps rather than interspersing them throughout the day allows the computer teacher to make the necessary modifications in the technology and specifications for young children. However, the chairs are still too big and the other materials in the room often inappropriate. Take along charts and posters of the critical elements of the units when you go to make it more familiar for the children.

CLASSROOM AND COMPUTER TEACHERS WORKING TOGETHER

Some of the best integration of technology into the classroom takes place when the classroom teacher and computer teacher work together. In some instances, when computers are in the classroom, the computer teacher can teach the software productivity packages while the students are in the lab. The classroom teacher then has the students use the software for projects in the classroom. When there is no computer in the classroom, the teacher can share the content and expectations with the computer teacher, who can match the software to the content and tasks.

LEARNING AND TEACHING EACH OTHER

In the above scenario, the computer teacher was not at all threatened by the classroom teacher. She did not see her job as that of a teacher in the computer lab who isolates computing skills from classroom experiences. Rather, she saw the need to connect the curriculum and the technology. She also saw one part of her job to be the education of the classroom teacher, showing her what could be done with various pieces of technology in the education of young children. Both adults are learning from and teaching each other.

Wireless Mobile Classroom

SCENARIO

Ms. B., a first-grade teacher only five years from retirement, had used computers for years, urged on by the parent of one of the boys in her classroom years ago. The school had had a computer lab, but that year, each teacher had received a brand new computer and a software bundle. Although Ms. B. had gladly had her students use the lab, and although she knew she wanted to use the computer, she was unsure how to use the new computer and software. She asked the parent volunteer for her help. Little did she know what was in store for her. The parent took the software home and, after exploring it with her four boys (ages 4–8), agreed with Ms. B. that the software was inappropriate for first graders. She loaded the boys in the car, went shopping, and bought some software that looked interesting. They took it home and tried it out. Living Books, Kidspiration, and The Amazing Writing Machine were all a success.

Last year, the same parent volunteer returned to the classroom with six wireless computers and a network hub to see how wireless computers might be used in a classroom. Ms. B. began to explain that these computers were just like the other computers except that they had no wires. One of the 6-year-olds raised his hand and said, "Ms. B., those are called laptops."

During the afternoon, children were working on beginning reading and phonics skills. A variety of centers were set up around the room. At the easel, children painted pictures and wrote the words to label them. At the writing center, children used colored markers to write words that were of a certain color. At the classroom computer center, each child was given one letter, blend, or diagraph and was to draw and label pictures that started with that letter on one Kid Pix slide. More advanced students used The Amazing Writing Machine to write stories, which they could change to rebus stories at the click of a button. At the art center, students made clay letters and words, wrote letters and words in salt trays, traced letters, and cut out Play-Doh letters with cookie cutters. The "ABC" song or "ABC Rock" sprang up spontaneously several times throughout the afternoon.

*At two round tables sat the wireless computers, three to a table, each table set for six. At one of the tables the students worked with Kidspiration Alphabet Examples, selecting a letter of the alphabet and then moving the mouse pointer over pictures, looking at the printed word, and deciding whether it started with the assigned alphabet letter. The other table had Little Explorers Picture Dictionary (available online at **www.enchantedlearning.com/Dictionary.html***) so students could see pictures, words, and definitions—a resource they could use for designing their own picture dictionary slideshows at the computer station using Kid Pix.*

This year, Ms. B.'s classroom was chosen as a demonstration classroom to receive a wireless mobile lab of 15 student computers and one teacher computer, a network hub, a projection unit, and a color printer. Now the class is both wired and wireless.

WORKING IN THE MOBILE AND WIRELESS CLASSROOM

Almost anything can be done in the wireless, fully equipped classroom, and all the computers can stay the way you want them. All the other learning materials are right there at your fingertips. Everything that can be done in the one-computer classroom can be done in the wireless, fully equipped classroom. Everything that can be done in the three to five computer classroom and in the computer lab can be done in the regular classroom setting. All of the technology is but an extension of paper, pencil, crayons, chalkboards, chalk, books, encyclopedias, dictionaries, television, bulletin boards, and planners.

What makes the wireless mobile classroom even more exciting is that it goes with you anywhere you want to go. Pack five of the computers in a rolling suitcase and take them on a field trip. Put five in a backpack and take them to the library to do some traditional research with encyclopedias and other reference books. Go outside to draw pictures of the school and playground, homes, and yards in the neighborhood. Explore the possibilities.

References

Davis, B. C., & Shade, D. D. (1994). *Integrate, don't isolate! Computers in the early childhood curriculum* [Online]. Available: www.ed.gov/databases/ERIC_Digests/ed376991.html

Dorrell, A. (2002). *Equipping the computer learning center* [Online]. Available: www.earlychildhood.com/Articles/index.cfm?FuseAction=Article&A=183

chapter 7

TONYA WITHERSPOON AND JERI CARROLL

Selecting Software and Peripherals

Many times when teachers enter a classroom, computers, peripherals, and software are already available. When that's the case, the teachers may have some say in any additional pieces that can be purchased. Likewise, if no technology is available in the early childhood classroom, teachers may help select hardware, software, and peripherals. Typically one might think to purchase the hardware first, but with young children, the first selection should center on the software that is considered to be most appropriate for the children (Thouvenelle, 2002). Because there are so many peripherals appropriate for extending technology experiences for young children, peripherals should be selected after the software, making choosing the hardware to support the peripherals the last decision. This chapter will provide guidance in selecting software and peripherals.

Selecting Software for Early Childhood Classrooms

According to the National Association for the Education of Young Children (NAEYC; 1996), "Developmentally appropriate software offers opportunities for collaborative play, learning, and creation." Teachers naturally want to take advantage of the educational possibilities that this software provides. Currently, however, there is an explosion of software titles for young children on the market, making selection difficult. The good news, according to Diane Kendall (2002), author of *Creating a Classroom Software Library,* is that coming up with the right titles for your classroom software collection isn't all that different from picking out good books for your library.

Susan Haugland (2000), author of *Computers in the Early Childhood Classroom,* cautions that while many early learning software titles are available, and appropriate for both school and home, some are better for young children than others. As with selecting books, workbooks, board games, and educational toys, teachers must consider many factors when choosing software for the classroom, such as the following:

- Multiple skill levels
- Multiple means of communication (visual and auditory): graphics, text, color, speaking, sounds, music, animation
- Hypermedia (linking to other resources)
- Clicking and moving the mouse
- Ease of use
- Navigation

- Multiple and complementary subject areas
- Skill reinforcement (but beware of too much emphasis on skill and drill software)

SOFTWARE REVIEWS

Before purchasing software for the classroom, you may want to read reviews to help you make your selections. Several software review resources are available online. Some reviews are specific to young children:

Kids Click: www.kidsclick.com/schools.htm
SuperKids Educational Software Review:
    www.superkids.com/aWeb/pages/reviews/subjects.shtml
Kids Domain Software Reviews for Ages 2–5:
    www.kidsdomain.com/review/kdr/_age2to5-index.html

FREE SOFTWARE DOWNLOADS

Some software suitable for the early childhood classroom can be downloaded for free from the Internet:

Edmark: www.riverdeep.net/products/downloads/free_downloads.jhtml
Kids Domain: www.kidsdomain.com/down/index.html
Inclusive Technology: www.inclusive.co.uk/downloads/downloads.shtml
Scribbles: www.scribbleskidsart.com/generic.html?pid=105

INTRODUCING STUDENTS TO SOFTWARE

The Montessori approach to introducing new activities is appropriate to use with software. This approach begins with giving students demonstrations of what they can expect, followed by exploration time. Montessori saw that "children worked better when left to themselves with a minimum of adult interference, for children are not small adults but essentially creatures of a different order, and too much adult interaction upset their own rhythms of work" (Carinato, Cluxton, McCarrick, Motz, & O'Connor, 1999, p. 7). Students do initially need to be taught how to use and respect the software (along with disks, Zip disks, CDs, and the Internet), and also require assistance in systematically exploring and using it.

For each piece of software, give a simple group demonstration with the image projected large so that all can see. An electronic whiteboard or projection through the television works well. Following the demonstration, monitor the children's use to make sure they are on their way. After providing a time of independent exploration, avoid having a child interact with the computer only—use the computer as a collaborative tool for students to share and discuss ideas and to tackle problems together. Remain available, but encourage students in their own analysis of problems before asking for help. Walking a regular path around the computers assures students that you are there and allows you to offer guidance if needed, but also fosters independence, as it lets children decide when to ask for help.

Many software programs have many different levels of menus and tools. In the early childhood classroom it is best to introduce the tools and menus a few at a time. Always teach the tools along with a working project. Giving them free exploration without some direction does not show the children how to be productive with the tools. After they have been shown several tools and how they work, provide a free day to allow them to explore other ways the tools might be used.

INTRODUCING SOFTWARE IN STEPS (EXAMPLE USING KID PIX)

1. Open Kid Pix and start a new project.
2. Select two tools to use (such as draw and fill).
3. Demonstrate one.
4. Demonstrate the other.
5. Show how to save to a disk or hard drive.
6. Allow some time for children to learn to use the tools on their own.
7. Repeat the sequence above using two different tools each time, such as
   - Adding text and voiceover
   - Checking spelling and adding motion

For example, in the **Health and Nutrition** unit (see the **Food** theme) students are asked to create a healthy meal. If time allows and students want to practice more, they could create a healthy breakfast, lunch, and dinner. Using Kid Pix, the instructions might be to use the circle tool to draw a plate and the stamp tool to stamp a healthy meal on the plate. Other tools could be used to complete this lesson, but assigning students to use specific tools allows them to more thoroughly explore how those tools are used. If the class is using many different tools it is also harder to give instructions and share ideas. Students can communicate and share ideas more easily if they are limited to just a couple of tools at a time.

Encourage students to explore all aspects of the tools they are assigned. For example, the circle created by the circle tool can be filled with different colors and patterns. When the shift key is held down while using the circle tool, a perfect circle is created. The stamp can be changed by choosing Goodies and picking a stamp set. The stamp's colors and shapes can also be changed. Each stamp can be stamped three different sizes by holding down different keys while stamping.

SOFTWARE TYPES

Several ways to use various types of software were outlined in the resource units (section 2). In this chapter, we provide an introduction to these tools. Spreadsheets and graphing software provide ways to analyze and present numbers and information. Word processing programs offer a means to communicate with others. Text to voice and voice to text software expand communication options. Graphics software allows picture storytelling for prewriters and story embellishment for more experienced writers. The Internet provides a way to research topics for new information and reinforce skills. With the addition of communications software, the Internet allows written, verbal, and visual communication without geographical constraints. Students can build skills with various subjects using content software.

SPREADSHEETS AND GRAPHS

A children's graphing program can help students make generalizations about data and observe similarities and differences. Students can compare information about physical characteristics, family size, favorite things, types of vehicles, kinds of trees, food consumed, and so forth. An electronic graphing program provides the opportunity to record and display the data quickly and to translate the data into various graphical forms including pie charts and bar graphs.

Students can be introduced to spreadsheets by first using an electronic graphing program to record and experiment with data. The graphical display of data gives concrete meaning to numbers. Spreadsheets allow students to quickly change variables and engage in prediction and comparison. Children love to see their ideas recorded and contributing to an overall discussion. Two examples of graphing and data analysis software designed for young children are The Graph Club, by Tom Snyder Productions, and Tabletop Jr., by Broderbund.

TEACHERS USING SPREADSHEETS AND GRAPHS

Teachers can use spreadsheets and graphs in many ways for themselves, including the following:

- Recording attendance and grades
- Creating benchmark checklists
- Monitoring the teaching of standards
- Monitoring the assessment of standards
- Monitoring student accomplishment of standards
- Creating a sortable table of software, books, themes, lessons, and so forth

STUDENTS USING SPREADSHEETS AND GRAPHS

Young children can use spreadsheets and graphs in many ways, too, such as the following:

- Graphically representing numbers
- Sorting and categorizing information
- Comparing numbers, weights, temperatures, and so on
- One-to-one matching
- Determining more than and less than, greater than and fewer than

WORD PROCESSING

Word processing can be used with young children in many effective ways. Children can write alphabet letters, words, sentences, and stories. Pictures can be embedded in a document to act as an inspiration for creative writing. As their skills increase, children can create stories and add clip art, graphics, and photos. Adding special fonts such as D'Nelian can be a great tool for the early childhood educator. The fonts can be changed to meet the school or district practices. After installing these fonts, teachers can print sentence strips, name strips, and other materials in a font that young children can read more easily.

Several word processing software packages are designed especially for young children: Kid Pix, by Broderbund (English/Spanish); The Amazing Writing Machine, by Broderbund; Storybook Weaver Deluxe, by Riverdeep (English/Spanish); Easy Book Deluxe, by Sunburst; and Clicker 4, by Crick Software. Kidspiration, by Inspiration Software, Inc., is a prewriting, brainstorming, and categorizing piece of software closely related to the language arts.

TEACHERS USING WORD PROCESSING

Teachers can use word processing in a variety of ways:

- Writing newsletters (with columns)
- Designing worksheets
- Making flashcards
- Creating board games
- Creating bulletin board headers and wall charts
- Limiting Internet usage with linked instructional stories (iStoryQuests)
- Creating scrapbooks
- Creating young children (baby) books as an approach to documenting assessment
- Writing sentence strips for story sequences

STUDENTS USING WORD PROCESSING

The ways students can use word processing seem limitless. Consider these and think of others:

- Creating invented spelling
- Writing words
- Writing words and having them read back to the child
- Making a scrapbook
- Creating digital portfolios
- Writing and illustrating stories
- Listing steps in a process
- Creating ABC books
- Creating picture dictionaries

- Writing procedures
- Exploring creative writing
- Making books

TEXT TO VOICE

Several early childhood word processing programs have a text-to-voice feature. This feature allows the computer to read back what the child has typed. Clicker 4 software allows children to write sentences by choosing pictures or words from teacher-selected grids. Children click on the pictures and words to hear them spoken. After they select the words and create a sentence, the sentence can be read back to them. Amazing Writing Machine and Storybook Weaver help students create books that can be printed in several different formats. Children feel a sense of accomplishment when their writing is published in a format similar to the books they regularly read.

VOICE TO TEXT

Software is also available that changes spoken words into text. This software is fairly expensive and must be "trained" to recognize individual voices. Although it is not a good choice for routine classroom activities it can be very beneficial for a student with special needs. In the future, voice-to-text software will become more user-friendly, reliable, and affordable for the classroom.

DRAWING SOFTWARE

For emerging readers, drawing software is used to record their thinking. They can use tools in the software to reinforce patterning, produce graphic effects, draw pictures, and create slideshows. Several units in this book use Kid Pix to create slideshows to display student ideas. For example, students create a Kid Pix illustration of what a parent or relative does for work and a slide of their favorite job. In this way, children explore the Kid Pix tools in the context of demonstrating their understanding of employment. Envisioning themselves in the workplace helps young children conceptualize their place in the world. The class slideshow is a way to share their ideas and see the ideas of others. Students love to replay the slideshow at the computer center as well as share it with parents and friends at open house.

GRAPHICS

Graphics programs for children come in three varieties: paint and draw (discussed previously), digital photography, and clip art and multimedia. Separate graphics programs can be used to create and edit graphics, but many productivity software titles also have built-in graphics tools. Photoshop LE and GraphicConverter are digital photo-editing and drawing programs. Microsoft Word, Excel, and PowerPoint all have built-in graphic tools.

To effectively use or manipulate graphics it is necessary to learn how to crop, resize, add text or effects, and insert the item into a word processing document or a slideshow.

GraphicConverter is a shareware graphic conversion program for the Mac that can be downloaded from the Web (**http://lemkesoft.com/gcdownload_us.html**). With it, you can easily create an automated slideshow. Additional features allow captions, timed sequencing of the pictures, looping of the photos, and more.

TEACHERS USING GRAPHICS

Regardless of the graphics program selected, teachers can use graphics in many ways:

- Taking screenshots to make task cards
- Creating labels for classroom places and supplies
- Taking photos in the classroom to document skills
- Creating bulletin boards
- Documenting field trips
- Creating digital or virtual field trips
- Designing programs for performances
- Making vocabulary cards
- Creating song and poem posters
- Editing or enhancing photos as a basis for a common experience about which to talk and write

STUDENTS USING GRAPHICS

Again, regardless of the graphics program selected, children can use graphics in many ways. Children can create the following items with a graphics program:

- ABC books
- Number books
- Rebus stories
- Illustrated stories
- Magnets for gifts
- Labels for supplies
- Folding books
- Thank you cards
- Invitations
- Postcards
- Cookbooks
- Iron-on pictures
- Slideshows

INTERNET SOFTWARE

You might be wondering why the Internet is listed in the software section. It doesn't seem like it is software. It isn't, but you do need software to use the Internet. The Internet is a worldwide network of connected computers. To connect to the Internet you must have a computer, an Internet service provider (a company that provides a telephone line or cable to connect), and, initially, one piece of software—a browser such as Internet Explorer or Netscape Navigator.

It is important to keep your browser updated regularly. The numbers after the name of your browser tells you which version it is. You can download free updates to your browser from the Internet. These updates are important for the computer to be able to view and receive up-to-date information on the Web.

In addition to the browser, a variety of software programs enhance the usefulness of the Web. These packages allow Web browsers to display graphics, movies, and other multimedia. The following sections discuss software you may want to become familiar with to get the most out of your use of the Internet.

PLUG-INS   As sound, graphics, animation, and video have improved, interactivity has greatly increased, making the Internet an exciting and motivating tool for young children. To access these features and use the Internet in an early childhood classroom, several additional pieces of software, called plug-ins, must be downloaded. Be aware that your school is probably using software to filter out inappropriate Web sites. This software may not allow you to download the plug-ins yourself. You may be required to have your technology administrator download them for you.

If you are downloading a plug-in yourself, be sure to choose the one most appropriate for your operating system. To find out what your operating system is, on a Macintosh click on the desktop, then click on the apple and pull down to About This Computer. The system number is listed under "version." On a Windows machine, go to the Control Panel and select System. Complete the process by downloading the file that matches your operating system to your desktop and following the installation instructions. Some of the most popular plug-ins to download free include:

Macromedia Shockwave Player:
    www.macromedia.com/software/shockwaveplayer/
Macromedia Flash Player: www.macromedia.com/software/flashplayer/
Adobe Acrobat Reader: www.adobe.com/products/acrobat/readstep2.html
Apple QuickTime: www.apple.com/quicktime/download/
RealPlayer by RealNetworks:
    http://home.netscape.com/plugins/get_real.html?cp=pi1

CONNECTION   Another consideration when using the Internet with young children is the speed of
SPEED   the Internet connection. The sites that have sound, motion, and interactivity require higher connection speeds. It is a good idea to test the adequacy of the speed of the connection by accessing the desired sites from the computers you will be using with

children. Keep in mind that if the entire class clicks on the same site at the same time, the situation is similar to having the whole class push through a door at once instead of lining up and walking in order. To avoid this congestion, choose several Internet sites and stagger the site use by giving different groups of children different sites to access or a different order for clicking on things within the site. Additionally, having several sites in mind is a good idea in case one of the sites is down or you have trouble connecting.

If your connection speed is slow, an alternative way to share an Internet site with the class is to use a software program to save or download the site to your hard drive. This folder can then be transferred to a CD or saved on a Zip disk and transferred to all of the computers you will have children using. WebWhacker EE, by Blue Squirrel, is a popular software title that will complete this function.

Remember, when you download sites, that all information published on the Web is protected by copyright. To use it in your class as a demonstration or with students is considered fair use in most cases. A safe way to make sure you can use it is to write to the author for permission. The Four Factor Fair Use Test provides guidelines for using copyrighted information (**www.utsystem.edu/ogc/intellectualproperty/ copypol2.htm#test**). It can help you determine fair use of material protected by copyright. The test asks:

- What is the character of the use? (Nonprofit through commercial)

- What is the nature of the work to be used?

- How much of the work will you use? (Small amount to more than a small amount)

- What effect would this use have on the market for the original or for permissions if the use were widespread? (Little to infringing on sales and/or royalties)

INTERNET USE IN THE CLASSROOM Web sites are used extensively in this book's units to provide additional information and to illustrate places that cannot realistically be visited. In the **Food** theme, students obtain grocery price information. In the **Communities** theme, they find and use maps. For some units they take a virtual tour. For example, the virtual tour of the International Space Station provides students with access to information and experiences they cannot obtain locally. Some units provide online games that reinforce content or skills.

Sometimes finding Web sites that are appropriate for young children can be difficult. Some general sites to use when looking for Internet support for instruction are:

Ben's Guide to U.S. Government for Kids: **http://bensguide.gpo.gov/**
Canadian Kids Page: **www.canadiankids.net/ck/default.jsp**
Create a Graph: **http://nces.ed.gov/nceskids/graphing/**
Little Explorers Picture Dictionary (offered in several languages—English, German, French, Italian, Japanese, Portuguese, and Spanish): **www.enchantedlearning.com/Dictionary.html**
Mr. Rogers' Neighborhood: **http://pbskids.org/rogers/**

Zelo Nursery Rhymes: www.zelo.com/family/nursery/index.asp
PBS Kids: http://pbskids.org
Peter Rabbit: www.peterrabbit.com
Sesame Workshop (Sesame Street): www.sesameworkshop.org
Seussville: www.seussville.com/seussville/
NIEHS Kids' Pages (songs): www.niehs.nih.gov/kids/musicchild.htm

INTERNET2

A new high-speed Internet network has emerged called Internet2, whose origins are similar to the Internet's. While the Internet first began with government and educational institutions, Internet2 is a collection of government, education, and industry entities working together to test the use of extremely high-speed connections and applications that might take advantage of the improved velocity. Internet2 has already been very successful as a communications line, facilitating connections that would, for example, allow a quartet to play together from four different locations around the world, with the resulting music sounding as if the listener were in a concert hall.

COMMUNICATION SOFTWARE

Computer technology has granted us the power to communicate in different and exciting ways. E-mail allows us to write when and where it is convenient and to quickly receive a response from across the world. Communication software is rapidly advancing to include graphics, sound, and video. For example, children can send Grandma and Grandpa, who live across the country, a video thank-you note just minutes after opening a birthday present.

This type of communication is opening up the world to early learners. They can see, hear, and interact with people and places that they might never have been introduced to without technology. Busy teachers can communicate with others to learn policies, get lesson ideas, and exchange information during the school day without interrupting their class. With young children, all online communication should be closely monitored. Legal and ethical issues surrounding safe use of online communication with young children are discussed in chapter 9.

A required piece of software is an e-mail program. Some e-mail can be delivered and received through your Internet browser. This is called Web mail. Some popular Web mail programs that are presently free are MSN Hotmail and Yahoo Mail. Some Internet service providers include the feature of accessing e-mail through your browser, while others require that you use an additional piece of software to write and receive your e-mail. Popular e-mail software includes Eudora, Entourage, Outlook, Outlook Express, and Lotus Notes.

Another types of communication software is courseware, such as Web CT or Blackboard, that delivers online courses and provides communication and collaboration spaces. Additionally, many different types of Web cams and software are available to use for videoconferencing. Some popular ones are NetMeeting, iVisit, and CU SeeMe.

CONTENT SOFTWARE

Several types of productivity software such as those listed previously are discussed in the resource units (section 2). Content software is also discussed in the units, and several products are listed in the following sections.

LANGUAGE ARTS AND READING

Several excellent products are available for reading and the language arts. Reader Rabbit software, by Learning Company (**www.readerrabbit.com/products/cdromproducts.asp**), combines interactive stories and games while allowing children to learn and get feedback. Living Books, by Broderbund (**www.livingbooks.com**), are popular and classic stories written by leading authors. They have been created for the computer to read aloud with sounds, animation, and interactivity. Following are several titles in the Living Books series:

Arthur's Birthday (English, Spanish), Marc Brown
Arthur's Teacher Trouble (English, Spanish), Marc Brown
D.W. the Picky Eater, Marc Brown
Just Me and My Mom, Mercer Mayer
Just Me and My Dad, Mercer Mayer
Just Grandma and Me (English, German, French, Spanish), Mercer Mayer
Just Me and My Grandpa, Mercer Mayer

MATH

The Graph Club, Tom Snyder Productions
Roamer Robot, TerrapinLogo
Tabletop Jr., Broderbund
TimeLiner, Tom Snyder Productions

SCIENCE

Bill Nye the Science Guy, Pacific Interactive
Dry Cereal, KidsClick Software
Elmo's Deep Sea Adventure, Mattel Interactive
Falling in a Black Hole, The Space Place
Magic School Bus, Microsoft/Scholastic
My Amazing Human Body, DK Interactive Learning
Sammy's Science House, Edmark
Space Academy GX, Edmark

SOCIAL STUDIES

Berenstain Bears Collection, Jan and Stan Berenstain (*Get in a Fight* & *In the Dark*; English, Spanish), Living Books
Choices, Choices: Kids and the Environment, Tom Snyder Productions
Choices, Choices: On the Playground, Tom Snyder Productions
A Community at Work, Clearvue/eau
Community Construction Kit, Tom Snyder Productions
Diorama Designer, Tom Snyder Productions
Economics in Our Age: Factors of Production and Economic Systems, Clearvue/eau

Economics in Our Age: Goods and Services, Clearvue/eau
Economics in Our Age: Supply and Demand, Clearvue/eau
Neighborhood Map Machine, Tom Snyder Productions
Space Academy GX, Edmark
Space: A Visual History of Manned Spaceflight, Sumeria
This Is Your Government: Good Citizen, Clearvue/eau
Thomas and Friends, Trouble on the Tracks, Infogrames
Travel the World with Timmy, Edmark

Selecting Peripherals for Early Childhood Classrooms

Many technology peripherals can be added to the classroom whether there is one computer for the entire classroom or one computer for each child in the class. The peripherals extend the use of technology into areas where the computer alone cannot go. The addition of each new peripheral multiplies the possibilities for teacher and student use.

In classrooms of young children, however, keep in mind that the addition of an abundance of materials, whether they be traditional materials or technology-related materials, can cause visual overload and academic fatigue. If they are a part of the classroom to begin with, students learn to accept them just as they would any other learning materials. If they are added to an existing environment, the old is often temporarily pushed aside for the new. Too many new materials introduced in too short a time is like eating too many chocolate cookies at once.

PRINTERS

Color inkjet printers can not only print your classroom documents and newsletters but can also print on many specialty papers. Several special papers made for printers are available, such as photo paper, greeting cards or card stock, sticker paper, T-shirt iron-ons, shrink art paper, fabric, bumper stickers, body tattoos, calendar kits, and much more. With these specialty papers and a color inkjet printer you can turn your computer into a printing shop.

GRAPHICS TECHNOLOGIES

DIGITAL CAMERA OR SCANNER

Digital cameras can be used to take pictures of students in action, student work, classroom displays, field trips, classroom procedures, playground activity, and so forth. Scanners can be used to scan students' work or scan photos taken with a 35mm camera. The pictures can be presented in a slideshow to the class or added to newsletters or Web pages and shared with the school, family, and friends.

WEB CAM

A Web cam is a digital camera that is connected to the computer by a cable. It can be used to take still photos, movies, or time-lapse photos. It can also be set up as an Internet Web cam that delivers live images or movies over the Internet. The pictures and movies are automatically stored on the computer the Web cam is hooked to. Being connected to the computer allows a little more freedom in the number of pictures or movies recorded because the storage capacity of a hard drive is much bigger than the memory cards on a digital camera. It does, however, confine you to taking pictures in your classroom or within reach of the Web cam's cable. A Web cam can be hooked to a laptop for more portability. Some Web cams can be separated from their stand and cord and used with a memory card as a portable digital camera.

An example of how a Web cam can be used in the classroom is to set it up to take pictures ever five minutes while a butterfly is coming out of its chrysalis. This allows the students to watch the process over and over again or to record the butterfly during the night or weekend when students are not in class and would miss this amazing event.

Other possibilities for a Web cam:

- Taking pictures of what your hamster does at night while you're away from the classroom
- Taking a time-lapse movie of the sun coming up or setting outside your classroom window
- Taking pictures of the cars going through the parking lot or along the street and then watching the movie to count the types, colors, numbers, and so on
- Taking step-by-step pictures of any science experiment or demonstration to refer to later
- Setting up your Web cam as an Internet Web cam, allowing parents or others to log on and see experiments or other things happening in your classroom live
- Videoconferencing with other classrooms, teachers, or parents

TEXT READING

Adding a pen scanner and text-reading software to the classroom may help beginning readers as well as those with special needs. Swiping a pen scanner across the letters of a book, a magazine, or a child's writing sample conveniently digitizes the text or handwriting and places the information into a digital text file. The text can then be uploaded to a desktop, laptop, or PDA by synching with a connecting cord or beaming to an infrared receiver. After the text is transferred to a computer, screen-reading software can be used to read the story or information aloud to the students.

PROJECTION

Projection equipment includes TV scan converters, data projectors, and interactive whiteboards or SMART Boards. Projecting the computer screen onto a larger surface so that the entire class can see and share allows teachers to:

- Demonstrate and present topics incorporating Internet resources or content software

- Demonstrate lessons to a whole group before students work in centers or the lab
- Share slideshows and presentations with the entire school or parents at a program
- Share one CD or software package with a group
- Introduce a topic or skill and work as a group to collaborate and discuss dynamically
- Share a 3-D object with a large group using the optional camera arm of a projector

PERSONAL DIGITAL ASSISTANTS

Personal digital assistants (PDAs) such as Palm Pilots and Handsprings are small handheld computers that are inexpensive and portable. Additional keyboards, cameras, voice recorders, and motion, temperature, and other sensors and probes can be purchased. Files can be transferred and shared easily be "beaming" or transferring the file using an infrared port similar to the one on a TV remote control. Files can also be synchronized with or uploaded to your desktop or laptop computer and used in your favorite word processing or spreadsheet program. Young children adapt to these quickly. The PDA fits in their hand very easily; most children are very well-acquainted with Game Boys and other small digital game devices, so the PDA and its small screen and buttons are very familiar.

Many educational software companies are creating a PDA version of their software that allows use of the software on the handheld or on a desktop or laptop, and can synchronize the information between the PDA and the desktop or laptop, allowing for great mobility. Teachers can grade papers in their laps sitting in front of the TV, record the grade in their handheld, and synch the next morning with their classroom computer grading program. Students can take a PDA on a field trip, taking pictures and recording their voice as they make observations, and then synch with the classroom computer so that the pictures and voice recordings can be inserted into a Kid Pix slideshow to share with the class.

TEACHERS USING PDAS

Teachers can use PDAs in the following ways:

- Portable grade and attendance books
- Digital check-sheets for standards taught and assessed
- Portable note-taking devices
- Voice recorders
- Cameras to document classroom activities for assessment
- Tools for easily transferring information and data between teachers

STUDENTS USING PDAS

Students can use PDAs for the following purposes:

- Personal flashcards with sound and graphics
- Timers
- Portable metronomes
- Portable talking books
- Devices for recording information by voice on a field trip or excursion
- Devices for recording information with photos on a field trip or excursion
- Tools for recording data using sensors

EXTERNAL STORAGE

CD BURNER

As you and your students create slideshows, make presentations, take photos, and so forth, your hard drive space will begin to run out and you will want an easy way to save and store files, and to share them with parents and others. A CD burner allows you to save files to a CD, which can then be archived or shared with any other computer that has a CD drive. You will need blank CD-R (CD-Recordable) or CD-RW (CD-Rewritable) discs to record on. Blank CD-Rs and CD-RWs can be purchased fairly inexpensively in small or large quantities. Some CD-Rs and CD-RWs come with their own jewel cases and labels, while others can be purchased separately, allowing you to choose the kind of case and label you would like. Students can design and print labels and jewel case covers to go with their CDs. Student presentations can be placed in the library for other students to check out and view or sent home with students to share with parents on home computers. This is also an excellent way to begin a student portfolio.

OTHER EXTERNAL STORAGE DEVICES

An external hard drive, Zip drive, PCI card, or pen-shaped drive can be useful to store, archive, and share files with others. External hard drives can be connected, disconnected, and moved to other computers, allowing large video or graphic files to be shared without taking up any data transfer time. Zip drives use Zip disks that hold 100 to 250 megabytes of data at a time. A pen drive hooks up to a computer through its USB port, allowing files to easily be shared and taken back and forth from school to home by teachers or students.

Additional high volume external drives are available that use firewire technology. This connection, similar in appearance to a USB connection and often used to download video from a digital camera, does not require a power cable. It is particularly usable with very young children to avoid multiple cable connections.

ROAMER ROBOTS

A Roamer Robot is a moving, turning microcomputer that students can program with Logo commands. Students working in groups can learn about patterns, measurements, predictions, and logic using Roamer. Lesson ideas can be found in the On the Go theme.

DIGITAL MICROSCOPES

A digital microscope takes the image you would see in a standard microscope and sends it to the computer monitor. Intel makes an inexpensive microscope that works well. For very young children, looking at a computer screen is much easier than trying to peer through a conventional microscope viewfinder. A digital microscope also allows teachers to share one microscope image with the entire class.

References

Carinato, M. E., Cluxton, A. J., McCarrick, A., Motz, M., & O'Connor, M. (1967; reprint 1999). *Montessori matters.* Cincinnati, OH: Sisters of Notre Dame de Namur.

Haugland, S. (2000). *Computers in the early childhood classroom* [Online]. Available: www.earlychildhood.com/Articles/index.cfm?FuseAction=Article&A=239

Kendall, D. S. (2002). *Creating a classroom software library* [Online]. Available: www.earlychildhood.com/Articles/index.cfm?FuseAction=Article&A=199

National Association for the Education of Young Children (NAEYC). (1996). *Technology and young children—Ages 3 through 8* [Online]. Available: www.naeyc.org/resources/position_statements/pstech98.htm

Thouvenelle, S. (2002). *Planning for technology in the classroom* [Online]. Available: www.earlychildhood.com/Articles/index.cfm?FuseAction=Article&A=24

chapter 8

JERI CARROLL

Using the Internet— Search, Sort, Save, and Select

The Internet provides a wealth of information just like any good library or school supply store. To find something, you must have an idea of what you want before you start. When you go to the library, you have some idea of your wishes, whether it is a title, author, or topic. The Internet is very much the same—and yet different. No more flipping card after card in a card catalog. With a title, author, or topic, a good search engine will do the work for you. In fact, the Internet can provide many research opportunities not otherwise available to early childhood educators (Hinchliffe, 1996). This chapter discusses techniques for searching the Internet, sorting and saving the results, and selecting the saved items for use in the classroom.

Searching

SEARCH ENGINES

Search engines are tools that help categorize and index the information found on the millions of Web sites and allow easy retrieval. Because there is so much information, search engines usually retrieve thousands of possible Web sites to fit any one topic. To find what you're looking for, you need to know a little about how search engines work and how to use them effectively.

Search engines find the Web sites and categorize or index them in several ways. One way is by using a software program called a spider or Web "bot." Spiders and Web bots search or "crawl" the Internet, collecting all the possible hyperlinked paths between Web pages and indexing the Web addresses found with the keywords or titles that are contained on the pages. This makes for a very comprehensive listing of Web pages but also provides no way to sort the relevance of those pages.

Another way to index and classify Web pages is for humans to actually read the information on a Web page and categorize it into topics. This is extremely time consuming and costly but provides a better listing of Web sites because they are not just gathered by the keywords that are found within their pages but also indexed by the relevance the information has to the topic. For example, searching for a good Web site to find pictures of cows using the keyword "cows" might land you on a site by the National Dairy Council, a slaughtering house, a sales site of cow hutches or figurines, a zoo, or a personal farm Web site. Using a directory search that looks for farm pictures of cows might bring several pages with exactly what you are looking for if that topic is included in the directory of possible topics.

A *keyword search engine* looks for your words anywhere on the page and provides an extensive, seemingly unlimited listing of sites. An example is AltaVista (www.altavista.com).

A *directory search engine* acts more like a subject guide, organizing information by topics and subtopics. Yahoo (www.yahoo.com) is one of the largest and most popular. Ask Jeeves (www.askjeeves.com) is similar, but allows asking questions in everyday language.

A *metasearch engine* allows you to search several search engines at the same time. However, you will have less control over the search. Metasearch engines include Google (www.google.com), Hotbot (www.hotbot.com), and Dogpile (www.dogpile.com).

A good place to start a search is Kid's Search Tools (www.rcls.org/ksearch.htm), where you will find a variety of search tools on one page. Mike Menchaca (2002) has explained each of these more thoroughly in ISTE's *NETS•S Curriculum Series– Multidisciplinary Units for Grades 3–5* (pp. 29–34).

COMMUNICATING WITH SEARCH ENGINES

Knowing a little about using search engines will improve your results and save you time on your searches. For example, putting phrases inside of quotation marks tells a search engine to look for the entire phrase on a page instead of just finding the words making up the phrase individually. Using boolean operators such as *and*, *or*, and *not* can help narrow and refine your search. If you're searching for lesson plans for early childhood, you could type this into a search engine: "lesson plans" and "early childhood." The search engine would look for those two phrases on the same Web page but would overlook pages that had the words "lesson," "plans," "early," and "childhood" separately. Here is a link that explains boolean logic: http://adam.ac.uk/info/boolean.html#bool.

KidsClick! has an advanced search feature that allows searching for specific reading levels and the number of pictures versus text on a page (http://sunsite.berkeley. edu/KidsClick!/search.html). These features can be extremely helpful for the early childhood teacher searching for appropriate sites to use with emerging readers.

Each search engine usually has an advanced section or help section that explains in detail how to use the specific search engine. Yahoo is an excellent example. This page explains how Yahoo works and has a tutorial: www.yahooligans.com/tg/ search.html.

CONTENT-SPECIFIC SEARCH ENGINES

Content-specific search engines contain listings of very specific information. Some examples:

MapQuest: http://mapquest.com
Bartlett's Quotations: www.bartleby.com/100/
Library of Congress Online Catalog: http://catalog.loc.gov/

Merriam-Webster OnLine: www.merriam-Webster.com
Kid's Image Search Tools: www.kidsclick.org/psearch.html

SEARCHING BY EARLY CHILDHOOD EDUCATORS

What appears to be the easiest thing to do is to determine a topic of interest or importance to your group (such as transportation), pull up a search engine (Yahoo), type the word in, and see what you get. Frequently the results are sites for adults (such as Web sites for the Department of Transportation, National Transportation Safety Board, or State Transportation). Interesting, perhaps, but of little use for PK–2 teachers.

Note: The number of sites listed and their categorization in this discussion are subject to change as Yahooligans collects more sites and refines its classification scheme.

Using a site designed for children will yield different results. For example, a search using Yahooligans for the keyword transportation reveals 29 sites, all related to transportation and far more suitable for children.

To keep track of the sites in your research, open a word processing document. This document will help you identify and sort the sites you want to use, and is sometimes called a *hotlist*. It will likely contain several topics related to one common topic. Transfer the title of the site and the URL to the document to provide a quick way to recall the site. Add a simple statement describing the site. The statement may provide the most useful information for jogging your memory of the site at a later date. As the collector, you determine that statement. You can write it yourself or quote it from the site.

Following are three example sites from the transportation search on Yahooligans. The first example (Air Transportation) first names the source of the site, incorporates a quote from the site, and then provides a statement of how it might be useful to young children.

EXAMPLE SEARCH RESULTS FROM YAHOOLIGANS

Air Transportation (Gallery 102): www.nasm.si.edu/galleries/gal102/gal102.html
The Smithsonian gallery "contains airplanes from the formative years of air transportation in the United States." Eight pictures of historical aircraft and their uses are provided. Reading level is above Grade 2.

Transportation and Public Transit: An Online Lesson:
www.transitpeople.org/lesson/trancovr.htm
Five chapters about transportation (early transportation, the train era, the car era, the problem with cars, and public transit) present information and pictures, followed by a quiz. Grades 2–4 reading level.

Transportation Timeline: www.gsu.edu/other/timeline/trans.html
This site offers 10–15 critical inventions listed by date, inventor, and invention. Grades 2–4 reading level.

MORE SEARCHING

Note the third example, Transportation Timeline. When you visit this Web site, you'll see at the bottom of the page an interesting link—Return to Timeline Index—which takes you to a page titled Events in Science, Mathematics, and Technology (www.gsu.edu/other/timeline.html). When you are searching for sites for kids, keep your eye out for this kind of information. It might be just what you or one of your colleagues is looking for in the future.

When you're in the middle of a search and you find something like this that is interesting but not exactly what you are currently looking for, you might ask yourself, Do I want to save it now? Gathering the pertinent information may cause a slow down in the task at hand, but will likely save a lot of time later. To save the information, open another word processing document, paste the site name, URL, and statement on the new page, title it something simple that will show up quickly in a search (in this case, Timelines), save the new document, and place it in a folder with a descriptive name, such as Interesting Web Sites.

Sorting

In your original word processing document, to sort the three example sites you would type in subcategories, such as Transportation (General) and Air Transportation (Specific), and then cut and paste the sites into their appropriate subcategories, as in the following example.

SORTED SEARCH RESULTS

Transportation (General)

Transportation and Public Transit: An Online Lesson: www.transitpeople.org/lesson/trancovr.htm
Five chapters about transportation (early transportation, the train era, the car era, the problem with cars, and public transit) present information and pictures, followed by a quiz. Grades 2–4 reading level.

Transportation Timeline: www.gsu.edu/other/timeline/trans.html
This site offers 10–15 critical inventions listed by date, inventor, and invention. Grades 2–4 reading level.

Air Transportation (Specific)

Air Transportation (Gallery 102): www.nasm.si.edu/galleries/gal102/gal102.html
The Smithsonian gallery "contains airplanes from the formative years of air transportation in the United States." Eight pictures of historical aircraft and their uses are provided. Reading level is above Grade 2.

Resuming the Search

Return to the search results on Yahooligans and to the following site: Estonian Railway Museum (www.jaam.ee/eng/history.rw.2.php). It is an interesting site, but not something appropriate to use with young children. Most likely you wouldn't add it to your hotlist or Interesting Web Sites folder.

The next site, U.S. Department of Transportation (www.dot.gov), could have a children's site like many federal offices do. Unfortunately, when you access the site there is no children's link, but a click on the Safety button does provide several organizations associated with transportation safety (general, air, land, and sea). Doing a search using the site's search function with keywords children or kids locates nothing of use.

Return to the Yahooligans search page to examine the following site:

Garrett A. Morgan Program: http://education.dot.gov/

At the top is a link to "Kid's Pages" of Agencies of the Department of Transportation, which provides a page with 12 links to specific administrations, boards, and other entities. For the purposes of the transportation units, the one that appears to be the most closely applicable to children's needs might be the National Highway Traffic Safety Administration (www.nhtsa.dot.gov/kids/).

Within this site is an area called Safety City. Randomly examining the icons results in the following list of potentially usable sites. This illustrates another useful search method. You can find many appropriate sites by exploring one good central location in addition to using a search engine.

As you collect these additional items for your hotlist on transportation, add information on the content and reading level. They can be sorted as you see fit, perhaps using the subcategory "Safety."

Bike Tour: www.nhtsa.dot.gov/kids/biketour/index.html
On this page, clear directions for bike safety are provided. Early reading levels (Grades 1–3). Use screen reader software for younger readers.

Safety School: www.nhtsa.dot.gov/kids/safeschool/index.html
The Safety School page provides a safety challenge for children, teacher resources pages, and information about Garrett Morgan, who invented traffic lights. Early reading levels (Grades 1–3). Use screen reader software for younger readers.

Garrett A. Morgan: Father of the Stoplight: www.nhtsa.dot.gov/kids/safeschool/morgan2.html
This page provides an interesting biography of the African American inventor. Early reading levels (Grades 1–3). Use screen reader software for younger readers.

Crash Testing Grounds: www.nhtsa.dot.gov/kids/research/crashtest/index.html
This page describes the car crash in terms of three collisions: the car's collision, the human collision, and the human body's collision. Early reading levels (Grades 1–3). Use screen reader software for younger readers.\

Seat Belts: www.nhtsa.dot.gov/kids/research/seatbelt/index.html
This page provides information about the use of seat belts, the various types, and how they work. Early reading levels (Grades 1–3). Use screen reader software for younger readers.

Saving

As the exploration of Safety City comes to an end, select the back button. This exercise has hit only one of the 12 links from the "Kid's Pages" of Agencies of the Department of Transportation. Because this site has many resources, consider marking it as one of your favorites using the functions on your Web browser. In your word processing document, be sure to include a statement about the appropriate grade level for the sites (such as "Early reading levels [Grades 1–3]. Use screen reader software for younger readers.").

Think about organizing what you have discovered in more than one way. For instance, the information could become part of a file on traffic safety, organized alphabetically and saved as "Traffic Safety." Or, it might be appropriate to add the sites to other hotlists or resource units. For example, the Safety School site could be used for the **My School** unit, and the Bike Tour site could be applied to the **My Neighborhood** unit. The other 11 sites are left for another time when there is more opportunity for exploring. You might create a "digital sticky" and post that reminder on your desktop.

Selecting

How are Web sites selected to use with students in the classroom? The answer to that question depends on the lesson topic, the standards you wish to address, the age of the children in the classroom, the skill level (academic and computer) of the students, and the computer configuration in the classroom. Assume the lesson topic, the age of your students, and their skill level are known. Simply collect several possibilities from your hotlists and match them to your needs. For example:

EXAMPLE 1

The topic? Fruits and vegetables. The age? PK. The skills? Beginning mouse skills. One of the following might be appropriate:

> Fabo's Bananaland Dot-to-Dot: **www.bananaland.com.au/games.php**
> Healthy Kids Concentration Game: **www.state.tn.us/health/java/concentration/**
> Mr. Potato Head Face Game:
> **www.hasbropreschool.com/default.asp?x=mph_act_facegame**

The first site helps students learn mouse skills. It has very little to do with food groups. The second helps students with mouse skills, memory, and matching. The third requires mouse skills (drag and drop).

EXAMPLE 2

The topic? Transportation safety. The age? Second grade. The skills? Reading (Grades 2–3). One of the following might be appropriate:

> Crash Testing Grounds: **www.nhtsa.dot.gov/kids/research/crashtest/index.html**
> Meet the EMS Team: **www.nhtsa.dot.gov/kids/ems/MeetEMS/**
> School Bus Safety: **www.nhtsa.dot.gov/kids/bussafety/index.html**

Conclusion

The searches conducted for this chapter took less than an hour. If you are using one search term or one search engine and you don't get results in the first five minutes, switch the term or the search engine. Save and share your hotlists with others in a file or on a class or school Web site.

References

Hinchliffe, L. J. (1996). *Early childhood teacher education students learn about the Internet* [Online]. Available: www.ed.gov/databases/ERIC_Digests/ed395714.html

Menchaca, M. (2002). Search engines explained. In *Multidisciplinary units for Grades 3–5* (pp. 29–34). Eugene, OR: ISTE.

chapter 9

JERI CARROLL AND TONYA WITHERSPOON

Ethical, Legal, and Human Aspects of Technology

Protecting children while they are using technology and teaching them safe practices and ethical behavior are the concerns of this chapter. We begin by presenting ISTE standards that focus on these issues, followed by a discussion of Internet filters, laws related to Internet use, the digital divide, and netiquette. The chapter concludes with an analogy to safe travel and encourages teachers to teach Internet safety in a way similar to teaching about "stranger danger" (reporting unsavory characters) and child abuse and neglect (reporting uneasy and uncomfortable feelings, and abuse).

The last three sections of this chapter—entitled Laws Related to Internet Use; Social, Ethical and Human Issues Related to Internet Use; and Traveling the Superhighway with Students—are reprinted from *Linking Technology and Curriculum: Integrating the ISTE NETS Standards into Teaching and Learning*, by J. A. Carroll and T. L. Witherspoon (2002), with permission from Pearson Education, Inc., Upper Saddle River, New Jersey.

ISTE Standards

Both the ISTE National Educational Technology Standards for Students (NETS•S) and the ISTE National Educational Technology Standards for Teachers (NETS•T) contain a standard that addresses the social, legal, ethical, and human issues associated with technology use. These standards and their Web sites are as follows:

Student Standard

ISTE NETS•S: http://cnets.iste.org/index2.html

2. Social, ethical, and human issues

- Students understand the ethical, cultural, and societal issues related to technology.

- Students practice responsible use of technology systems, information, and software.

- Students develop positive attitudes toward technology uses that support lifelong learning, collaboration, personal pursuits, and productivity.

Teacher Standard

ISTE NETS•T: http://cnets.iste.org/index3.html

VI. Social, Ethical, Legal, and Human Issues: Teachers understand the social, ethical, legal, and human issues surrounding the use of technology in PK–12 schools and apply that understanding in practice. Teachers:

- model and teach legal and ethical practice related to technology use.
- apply technology resources to enable and empower learners with diverse backgrounds, characteristics, and abilities.
- identify and use technology resources that affirm diversity.
- promote safe and healthy use of technology resources.
- facilitate equitable access to technology resources for all students.

Implementing the above standards in the classroom is a complex task that involves researching district expectations, modeling appropriate behavior on the part of the teacher, instructing children on the appropriate handling of electronic resources including citations, and continual monitoring of changes in the law. Educational uses of technology resources are still under scrutiny by the public and are a concern with some parents. It is the responsibility of the classroom teacher to educate both the children in the classroom and the parents at home on classroom expectations and ethical and legal responsibilities, and to facilitate and monitor the social and human concerns that come with classroom technology use.

Internet Filters

There are many ways to sift or filter through information on the Internet to decide whether it is safe, accurate, or appropriate to use in classrooms. Once inappropriate sites are located and filtered, they can be blocked from being displayed on classroom computers. Specific functions when using the Internet such as file sharing, downloading, and uploading can be blocked as well. Laws have been put into place to require that some filtering measures be taken in public schools. Your school or district acceptable use policies (AUPs) may require additional filtering. Check with your building or district technology AUP and technology support personnel to find out whether filtering is done in your building or district and whether you are expected to provide filtering in your classroom.

CHILDREN'S INTERNET PROTECTION ACT

The Children's Internet Protection Act (CIPA), which went into effect April 20, 2001, requires schools and libraries receiving certain types of federal funds to have safe-use Internet policies and to use Internet filtering to protect children from pornography. Despite some legal challenges, "most schools must still comply with a federal law requiring them to install filtering software to prevent children from viewing Internet pornography on school computers," Mark Walsh (2002) explains in *Education Week* (www.edweek.org/ew/newstory.cfm?slug=40filter.h21&keywords=CIPA).

DISTRICT AND SCHOOL FILTERING

Filtering software can be installed in the following locations: the computer in the classroom, the server in the building that your computer goes through to get to the Internet, or the server at some other building that your district or Internet provider uses to give you access to the Internet. This software can filter out and block specific Web addresses that have been found inappropriate, inappropriate keywords within a Web page, or specific applications that may be used over the Internet such as software for chat, downloading music files from other computers, or uploading Web pages to a Web server.

CLASSROOM FILTERING

Typically the filtering that is required of classroom teachers centers on the supervision of computer use. Teachers need to be diligent in supervising students when they are using the Internet. Tools and strategies are available that can help sort and filter through information to find appropriate material for students. Web portals, WebQuests, and child-friendly search engines are some tools that help supervise students while they are online. Teachers must instruct students on what to do if they come upon an inappropriate site, as well as assist students and parents in understanding how to stay safe online at home, where filtering may not be provided. The establishing of the "dot kids" domain name, which will provide pre-screened Web sites appropriate for children, should make some of the classroom filtering issues less difficult.

WEB PORTALS Web portals are Web sites that offer "one-stop shopping" by providing a clearinghouse of links to information on certain topics. Web portals are run by humans (not computers!) and contain hand-selected sites on specific topics. A few examples are:

Abcteach: www.abcteach.com
A to Z Teacher Stuff: www.atozteacherstuff.com
Blue Web'N: www.kn.pacbell.com/wired/bluewebn/index.html
Preschool Education: www.preschooleducation.com

WEBQUESTS WebQuests are similar to Web portals but are created by teachers. A WebQuest is a lesson built around a preselected set of links to use with students on a particular topic. For example:

A Quest for Zoo Animals: www.berksiu.k12.pa.us/Webquest/Dries/default.htm
Barnyard Friends: A Primary WebQuest:
www.plainfield.k12.in.us/hschool/Webq/Webq43/shannon.htm
Heroes and Legends for Kindergarten:
http://oncampus.richmond.edu/academics/as/education/projects/Webunits/khistory/home.htm

CHILD-FRIENDLY SEARCH ENGINES

Child-friendly search engines are either filtered with software that blocks certain keywords or Web addresses or filtered by people who have determined certain sites must be blocked from children. This filtering allows these search engines to search the Web and automatically block inappropriate sites. A few examples include:

Yahooligans!: www.yahooligans.com
KidsClick!: http://sunsite.berkeley.edu/KidsClick!/
Ask Jeeves Kids: www.ajkids.com
One Key: www.onekey.com/live/index.htm

A WORD OF CAUTION ABOUT FILTERS

Internet filters are a necessary tool to help us sort and sift through the huge amounts of information available on the Internet and find appropriate sites for students. They will not replace teacher or parent supervision. Teachers must be very careful not to let Internet filters give a false sense of security and replace the teaching and learning of appropriate use of the Internet.

Filters not only limit access to inappropriate sites and inappropriate information, but may also block sites one may wish access to. For example, a filter that blocks out any sites using the keyword "sex" will block all sites that give information about how the female sex of an animal is different from the male or other sites that use the word "sex" in an appropriate way. Even if filters help us block inappropriate sites, the teacher must decide whether the sites that are accessible are educational or have a place in the classroom or curriculum.

And finally, teachers must be careful when using the Internet at home without the same filters that are in place at school. Web sites found at home without using filters might not be available to students at school. Some file downloads and other types of applications blocked by filters will not allow teachers to perform some necessary procedures at school without asking for tech help. For example, when plug-ins or drivers are required to be downloaded from the Internet, some filters will block this type of activity, thus preventing a valuable site from being viewed in the classroom.

CYBER SQUATTING AND PORN NAPPING

According to the Online Internet Institute (OII: 2002, www.oii.org/html/definitions. html), "Cyber squatting is the practice of registering a desirable domain name in the hope that you will be able to sell it to someone else for a much inflated price." The OII further states, "Porn-napping is a relatively new form of cyber squatting where someone waits for a desirable name registration to expire. They then pick it up, turn the front page into a portal for pornography, and offer the domain for sale in the hopes that the original owner or someone else will rescue the once respectable site from the grips of pornography."

Educators should be aware that Internet sites previously deemed safe may be hijacked for inappropriate uses. Many .edu domains (URLs) are expiring and being purchased by porn, casino, and other companies, which is frightening because .edu sites are linked all over the Internet to educational and teacher sites. Many educational sites are maintained by busy educators who do not take the time to check their list of "great links," which means that they could be unwittingly linking to former educational URLs that are now porn sites. Some companies are preying on the traffic they can nab from unsuspecting kids, families, and teachers. Other companies are hoping that they can try to blackmail the original owner of the URL into paying a high price to get it back. The Web site at **www.oii.org/html/porn-napping.html** provides an overview of the problem and lists sites that have been taken over (OII, 2002).

SUPERVISION

John Schwartz (2002) in the *New York Times* notes that "one of the most thorough reports [*Youth, Pornography, and the Internet,* National Research Council, 2002] ever produced on protecting children from Internet pornography has concluded that neither tougher laws nor new technology alone can solve the problem" even though certain "sexually explicit materials (obscenity, child pornography) enjoy no First Amendment protection at all" (National Research Council, 2002, Section 14.1.3, **www.nap.edu/catalog/10261.html**).

The *Youth, Pornography, and the Internet* report states (National Research Council, 2002, Section 14.3, **www.nap.edu/catalog/10261.html**):

"Technology solutions seem to offer quick and inexpensive fixes that allow adult caregivers to believe that the problem has been addressed, and it is tempting to believe that the use of technology can drastically reduce or even eliminate the need for human supervision.... Public policy aimed at eliminating sources of sexually explicit material can affect only indigenous domestic sources, and a substantial fraction of such materials originates overseas. Nor is technology a substitute for education, responsible adult supervision, and ethical Internet use."

"The most important finding of the committee is that developing in children and youth an ethic of responsible choice and skills for appropriate behavior is foundational for all efforts to protect them—with respect to inappropriate sexually explicit material on the Internet as well as many other dangers on the Internet and in the physical world. Social and educational strategies are central to such development, but technology and public policy are important as well—and the three can act together to reinforce each other's value."

The most valuable filter is *you*. The most important person involved in the legal, ethical, social, and human issues surrounding the use of the Internet with young children is the responsible adult, parent, or teacher. Be aware. Be decisive. Be an advocate.

Several U.S. laws govern our use of the Internet: the Children's Online Privacy Protection Act (COPPA), the Children's Internet Protection Act (CIPA), and the Family Educational Rights and Privacy Act (FERPA). In addition, laws addressing copyright have been extended to technology sources. Many of these laws, however, are being contested based on the First Amendment right of free speech. It is critical to check your own school policies related to COPPA, CIPA, and FERPA.

Laws Related to Internet Use

Note: The information in the remainder of this chapter has been reprinted with permission. Minor edits have been made to the text.

CHILDREN'S ONLINE PRIVACY PROTECTION ACT

The Children's Online Privacy Protection Act, which went into effect April 21, 2000, affects U.S. commercial Web sites and third-party commercial Web sites that schools permit their students to access. COPPA requires "operators of Web sites or online services directed to children and operators of Web sites or online services who have actual knowledge that the person from whom they seek information is a child (1) to post prominent links on their Web sites to a notice of how they collect, use, and/or disclose personal information from children; (2) with certain exceptions, to notify parents that they wish to collect information from their children and obtain parental consent prior to collecting, using, and/or disclosing such information; (3) not to condition a child's participation in online activities on the provision of more personal information than is reasonably necessary to participate in the activity; (4) to allow parents the opportunity to review and/or have their children's information deleted from the operator's database and to prohibit further collection from the child; and (5) to establish procedures to protect the confidentiality, security, and integrity of personal information they collect from children." The act also provides a safe harbor for operators following Commission-approved, self-regulatory guidelines (COPPA, 1998, www.ftc.gov/os/1999/9910/64fr59888.htm).

Nonprofit sites are not included in the act; however, many are voluntarily complying. A key component of COPPA is that sites must have a privacy policy disclosing what information is being collected, how it is being used, and with whom they will share the information. A second component requires that when personal information (name, address, phone, and e-mail address) is collected from a child under the age of 13, parents must be informed and their consent given. The third component deals with Internet safety. Children under the age of 13 must have parental consent to use communication technologies prior to use (chat, e-mail, instant messaging, e-pals, discussion boards, videoconferencing, etc.).

CHILDREN'S INTERNET PROTECTION ACT

The Children's Internet Protection Act went into effect April 20, 2001, requiring that schools and libraries that receive certain types of federal technology funding have safe-use Internet policies. The policies require the use of Internet filtering software to screen material that is inappropriate (obscene) or harmful to minors and the monitoring of student Internet use. Free speech challenges to this law have been made with regard to libraries, but there are none yet on the CIPA requirements for schools. Schools and libraries were to begin addressing the provisions in the law July 1, 2001, indicating whether they had complied, were in the process of complying, would be compliant by the next year, or need not comply (www.neirls.org/consulting/lawfilter.htm).

FAMILY EDUCATIONAL RIGHTS AND PRIVACY ACT

The Family Educational Rights and Privacy Act, which protects the privacy of student education records, applies to all schools that receive funds under an applicable program of the U.S. Department of Education. FERPA gives parents certain rights with respect to their children's education records, and the rights transfer to the student at age 18 or when the student attends a school beyond the high school level. Schools must notify parents and eligible students annually of their rights under FERPA. Those rights include (**www.ed.gov/offices/OM/fpco/ferpa/index.html**):

- Parents or eligible students have the right to inspect and review the student's education records maintained by the school.
- Parents or eligible students have the right to request that a school correct any records they believe to be inaccurate or misleading.
- Generally, schools must have written permission from the parent or eligible student to release any information from a student's education record, and parents have a right to deny that release.

Personally identifiable information includes the student's name, address, Social Security number, or any other information that makes the student's identity easily traceable. Teachers must be cautious about posting student work or student information online and take care in the use of electronic communication in general.

COPYRIGHT AND FAIR USE

Copyright protects authors of "original works of authorship," including literary, dramatic, musical, artistic, and certain other intellectual works. This protection gives the owner of copyright the exclusive right to, and to authorize others to, reproduce the work, prepare derivative works, distribute copies, perform the work, display the work, and in the case of sound recordings, to perform the work by means of digital audio transmission. The penalties for infringement are very harsh. According to the U.S. Copyright Office (2000), "It is illegal for anyone to violate any of the rights provided by the copyright law to the owner of copyright." These rights, however, are not unlimited, and there are specified exemptions from copyright liability. One major limitation is the doctrine of "fair use" (**www.loc.gov/copyright/circs/circ1.html#wci**). However, determining "fair use" is fuzzy. A comprehensive set of links associated with copyright and fair use resources on the Internet is available at **http://groton.k12.ct.us/mts/pt2a.htm**.

A FURTHER WORD OF CAUTION

Remember, information on the Internet is not just available or published in the U.S. Our laws do not cover everything that is on the Internet. Because of this, parents and teachers must be responsible in what they require of students to ensure that they are protected online.

Social, Ethical, and Human Issues Related to Internet Use

Beyond the legal issues, there are other social, ethical, and human issues related to Internet use. These include the digital divide and social etiquette.

DIGITAL DIVIDE

Within any classroom, there are students who have more than others—money, intelligence, or material goods. In addition, according to the Digital Divide Network (2002), there "has always been a gap between those people and communities who can make effective use of information technology and those who cannot. Now, more than ever, unequal adoption of technology excludes many from reaping the fruits of the economy." The term *digital divide* refers to the gap between those who can effectively use new information and communication tools, such as the Internet, and those who cannot (www.digitaldividenetwork.org/content/sections/index.cfm?key=2).

Some solutions to the digital divide in the news worldwide recently include:

- E-branch libraries (library kiosks placed in schools, grocery stores, and malls) that provide patrons with computers and phone-line Internet access to libraries (www.digitaldividenetwork.org/content/news/index.cfm?key=413).
- The distribution of at least 100,000 high-capacity computer game consoles equipped with satellite links to schools and in homes in developing countries (www.digitaldividenetwork.org/content/news/index.cfm?key=412).
- A proposal backed by European Union telecoms ministers to provide Internet access to every citizen's house. The plan, which proposes to update existing so-called universal service provisions for access to voice telephony and fax lines, requires operators to guarantee "functional" Internet access even in unprofitable regions, such as remote geographical locations (www.digitaldividenetwork.org/content/news/index.cfm?key=395).

For further information, see these two Web sites dedicated to information on the digital divide:

Closing the Digital Divide: www.digitaldivide.gov
Digital Divide Network:
www.digitaldividenetwork.org/content/sections/index.cfm

ASSESSING AND ADDRESSING THE DIGITAL DIVIDE IN CLASSROOMS

To give assignments that students can complete, it is necessary to find out what technology students have access to at home, in public places, at boys' and girls' clubs, at friends' and relatives' homes, and so forth. Having students help you develop a list of all the technologies they can think of to place in one column and providing several columns for use (home, library, school, relative, other) will let you know the extent of the digital divide in your class of students. Seeking appropriate accommodations to include all students in the activities of the classroom is a responsibility all teachers have (Jordon & Stuve, 2000).

NETIQUETTE

As students use the Internet for communication, rules of etiquette need to be examined. Network etiquette, or *netiquette*, according to Virginia Shea (1994, 2000; www.albion.com/netiquette/introduction.html), author of a book of the same name, is "a set of rules for behaving properly online." Shea's core rules include:

- Remember the human. (Never forget that the person reading your mail or posting is, indeed, a person, with feelings that can be hurt.)
- Adhere to the same standards of behavior online that you follow in real life. (Be ethical and don't break the law.)
- Know where you are in cyberspace. (Netiquette varies from domain to domain, personal to professional, business to education, etc.)
- Respect other people's time and bandwidth. (Be brief, to the point, and considerate.)

Traveling the Superhighway with Students

ADDRESSING SOCIAL, LEGAL, ETHICAL, AND HUMAN ISSUES ONLINE

For some time, the Internet has been referred to as the Information Superhighway. As in real life, hackers, trespassers, and robbers wreak their havoc as one travels the superhighway. Advice to world travelers often includes words of wisdom such as "Don't go into dark alleys," "Stick with the group," and "Be wary of strangers." These words of wisdom, along with others, are chosen to outline the following legal and ethical issues associated with Internet use.

OBTAINING A PASSPORT: SCHOOL INTERNET USE POLICIES

To protect students online is both a legal and ethical issue. Remember to do these things before traveling with students:

- Locate the school's Internet safe-use policies and make sure parents have given students permission to use the Internet.
- Preview the Internet sites you want your students to use.
- Post a set of safe sites (like visas to visit other countries) on your Web site.
- If you search for sites on your home computers, remember to try them on the school computers. Schools and districts are establishing firewalls to lock out inappropriate information for students. Filtering software at school may lock you out of a site you can visit at home.

REPORTING SUSPECTED INTRUDERS: STRANGER DANGER

As with real-life strangers, students need to be wary of child predators on the Internet and be instructed to report any unwanted, uncomfortable, or unsolicited approaches by strangers. Recent legislation indicates how serious our government is about the protection of children online. COPPA and CIPA provide guidelines and consequences for protecting children online. No one can ask students under the age of 13 to report personal information to them. That doesn't mean that it won't happen. It just means that it is against the law to do so.

- Train students in their online rights. No one online is to ask them for identifying information and they are not to give it without their parent's consent.

- Remind students to report when they think someone has requested any information from them. "Think" is the key word here, just as "suspected" child abuse must be reported.

- Students should not have to confirm that information has been solicited. It will be up to others to determine that. Suspicion is enough to warrant a report to the teacher.

- As with all infractions of the law, students need to be encouraged to report their findings to the proper authorities and feel comfortable doing so.

MINDING AND ESTABLISHING ROAD BLOCKS

When traveling, we sometimes run into roadblocks that have been put there for our protection. Do we move the barricades or do we take the detour? The same is true for the superhighway. Often a notice will appear that you are leaving or entering a secure site.

- Teach students about roadblocks. They are there for student protection.

- Teach students what to do about roadblocks: Do Not Enter!

- If students come upon a sign telling them they are leaving a safe site, ask them to seek permission from you to leave the site, and then monitor the next sites closely to see what is outside the protected site.

When traveling, we often take the wrong road and end up at places we didn't want to go. Or we might find a fallen rock that impedes travel. When that happens, we often give future travelers a cautionary word or report the problem to the authorities. CIPA requires the use of filtering software, but until firewalls are in place, it is the teacher's responsibility to monitor students. Offensive or unsafe Internet sites can be entered by accident when we have no intention of going there. The simple, innocent mistake of using the wrong domain designator (.com rather than .edu) can place us in embarrassing situations. The same can happen with our students.

To help students cope when these things happen:

- Teach students what to do when accidents occur or potential accidents are about to happen. Report accidents to proper authorities!

- Warn the next students who travel the paths leading to this unsavory site to be cautious. (Remember, too, that telling students about issues like this might only arouse their curiosity.)

ASSURING PRIVATE HOUSING

When traveling, we look for secure and safe housing. Safety and privacy also need to be considered on the Internet. Secure files, secure computers, and secure information all seem to be targets for those "highwaymen" who see hacking as creative thinking and problem-solving activities. The Family Education Rights and Protection Act guarantees students and families privacy. Each district has a policy designed to require its employees to be in line with this act. All teachers need to know and follow these policies. Typically, teachers should:

- Know and follow district policies related to FERPA.
- Be careful with grades. Grades should not be reported or accessible to anyone except appropriate school personnel and family members.
- Use the appropriate software. Grades can be safely posted within courseware.
- Make every effort to keep confidential information confidential.
- Keep children's personal information safe. Online publishing of student work should contain no identifying information other than the first name, the school, and in some instances, the grade level.

AVOIDING HIGHWAY ROBBERY

Robbery occurs in society, along the information highway, and in schools. Information protected by copyright has long been in schools, first entering with textbooks, and more recently with software and technology tools. As it has become easier and easier to do, copying of information protected by copyright has occurred more frequently. Often the perpetrator has done so with good intent—to share something exciting with a colleague, to allow more students to use an exciting product, or to make sure students had a copy if things got lost or stolen. However, the copyright is there to protect the author and publisher and the long hours, time, and expense they put into the product. Recent litigation reported in the national news shows the severity of these highway robberies and the potential losses of revenue for many people and companies.

Teachers and students alike should understand issues associated with "fair use":

- Teach students copyright and fair use policies.
- Warn students against copying information for which there is a copyright.
- Students can use the information from Internet sites just the same as they can use information from books, magazines, journals, and so forth. Teach students how to identify the use of information appropriately rather than plagiarizing it.
- Teach students how to ask permission to use information, graphics, icons, and so on. A request can be sent to the author or organization describing the desired use and seeking permission.
- When identifying information is not available and when there is no copyright, citing the source of the information is critical. Using the URL and the date of acquisition provides legitimate documentation.

■ In teacher education you may need to cite electronic sources. See APA Style: Electronic Resources: www.apastyle.org/elecref.html.

PROTECTING YOUR VALUABLES

Many software and technology tools allow a backup file to protect the originals. In schools this could translate to a library of originals and copies kept in separate CD notebooks, with copies being checked out for use and originals kept secure. Then, to keep the copies secure:

■ Software can be installed on classroom computers using the copy while the original is kept secure and away from those who might want to copy it. Once the program is installed, the teacher using the copy should keep it in his or her possession so that only legitimate copies are in use.

■ When use is completed, the software or tool should be removed from the hard drive, and the copy returned to the CD library.

■ When a legitimate copy is available in the school library of software, the program can be used.

WRITING HOME

In mail delivery, we have come a long way since the pony express, mail trains, airmail, and overnight delivery of letters. Now, instantly, colleagues around the world can converse and collaborate in many ways. Remember:

■ Children younger than 13 must have parental consent to use communication technologies (chat, e-mail, instant messaging, e-pals, discussion boards, videoconferencing, etc.) prior to use (COPPA).

■ It is good to inform or seek permission from parents of other [older] students also.

■ Children must be taught the social graces of online communication.

USING INTERNET ETIQUETTE

The Internet as a communication tool is a lot faster than the pony express of old. Messages and responses are delivered around the world in a matter of minutes, rather than days, weeks, or months. However, Internet etiquette (netiquette), still exists.

■ Begin "letters" with the name, an address, a date (many e-mail programs provide the date and time automatically, to the minute), a topic, a salutation, a knowledge of the reader, a clear note, expectations, and a closing.

■ Rather than weighing the "pony" down with unwanted mail or exposing it to illness, one should avoid passing on junk mail, chain letters, and viruses. Check those chain letters. Although not necessarily illegal on the Internet, they can consume an enormous amount of time and space.

References

American Library v. U.S.A., No. 01-1303. (2002, May 31). United States District Court for the Eastern District of Pennsylvania. [Online]. Available: www.paed.uscourts.gov/documents/opinions/02D0415P.HTM

Carroll, J. A., & Witherspoon, T. L. (2002). *Linking technology and curriculum: Integrating the ISTE NETS standards into teaching and learning.* Upper Saddle River, NJ: Merrill/Prentice Hall.

Children's Online Privacy Protection Act (COPPA). (1998). 15 U.S. Code 6501–6506. [Online]. Available: www.ftc.gov/os/1999/9910/64fr59888.htm

Digital Divide Network. (2002). *Digital divide basics* [Online]. Available: www.digitaldividenetwork.org/content/sections/index.cfm?key=2

Jordon, M., & Stuve, G. (2000, August). Presented at the ISTE NETS for Teachers Writing Session, Wheeling, WV.

National Research Council. (2002). *Youth, pornography, and the Internet* [Online]. National Academies Press. Available: www.nap.edu/catalog/10261.html

Online Internet Institute (OII). (2002). *Porn-napping and cyber squatting* [Online]. Available: www.oii.org/html/porn-napping.html

Schwartz, J. (2002, May 3). No easy fixes are seen to curb sex-site access. *New York Times*, p. C6.

Shea, V. (1994). *Netiquette* [Online]. Albion. Available: www.albion.com/netiquette/introduction.html

U.S. Copyright Office. (2000). *Copyright basics* [Online]. Available: www.loc.gov/copyright/circs/circ1.html#wci

Walsh, M. (2002, June 12). Schools still required to install Internet filters. *Education Week* [Online]. Available: www.edweek.org/ew/newstory.cfm?slug=40filter.h21&keywords=CIPA

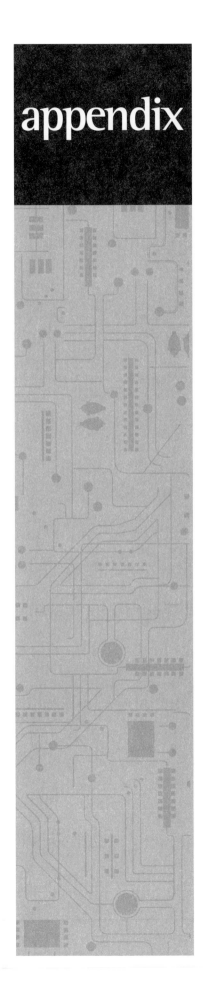

appendix

CLASSROOM IDEAS FOR MEETING THE STANDARDS

NATIONAL EDUCATIONAL TECHNOLOGY STANDARDS FOR STUDENTS (NETS•S)

NATIONAL EDUCATIONAL TECHNOLOGY STANDARDS FOR TEACHERS (NETS•T)

EARLY CHILDHOOD PROFESSIONAL PREPARATION GUIDELINES

ENGLISH/LANGUAGE ARTS STANDARDS

MATHEMATICS STANDARDS

SCIENCE STANDARDS

SOCIAL STUDIES STANDARDS

classroom
ideas

Classroom Ideas
for Meeting the Standards

ISTE PROFILES FOR TECHNOLOGY-LITERATE STUDENTS (PK–2)

All students should have opportunities to demonstrate the following performances. Numbers in parentheses following each performance indicator refer to the standards category to which the performance is linked. Sample ideas have been generated to show specific activities and tasks that might be used with young children. ISTE has developed performance indicators for all grade levels. The following list describes only the PK–2 indicators—the specific focus of this book.

Prior to completion of Grade 2, students will:

1. Use input devices (e.g., mouse, keyboard, remote control) and output devices (e.g., monitor, printer) to successfully operate computers, VCRs, audiotapes, and other technologies. (ISTE NETS•S, Standard 1)

EXAMPLES

- The skill of using the mouse is learned as students "mouse" over images to find new information, click, and click-and-drag. Rather than just participating in a practice exercise, children mouse over interesting and meaningful sites.

- Keyboarding skills are practiced as children learn to write their names, words, sentences, and eventually stories. Stickers and color codes provide visual clues.

- Digital cameras, scanners, and printers can be used by children with close supervision by adults.

- Young children are taught to respect and care for hardware and software. Task cards give directions. Flipcharts, books, and posters remind students of common tasks and procedures.

- Simple exploration of new content software allows the practice of simple computer skills. There is a maxim in working with young children: "Use familiar content in learning new skills; use familiar skills in learning new content."

2. Use a variety of media and technology resources for directed and independent learning activities. (ISTE NETS•S, Standards 1, 3)

EXAMPLES

- Students save files to a network folder or disk. They become familiar with the school's preferred storage devices such as memory sticks or cards, and Zip, floppy, or pen drives.

- Students use computers, cameras, scanners, printers, PDAs, digital sensors, robots (such as the Roamer), and other equipment.

- Students see technology used as teachers demonstrate tools, learning centers, and independent areas and as teachers use the technology for the many responsibilities associated with teaching.

- Students learn to select the appropriate tool for the job.

3. Communicate about technology using developmentally appropriate and accurate terminology. (ISTE NETS•S, Standard 1)

EXAMPLES

- Students learn the proper vocabulary for each piece of equipment and its relationship to other equipment.

- Students understand the technology terms in relation to known words or concepts: hard drive = filing cabinet, CPU = brain, and so on.

- Technology tools in the classroom are labeled.

- Technology tools outside the classroom and in the home can be identified (telephones, televisions, CD players, etc.).

- Attention to technology resources takes place when children are reading books, watching videos, and listening to CDs.

4. Use developmentally appropriate multimedia resources (e.g., interactive books, educational software, elementary multimedia encyclopedias) to support learning. (ISTE NETS•S, Standard 1)

EXAMPLES

- Students should understand that the computer is a tool that they can learn to control, not a piece of machinery that they must react to. Software such as the Living Books series allows the student to be active in the listening and learning process.

- Skill and drill software should be used appropriately and sparingly.

- Computer use is tied directly to curriculum standards. Students are aware of the purpose of the activity.

5. **Work cooperatively and collaboratively with peers, family members, and others when using technology in the classroom. (ISTE NETS•S, Standard 2)**

EXAMPLES

- Children work together at the computer (sharing the chair, taking turns with the mouse or trackpad, and using a kitchen timer, hourglass timer, or Big Clock [PDA software]).

- Students and teachers use e-mail to communicate with friends, families, and e-pals and send smilies and cyber hugs to friends and family.

- Teachers post upcoming and current events on a class Web page. Students select pictures of their projects to post.

- The helper chart includes responsibilities associated with technology jobs.

- Parents are trained and used as helpers in the classroom to support appropriate technology use.

- Students tell about technology projects as part of the class newsletter.

- Guests speakers talk about their technology use in jobs.

6. **Demonstrate positive social and ethical behaviors when using technology. (ISTE NETS•S, Standard 2)**

EXAMPLES

- Students learn digital and online manners.

- As with traditional class activities, copying a computer file or online work of others is clearly conveyed as inappropriate behavior. Students are able to state and demonstrate that whoever did the work should have his or her name on it.

- When students find information they want to use, they know to give the other person credit.

- Online perpetrators become another element of "stranger danger."

- Social interaction is not replaced with computers.

- Students and families are aware of the school's safe- and fair-use policies and have made the commitment to enforce those policies at home.

7. **Practice responsible use of technology systems and software. (ISTE NETS•S, Standard 2)**

EXAMPLES

- Rules for computer use are posted:
  i. No food, drink, or magnets around computers.
  ii. Wash and clean monitors, keyboards, hands, mice, and mousepads.
  iii. Use computers in pairs.
  iv. Ask for help when needed.

- Students use discarded discs to practice handling CDs and DVDs.

■ When responsible use is demonstrated by students, give them "mouse patrol" responsibilities in helping others.

■ Create a tech lab (similar to a housekeeping area). Use old machines for practice. Allow students to plug in the mouse, keyboard, and monitor to each other (but not to electricity). Add other tools that can be handled and practiced with for creative play and to pretend tech support.

8. **Create developmentally appropriate multimedia products with support from teachers, family members, or student partners. (ISTE NETS•S, Standard 3)**

EXAMPLES

■ Have students draw, write, record, take pictures, and so forth, and incorporate these multimedia pieces into a bigger piece.

■ Teachers and students make short videos of proper use of equipment.

■ Take photos of equipment and have students create labels.

■ Take photos or videos on field trips. When back in class, use the photos or videos to reinforce skills and knowledge. If children are absent, they can still "attend" the field trip. The photos and videos can be used in subsequent years to introduce the field trip and point out things to pay attention to. If the weather is poor in following years, the videos can become the field trip.

■ Have students each create one slide or portion of a larger classroom multimedia slideshow.

■ Eventually have students create a slide presentation themselves. Start small— three slides (beginning, middle, end). The title slide and credit slide make a five-slide presentation.

■ Send digital cameras home so that students may take pictures at home with family or encourage that pictures be brought to class to be scanned. Encourage parents to have pictures developed to CDs.

■ Model multimedia by creating an All About Me slideshow that is set to run during an open house or conference.

9. **Use technology resources (e.g., puzzles, logical thinking programs, writing tools, digital cameras, drawing tools) for problem solving, communication, and illustration of thoughts, ideas, and stories. (ISTE NETS•S, Standards 3, 4, 5, 6)**

EXAMPLES

■ Teachers demonstrate the use of resources in realistic settings while "thinking aloud" to further model the problem-solving process.

■ Teachers require students to use technology resources in classroom activities and learning centers.

10. Gather information and communicate with others using telecommunications, with support from teachers, family members, or student partners. (ISTE NETS•S, Standard 4)

EXAMPLES

- Students use online communication as a resource to find out information from others about topics and projects.

- Students observe teachers using technology tools in everyday tasks, such as recording attendance, printing lunch menus, and accessing weather reports.

- Students and teachers send messages to family, friends, administrators, and legislators.

NATIONAL ASSOCIATION FOR THE EDUCATION OF YOUNG CHILDREN POSITION STATEMENT

In the late 1990s two national organizations, the National Association for the Education of Young Children (NAEYC) and the International Society for Technology in Education (ISTE) worked to address issues of whether technology was appropriate for use with young children and which standards and objectives were achievable.

The NAEYC set the stage for the use of technology in early childhood classrooms with its 1996 position statement entitled *Technology and Young Children—Ages 3–8*: "Technology plays a significant role in all aspects of American life today, and this role will only increase in the future....Early childhood educators must take responsibility to influence events that are transforming the daily lives of children and families." Noting that the research points to the positive effect that technology can have on children's learning and development, NAEYC cautions, too, that it can be misused. It is up to the teachers to use their "professional judgment in evaluating and using this learning tool appropriately, applying the same criteria they would to any other learning tool or experience."

Each of the following numbered items is taken from the NAEYC's (1996) position statement. The bulleted points that appear after each item are some ways we see these statements being implemented in classrooms for young children.

1. NAEYC believes that in any given situation, a professional judgment by the teacher is required to determine whether a specific use of technology is age appropriate, individually appropriate, and culturally appropriate.

EXAMPLES

- Teachers need to examine computers, software, and online resources in much the same way they evaluate any other item for use in their classroom. The content knowledge and the computer skills required must be age, stage, and culturally appropriate.

- Learning to use the hardware and software ourselves allows us to see any problems young children might encounter.

2. **Used appropriately, technology can enhance children's cognitive and social abilities.**

EXAMPLES

- Observation is a critical piece of assessing young children's knowledge and skills. As you watch young children play Concentration online, you can tell the strategies used for matching, much the same way you can when they play the game offline.
- Young children can understand words in online and software resources with a little adult coaching, but screen-reading software allows the material to be read when an adult is not present.
- Voice-recording software allows teachers, parents, aides, or children to verbally record assignments and stories.
- When young children work in pairs at a computer, they learn from each other—cognitively and socially. The information is learned, but so are the social skills of sharing, communicating, asking questions, and working out problems.
- Working with younger or older children as peer mentors allows the children to learn from others or teach others what they know.

3. **Appropriate technology is integrated into the regular learning environment and used as one of many options to support children's learning.**

EXAMPLES

- Computers and technology are not the only source of learning, nor the primary source.
- Centers are set up for children where they can work independently or collaboratively on art, research, reading, science problems, or projects.
- Adults can still teach, read stories, and guide student's learning in many ways.
- Computers are set up as a center or used as an instructional vehicle.

4. **Early childhood educators should promote equitable access to technology for all children and their families. Children with special needs should have increased access when this is helpful.**

EXAMPLES

- Using computers regularly in the classroom provides an opportunity for all children to become familiar with technology.
- Adaptive devices (touch screens, screen readers, voice recording software, etc.) allow all children to work effectively, and allow those with special needs to work more effectively.

5. The power of technology to influence children's learning and development requires that attention be paid to eliminating stereotyping of any group and eliminating exposure to violence, especially as a problem-solving strategy.

EXAMPLES

- Screening all software and online resources requires that teachers examine the gender, ethnicity, and age of the people seen.

- Diversity in software and online resources should be readily evident.

- Just as schools are drug-free and weapon-free environments, the resources provided for students should also be.

6. Teachers, in collaboration with parents, should advocate for more appropriate technology applications for all children.

EXAMPLES

- Initially teachers may need to educate parents about the effective use of technology in classrooms. Some parents, however, may be the ones educating the teachers.

- Individually, together, or as a group, parents and teachers should communicate to their building, district, and state administrators their desire for appropriate technology for all children.

- As part of the IFSP and/or IEP process, children with special needs should be supplied with appropriate adaptive technologies.

7. The appropriate use of technology has many implications for early childhood professional development.

EXAMPLES

- Teachers need training in the use of technology with young children.

- Professional development specialists need to model the appropriate use of technology in their training sessions.

- Online learning allows teachers to go to school and learn academic and technology content at any time, independently through personal research or taught by professionals in online discussion groups, virtual chats, guided experiences, and courses.

nets
for
students

National Educational Technology Standards for Students (NETS•S)

1. BASIC OPERATIONS AND CONCEPTS
   - Students demonstrate a sound understanding of the nature and operation of technology systems.
   - Students are proficient in the use of technology.

2. SOCIAL, ETHICAL, AND HUMAN ISSUES
   - Students understand the ethical, cultural, and societal issues related to technology.
   - Students practice responsible use of technology systems, information, and software.
   - Students develop positive attitudes toward technology uses that support lifelong learning, collaboration, personal pursuits, and productivity.

3. TECHNOLOGY PRODUCTIVITY TOOLS
   - Students use technology tools to enhance learning, increase productivity, and promote creativity.
   - Students use productivity tools to collaborate in constructing technology-enhanced models, preparing publications, and producing other creative works.

4. TECHNOLOGY COMMUNICATIONS TOOLS
   - Students use telecommunications to collaborate, publish, and interact with peers, experts, and other audiences.
   - Students use a variety of media and formats to communicate information and ideas effectively to multiple audiences.

5. TECHNOLOGY RESEARCH TOOLS
   - Students use technology to locate, evaluate, and collect information from a variety of sources.
   - Students use technology tools to process data and report results.
   - Students evaluate and select new information resources and technological innovations based on the appropriateness to specific tasks.

6. TECHNOLOGY PROBLEM-SOLVING AND DECISION-MAKING TOOLS
   - Students use technology resources for solving problems and making informed decisions.
   - Students employ technology in the development of strategies for solving problems in the real world.

PERFORMANCE INDICATORS FOR TECHNOLOGY-LITERATE STUDENTS, GRADES PK–2

All students should have opportunities to demonstrate the following performances. Numbers in parentheses following each performance indicator refer to the standards category to which the performance is linked.

PRIOR TO COMPLETION OF GRADE 2, STUDENTS WILL:

- Use input devices (e.g., mouse, keyboard, remote control) and output devices (e.g., monitor, printer) to successfully operate computers, VCRs, audiotapes, and other technologies. (1)

- Use a variety of media and technology resources for directed and independent learning activities. (1, 3)

- Communicate about technology using developmentally appropriate and accurate terminology. (1)

- Use developmentally appropriate multimedia resources (e.g., interactive books, educational software, elementary multimedia encyclopedias) to support learning. (1)

- Work cooperatively and collaboratively with peers, family members, and others when using technology in the classroom. (2)

- Demonstrate positive social and ethical behaviors when using technology. (2)

- Practice responsible use of technology systems and software. (2)

- Create developmentally appropriate multimedia products with support from teachers, family members, or student partners. (3)

- Use technology resources (e.g., puzzles, logical thinking programs, writing tools, digital cameras, drawing tools) for problem solving, communication, and illustration of thoughts, ideas, and stories. (3, 4, 5, 6)

- Gather information and communicate with others using telecommunications, with support from teachers, family members, or student partners. (4)

National Educational Technology Standards for Teachers (NETS•T)

All classroom teachers should be prepared to meet the following standards and performance indicators.

I. TECHNOLOGY OPERATIONS AND CONCEPTS
Teachers demonstrate a sound understanding of technology operations and concepts. Teachers:

    A.   demonstrate introductory knowledge, skills, and understanding of concepts related to technology (as described in the ISTE *National Educational Technology Standards for Students*).

    B.   demonstrate continual growth in technology knowledge and skills to stay abreast of current and emerging technologies.

II. PLANNING AND DESIGNING LEARNING ENVIRONMENTS AND EXPERIENCES
Teachers plan and design effective learning environments and experiences supported by technology. Teachers:

    A.   design developmentally appropriate learning opportunities that apply technology-enhanced instructional strategies to support the diverse needs of learners.

    B.   apply current research on teaching and learning with technology when planning learning environments and experiences.

    C.   identify and locate technology resources and evaluate them for accuracy and suitability.

    D.   plan for the management of technology resources within the context of learning activities.

    E.   plan strategies to manage student learning in a technology-enhanced environment.

III. TEACHING, LEARNING, AND THE CURRICULUM
Teachers implement curriculum plans that include methods and strategies for applying technology to maximize student learning. Teachers:

    A.   facilitate technology-enhanced experiences that address content standards and student technology standards.

    B.   use technology to support learner-centered strategies that address the diverse needs of students.

    C.   apply technology to develop students' higher-order skills and creativity.

    D.   manage student learning activities in a technology-enhanced environment.

IV. ASSESSMENT AND EVALUATION

Teachers apply technology to facilitate a variety of effective assessment and evaluation strategies. Teachers:

A. apply technology in assessing student learning of subject matter using a variety of assessment techniques.

B. use technology resources to collect and analyze data, interpret results, and communicate findings to improve instructional practice and maximize student learning.

C. apply multiple methods of evaluation to determine students' appropriate use of technology resources for learning, communication, and productivity.

V. PRODUCTIVITY AND PROFESSIONAL PRACTICE

Teachers use technology to enhance their productivity and professional practice. Teachers:

A. use technology resources to engage in ongoing professional development and lifelong learning.

B. continually evaluate and reflect on professional practice to make informed decisions regarding the use of technology in support of student learning.

C. apply technology to increase productivity.

D. use technology to communicate and collaborate with peers, parents, and the larger community in order to nurture student learning.

VI. SOCIAL, ETHICAL, LEGAL, AND HUMAN ISSUES

Teachers understand the social, ethical, legal, and human issues surrounding the use of technology in PK–12 schools and apply that understanding in practice. Teachers:

A. model and teach legal and ethical practice related to technology use.

B. apply technology resources to enable and empower learners with diverse backgrounds, characteristics, and abilities.

C. identify and use technology resources that affirm diversity.

D. promote safe and healthy use of technology resources.

E. facilitate equitable access to technology resources for all students.

Early Childhood Professional Preparation Guidelines

1.0 CHILD DEVELOPMENT AND LEARNING

Programs prepare early childhood professionals who:

1.1 Use knowledge of how children develop and learn to provide opportunities that support the physical, social, emotional, language, cognitive, and aesthetic development of all young children from birth through age eight.

1.2 Use knowledge of how young children differ in their development and approaches to learning to support the development and learning of individual children.

　1.2.1 Demonstrate understanding of the conditions that affect children's development and learning, including risk factors, developmental variations, and developmental patterns of specific disabilities.

　1.2.2 Create and modify environments and experiences to meet the individual needs of all children, including children with disabilities, developmental delays, and special abilities.

1.3 Apply knowledge of cultural and linguistic diversity and the significance of socio-cultural and political contexts for development and learning, and recognize that children are best understood in the contexts of family, culture, and society.

　1.3.1 Demonstrate understanding of the interrelationships among culture, language, and thought and the function of the home language in the development of young children.

　1.3.2 Affirm and respect culturally and linguistically diverse children, support home language preservation, and promote anti-bias approaches through the creation of learning environments and experiences.

2.0 CURRICULUM DEVELOPMENT AND IMPLEMENTATION

Programs prepare early childhood professionals who:

2.1 Plan and implement developmentally appropriate curriculum and instructional practices based on knowledge of individual children, the community, and curriculum goals and content.

　2.1.1 Use and explain the rationale for developmentally appropriate methods that include play, small group projects, open-ended questioning, group discussion, problem solving, cooperative learning, and inquiry experiences to help young children develop intellectual curiosity, solve problems, and make decisions.

　2.1.2 Use a variety of strategies to encourage children's physical, social, emotional, aesthetic, and cognitive development.

　2.1.3 Demonstrate current knowledge of and ability to develop and implement meaningful, integrated learning experiences, using the central concepts and tools of inquiry in curriculum content areas including language and literacy, mathematics, science, health, safety, nutrition, social studies, art, music, drama, and movement.

　2.1.4 Develop and implement an integrated curriculum that focuses on children's needs and interests and takes into account culturally valued content and children's home experiences.

2.1.5 Create, evaluate, and select developmentally appropriate materials, equipment, and environments.

2.1.6 Evaluate and demonstrate appropriate use of technology with young children, including assistive technologies for children with disabilities.

2.1.7 Develop and evaluate topics of study in terms of conceptual soundness, significance, and intellectual integrity.

2.1.8 Adapt strategies and environments to meet the specific needs of all children, including those with disabilities, developmental delays, or special abilities.

2.2 Use individual and group guidance and problem-solving techniques to develop positive and supportive relationships with children, to encourage positive social interaction among children, to promote positive strategies of conflict resolution, and to develop personal self-control, self-motivation, and self-esteem.

2.3 Incorporate knowledge and strategies from multiple disciplines (for example, health, social services) into the design of intervention strategies and integrate goals from Individual Education Plans (IEPs) and Individual Family Service Plans (IFSPSs) into daily activities and routines.

2.4 Establish and maintain physically and psychologically safe and healthy learning environments for children.

2.4.1 Demonstrate understanding of the influence of the physical setting, schedule, routines, and transitions on children and use these experiences to promote children's development and learning.

2.4.2 Demonstrate understanding of the developmental consequences of stress and trauma, protective factors and resilience, and the development of mental health, and the importance of supportive relationships.

2.4.3 Implement basic health, nutrition, and safety management practices for young children, including specific procedures for infants and toddlers and procedures regarding childhood illness and communicable diseases.

2.4.4 Use appropriate health appraisal procedures and recommend referral to appropriate community health and social services when necessary.

2.4.5 Recognize signs of emotional distress, child abuse, and neglect in young children and know responsibility and procedures for reporting known or suspected abuse or neglect to appropriate authorities.

3.0 FAMILY AND COMMUNITY RELATIONSHIPS

Programs prepare early childhood professionals who:

3.1 Establish and maintain positive, collaborative relationships with families.

3.1.1 Respect parents' choices and goals for children and communicate effectively with parents about curriculum and children's progress.

3.1.2 Involve families in assessing and planning for individual children, including children with disabilities, developmental delays, or special abilities.

3.1.3 Support parents in making decisions related to their child's development and parenting.

3.2 Demonstrate sensitivity to differences in family structures and social and cultural backgrounds.

3.3 Apply family systems theory, knowledge of the dynamics, roles, and relationships within families and communities.

3.4 Link families with a range of family-oriented services based on identified resources, priorities, and concerns.

3.5 Communicate effectively with other professionals concerned with children and with agencies in the larger community to support children's development, learning, and well being.

4.0 ASSESSMENT AND EVALUATION

Programs prepare early childhood professionals who:

4.1 Use informal and formal assessment strategies to plan and individualize curriculum and teaching practices.

    4.1.1 Observe, record, and assess young children's development and learning and engage children in self-assessment for the purpose of planning appropriate programs, environments, and interactions, and adapting for individual differences.

    4.1.2 Develop and use authentic, performance-based assessments of children's learning to assist in planning and to communicate with children and parents.

    4.1.3 Participate and assist other professionals in conducting family-centered assessments.

    4.1.4 Select, evaluate, and interpret formal, standardized assessment instruments and information used in the assessment of children, and integrate authentic classroom assessment data with formal assessment information.

    4.1.5 Communicate assessment results and integrate assessment results from others as an active participant in the development and implementation of IEP and IFSP goals for children with special developmental and learning needs.

4.2 Develop and use formative and summative program evaluation to ensure comprehensive quality of the total environment for children, families, and the community.

5.0 PROFESSIONALISM

Programs prepare early childhood professionals who:

5.1 Reflect on their practices, articulate a philosophy and rationale for decisions, continually self-assess and evaluate the effects of their choices and actions on others (young children, parents, and other professionals) as a basis for program planning and modification, and continuing professional development.

5.2 Demonstrate an understanding of conditions of children, families, and professionals; current issues and trends; legal issues; and legislation and other public policies affecting children, families, and programs for young children and the early childhood profession.

5.3 Demonstrate an understanding of the early childhood profession, its multiple historical, philosophical, and social foundations, and how these foundations influence current thought and practice.

5.4 Demonstrate awareness of and commitment to the profession's code of ethical conduct.

5.5 Actively seek out opportunities to grow professionally by locating and using appropriate professional literature, organizations, resources, and experiences to inform and improve practice.

5.6 Establish and maintain positive, collaborative relationships with colleagues, other professionals and families, and work effectively as a member of a professional team.

5.7 Serve as advocates on behalf of young children and their families, improved quality of programs and services for young children, and enhanced professional status and working conditions for early childhood educators.

5.8 Demonstrate an understanding of basic principles of administration, organization, and operation of early childhood programs, including supervision of staff and volunteers and program evaluation.

6.0 FIELD EXPERIENCES

Programs prepare early childhood professionals who:

6.1 Observe and participate under supervision of qualified professionals in a variety of settings in which young children, from birth through age eight, are served (such as public and private; centers, schools, and community agencies).

6.2 Work effectively over time with children of diverse ages (infants, toddlers, pre-schoolers, or primary school-age), with children with diverse abilities, with children reflecting culturally and linguistically diverse family systems.

6.3 Demonstrate ability to work effectively during full-time (totally at least 300 clock hours) supervised student teaching and/or practica experiences in at least two different settings, serving children of two different age groups (infant/toddler, preprimary, or primary age) and with varying abilities.

6.4 Analyze and evaluate field experience, including supervised experience in working with parents, and supervised experience in working with interdisciplinary teams of professionals.

English language arts

English/Language Arts Standards

The vision guiding these standards is that all students must have the opportunities and resources to develop the language skills they need to pursue life's goals and to participate fully as informed, productive members of society. These standards assume that literacy growth begins before children enter school as they experience and experiment with literacy activities—reading and writing, and associating spoken words with their graphic representations. Recognizing this fact, these standards encourage the development of curriculum and instruction that make productive use of the emerging literacy abilities that children bring to school. Furthermore, the standards provide ample room for the innovation and creativity essential to teaching and learning. They are not prescriptions for particular curricula or instruction.

Although we present these standards as a list, we want to emphasize that they are not distinct and separable; they are, in fact, interrelated and should be considered as a whole.

1. Students read a wide range of print and nonprint texts to build an understanding of texts, of themselves, and of the cultures of the United States and the world; to acquire new information; to respond to the needs and demands of society and the workplace; and for personal fulfillment. Among these texts are fiction and nonfiction, classic and contemporary works.

2. Students read a wide range of literature from many periods in many genres to build an understanding of the many dimensions (e.g., philosophical, ethical, and aesthetic) of human experience.

3. Students apply a wide range of strategies to comprehend, interpret, evaluate, and appreciate texts. They draw on their prior experience, their interactions with other readers and writers, their knowledge of word meaning and of other texts, their word identification strategies, and their understanding of textual features (e.g., sound-letter correspondence, sentence structure, context, and graphics).

4. Students adjust their use of spoken, written, and visual language (e.g., conventions, style, and vocabulary) to communicate effectively with a variety of audiences and for different purposes.

5. Students employ a wide range of strategies as they write and use different writing process elements appropriately to communicate with different audiences for a variety of purposes.

6. Students apply knowledge of language structure, language conventions (e.g., spelling and punctuation), media techniques, figurative language, and genre to create, critique, and discuss print and nonprint texts.

Reprinted with permission from Standards for the English Language Arts, *p. 24. Copyright 1996 by the International Reading Association and National Council of Teachers of English. All Rights Reserved.*

7. Students conduct research on issues and interests by generating ideas and questions, and by posing problems. They gather, evaluate, and synthesize data from a variety of sources (e.g., print and nonprint texts, artifacts, and people) to communicate their discoveries in ways that suit their purpose and audience.

8. Students use a variety of technological and information resources (e.g., libraries, databases, computer networks, and video) to gather and synthesize information and to create and communicate knowledge.

9. Students develop an understanding of and respect for diversity in language use, patterns, and dialects across cultures, ethnic groups, geographic regions, and social roles.

10. Students whose first language is not English make use of their first language to develop competency in the English language arts and to develop understanding of content across the curriculum.

11. Students participate as knowledgeable, reflective, creative, and critical members of a variety of literacy communities.

12. Students use spoken, written, and visual language to accomplish their own purposes (e.g., for learning, enjoyment, persuasion, and the exchange of information).

math

Mathematics Standards

STANDARD 1: NUMBER AND OPERATIONS
Instructional programs from prekindergarten through Grade 12 should enable all students to—
- understand numbers, ways of representing numbers, relationships among numbers, and number systems;
- understand meanings of operations and how they relate to one another;
- compute fluently and make reasonable estimates.

STANDARD 2: ALGEBRA
Instructional programs from prekindergarten through Grade 12 should enable all students to—
- understand patterns, relations, and functions;
- represent and analyze mathematical situations and structures using algebraic symbols;
- use mathematical models to represent and understand quantitative relationships;
- analyze change in various contexts.

STANDARD 3: GEOMETRY
Instructional programs from prekindergarten through Grade 12 should enable all students to—
- analyze characteristics and properties of two- and three-dimensional geometric shapes and develop mathematical arguments about geometric relationships;
- specify locations and describe spatial relationships using coordinate geometry and other representational systems;
- apply transformations and use symmetry to analyze mathematical situations;
- use visualization, spatial reasoning, and geometric modeling to solve problems.

STANDARD 4: MEASUREMENT
Instructional programs from prekindergarten through Grade 12 should enable all students to—
- understand measurable attributes of objects and the units, systems, and processes of measurement;
- apply appropriate techniques, tools, and formulas to determine measurements.

STANDARD 5: DATA ANALYSIS AND PROBABILITY
Instructional programs from prekindergarten through Grade 12 should enable all students to—
- formulate questions that can be addressed with data and collect, organize, and display relevant data to answer them;
- select and use appropriate statistical methods to analyze data;
- develop and evaluate inferences and predictions that are based on data;
- understand and apply basic concepts of probability.

STANDARD 6: PROBLEM SOLVING

Instructional programs from prekindergarten through Grade 12 should enable all students to—

- build new mathematical knowledge through problem solving;
- solve problems that arise in mathematics and in other contexts;
- apply and adapt a variety of appropriate strategies to solve problems;
- monitor and reflect on the process of mathematical problem solving.

STANDARD 7: REASONING AND PROOF

Instructional programs from prekindergarten through Grade 12 should enable all students to—

- recognize reasoning and proof as fundamental aspects of mathematics;
- make and investigate mathematical conjectures;
- develop and evaluate mathematical arguments and proofs;
- select and use various types of reasoning and methods of proof.

STANDARD 8: COMMUNICATION

Instructional programs from prekindergarten through Grade 12 should enable all students to—

- organize and consolidate their mathematical thinking through communication;
- communicate their mathematical thinking coherently and clearly to peers, teachers, and others;
- analyze and evaluate the mathematical thinking and strategies of others;
- use the language of mathematics to express mathematical ideas precisely.

STANDARD 9: CONNECTIONS

Instructional programs from prekindergarten through Grade 12 should enable all students to—

- recognize and use connections among mathematical ideas;
- understand how mathematical ideas interconnect and build on one another to produce a coherent whole;
- recognize and apply mathematics in contexts outside of mathematics.

STANDARD 10: REPRESENTATION

Instructional programs from prekindergarten through Grade 12 should enable all students to—

- create and use representations to organize, record, and communicate mathematical ideas;
- select, apply, and translate among mathematical representations to solve problems;
- use representations to model and interpret physical, social, and mathematical phenomena.

science

Science Standards

Grades K–12

CONTENT STANDARD: UNIFYING CONCEPTS AND PROCESSES
As a result of activities in Grades K–12, all students should develop understanding and abilities aligned with the following concepts and processes:

- Systems, order, and organization
- Evidence, models, and explanation
- Constancy, change, and measurement
- Evolution and equilibrium
- Form and function

Grades K–4

CONTENT STANDARD A: SCIENCE AS INQUIRY
A1. Abilities necessary to do scientific inquiry:
- Ask a question about objects, organisms, and events in the environment.
- Plan and conduct a simple investigation.
- Employ simple equipment and tools to gather data and extend the senses.
- Use data to construct a reasonable explanation.
- Communicate investigations and explanations.

A2. Understanding about scientific inquiry:
- Scientific investigations involve asking and answering a question and comparing the answer with what scientists already know about the world.
- Scientists use different kinds of investigations depending on the questions they are trying to answer.
- Simple instruments provide more information than scientists obtain using only their senses.
- Scientists develop explanations using observations (evidence) and what they already know about the world (scientific knowledge).
- Scientists make the results of their investigations public; they describe the investigations in ways that enable others to repeat the investigations.
- Scientists review and ask questions about the results of other scientists' work.

CONTENT STANDARD B: PHYSICAL SCIENCE
B1. Properties of objects and materials
B2. Position and motion of objects
B3. Light, heat, electricity, and magnetism

CONTENT STANDARD C: LIFE SCIENCE
C1. The characteristics of organisms
C2. Life cycles of organisms
C3. Organisms and environments

Reprinted with permission from National Science Education Standards. Copyright 1996 by the National Academy of Sciences. Courtesy of the National Academy Press, Washington, D.C.

CONTENT STANDARD D: EARTH AND SPACE SCIENCE

D1. Properties of earth materials

D2. Objects in the sky

D3. Changes in earth and sky

CONTENT STANDARD E: SCIENCE AND TECHNOLOGY

E1. Abilities of technological design

E2. Understanding about science and technology

E3. Abilities to distinguish between natural objects and objects made by humans

CONTENT STANDARD F: SCIENCE IN PERSONAL AND SOCIAL PERSPECTIVES

F1. Personal health

F2. Characteristics and changes in populations

F3. Types of resources

F4. Changes in environments

F5. Science and technology in local challenges

CONTENT STANDARD G: HISTORY AND NATURE OF SCIENCE

G1. Science as a human endeavor:

- Science and technology have been practiced by people for a long time.
- Men and women have made a variety of contributions throughout the history of science and technology.
- Science will never be finished.
- Many people choose science as a career.

Social Studies Standards

Performance Expectations for the Early Grades

I. CULTURE

Social studies programs should include experiences that provide for the study of culture and cultural diversity, so that the learner can:

    a.   explore and describe similarities and differences in the ways groups, societies, and cultures address similar human needs and concerns;

    b.   give examples of how experiences may be interpreted differently by people from diverse cultural perspectives and frames of reference;

    c.   describe ways in which language, stories, folktales, music, and artistic creations serve as expressions of culture and influence behavior of people living in a particular culture;

    d.   compare ways in which people from different cultures think about and deal with their physical environment and social conditions;

    e.   give examples and describe the importance of cultural unity and diversity within and across groups.

II. TIME, CONTINUITY, AND CHANGE

Social studies programs should include experiences that provide for the study of the ways human beings view themselves in and over time, so that the learner can:

    a.   demonstrate an understanding that different people may describe the same event or situation in diverse ways, citing reasons for the differences in views;

    b.   demonstrate an ability to use correctly vocabulary associated with time such as past, present, future, and long ago; read and construct simple timelines; identify examples of change; and recognize examples of cause and effect relationships;

    c.   compare and contrast different stories or accounts about past events, people, places, or situations, identifying how they contribute to our understanding of the past;

    d.   identify and use various sources for reconstructing the past, such as documents, letters, diaries, maps, textbooks, photos, and others;

    e.   demonstrate an understanding that people in different times and places view the world differently;

    f.   use knowledge of facts and concepts drawn from history, along with elements of historical inquiry, to inform decision making about and action-taking on public issues.

Reprinted with permission from Expectations of Excellence—Curriculum Standards for Social Studies, *published by National Council for the Social Studies, 1994, p. 33–45.*

III. PEOPLE, PLACES, AND ENVIRONMENTS

Social studies programs should include experiences that provide for the study of people, places, and environments, so that the learner can:

    a.   construct and use mental maps of locales, regions, and the world that demonstrate understanding of relative location, direction, size, and shape;

b. interpret, use, and distinguish various representations of the earth, such as maps, globes, and photographs;

c. use appropriate resources, data sources, and geographic tools such as atlases, databases, grid systems, charts, graphs, and maps to generate, manipulate, and interpret information;

d. estimate distances and calculate scale;

e. locate and distinguish among varying landforms and geographic features, such as mountains, plateaus, islands, and oceans;

f. describe and speculate about physical system changes, such as seasons, climate and weather, and the water cycle;

g. describe how people create places that reflect ideas, personality, culture, and wants and needs as they design homes, playgrounds, classrooms, and the like;

h. examine the interaction of human beings and their physical environment, the use of land, building of cities, and ecosystem changes in selected locales and regions;

i. explore ways that the earth's physical features have changed over time in the local region and beyond and how these changes may be connected to one another;

j. observe and speculate about social and economic effects of environmental changes and crises resulting from phenomena such as floods, storms, and drought;

k. consider existing uses and propose and evaluate alternative uses of resources and land in home, school, community, the region, and beyond.

IV. INDIVIDUAL DEVELOPMENT AND IDENTITY

Social studies programs should include experiences that provide for the study of individual development and identity, so that the learner can:

a. describe personal changes over time, such as those related to physical development and personal interests;

b. describe personal connections to place—especially place as associated with immediate surroundings;

c. describe the unique features of one's nuclear and extended families;

d. show how learning and physical development affect behavior;

e. identify and describe ways family, groups, and community influence the individual's daily life and personal choices;

f. explore factors that contribute to one's personal identity such as interests, capabilities, and perceptions;

g. analyze a particular event to identify reasons individuals might respond to it in different ways;

h. work independently and cooperatively to accomplish goals.

V. INDIVIDUALS, GROUPS, AND INSTITUTIONS

Social studies programs should include experiences that provide for the study of interactions among individuals, groups, and institutions, so that the learner can:

a. identify roles as learned behavior patterns in group situations such as student, family member, peer play group member, or club member;

b. give examples of and explain group and institutional influences such as religious beliefs, laws, and peer pressure, on people, events, and elements of culture;

c. identify examples of institutions and describe the interactions of people with institutions;

d. identify and describe examples of tensions between and among individuals, groups, or institutions, and how belonging to more than one group can cause internal conflicts;

e. identify and describe examples of tension between an individual's beliefs and government policies and laws;

f.   give examples of the role of institutions in furthering both continuity and change;

g.   show how groups and institutions work to meet individual needs and promote the common good, and identify examples of where they fail to do so.

VI. POWER, AUTHORITY, AND GOVERNANCE

Social studies programs should include experiences that provide for the study of how people create and change structures of power, authority, and governance, so that the learner can:

a.   examine the rights and responsibilities of the individual in relation to his or her social group, such as family, peer group, and school class;

b.   explain the purpose of government;

c.   give examples of how government does or does not provide for needs and wants of people, establish order and security, and manage conflict;

d.   recognize how groups and organizations encourage unity and deal with diversity to maintain order and security;

e.   distinguish among local, state, and national government and identify representative leaders at these levels such as mayor, governor, and president;

f.   identify and describe factors that contribute to cooperation and cause disputes within and among groups and nations;

g.   explore the role of technology in communications, transportation, information-processing, weapons development, or other areas as it contributes to or helps resolve conflicts;

h.   recognize and give examples of the tensions between the wants and needs of individuals and groups, and concepts such as fairness, equity, and justice.

VII. PRODUCTION, DISTRIBUTION, AND CONSUMPTION

Social studies programs should include experiences that provide for the study of how people organize for the production, distribution, and consumption of goods and services, so that the learner can:

a.   give examples that show how scarcity and choice govern our economic decisions;

b.   distinguish between needs and wants;

c.   identify examples of private and public goods and services;

d.   give examples of the various institutions that make up economic systems such as families, workers, banks, labor unions, government agencies, small businesses, and large corporations;

e.   describe how we depend upon workers with specialized jobs and the ways in which they contribute to the production and exchange of goods and services;

f.   describe the influence of incentives, values, traditions, and habits on economic decisions;

g.   explain and demonstrate the role of money in everyday life;

h.   describe the relationship of price to supply and demand;

i.   use economic concepts such as supply, demand, and price to help explain events in the community and nation;

j.   apply knowledge of economic concepts in developing a response to a current local economic issue, such as how to reduce the flow of trash into a rapidly filling landfill.

VIII. SCIENCE, TECHNOLOGY, AND SOCIETY

Social studies programs should include experiences that provide for the study of relationships among science, technology, and society, so that the learner can:

a.   identify and describe examples in which science and technology have changed the lives of people, such as in homemaking, childcare, work, transportation, and communication;

b. identify and describe examples in which science and technology have led to changes in the physical environment, such as the building of dams and levees, offshore oil drilling, medicine from rain forests, and loss of rain forests due to extraction of resources or alternative uses;

c. describe instances in which changes in values, beliefs, and attitudes have resulted from new scientific and technological knowledge, such as conservation of resources and awareness of chemicals harmful to life and the environment;

d. identify examples of laws and policies that govern scientific and technological applications, such as the Endangered Species Act and environmental protection policies;

e. suggest ways to monitor science and technology in order to protect the physical environment, individual rights, and the common good.

IX. GLOBAL CONNECTIONS

Social studies programs should include experiences that provide for the study of global connections and interdependence, so that the learner can:

a. explore ways that language, art, music, belief systems, and other cultural elements may facilitate global understanding or lead to misunderstanding;

b. give examples of conflict, cooperation, and interdependence among individuals, groups, and nations;

c. examine the effects of changing technologies on the global community;

d. explore causes, consequences, and possible solutions to persistent, contemporary, and emerging global issues, such as pollution and endangered species;

e. examine the relationships and tensions between personal wants and needs and various global concerns, such as use of imported oil, land use, and environmental protection;

f. investigate concerns, issues, standards, and conflicts related to universal human rights, such as the treatment of children, religious groups, and effects of war.

X. CIVIC IDEALS AND PRACTICES

Social studies programs should include experiences that provide for the study of the ideals, principles, and practices of citizenship in a democratic republic, so that the learner can:

a. identify key ideals of the United States' democratic republican form of government, such as individual human dignity, liberty, justice, equality, and the rule of law, and discuss their application in specific situations;

b. identify examples of rights and responsibilities of citizens;

c. locate, access, organize, and apply information about an issue of public concern from multiple points of view;

d. identify and practice selected forms of civic discussion and participation consistent with the ideals of citizens in a democratic republic;

e. explain actions citizens can take to influence public policy decisions;

f. recognize that a variety of formal and informal actors influence and shape public policy;

g. examine the influence of public opinion on personal decision making and government policy on public issues;

h. explain how public policies and citizen behaviors may or may not reflect the stated ideals of a democratic republican form of government;

i. describe how public policies are used to address issues of public concern;

j. recognize and interpret how the "common good" can be strengthened through various forms of citizen action.